Vicissitudes
Histories and Destinies of Psychoanalysis

igrs books

Established by the Institute of Germanic & Romance Studies, this series aims to bring to the public monographs and collections of essays in the field of modern foreign languages. Proposals for publication are selected by the Institute's editorial board, which is advised by a peer review committee of 36 senior academics in the field. To make titles as accessible as possible to an English-speaking and multi-lingual readership, volumes are written in English and quotations given in English translation.

For further details on the annual competition, visit:
http://www.igrs.sas.ac.uk/publications/igrs-books/igrs-books-annual-competition

Editorial Board

Dr Jordana Blejmar (Hispanic)
Ms Maria-José Homem (Portuguese)
Professor Bill Marshall (French)
Dr Katia Pizzi (Italian)
Dr Anne Simon (Germanic)
Dr Godela Weiss-Sussex (Germanic)

igrs books Volume 7

Volume Editor
Professor Naomi Segal

Vicissitudes
Histories and Destinies of Psychoanalysis

Edited by

Naomi Segal and Sharon Kivland

SCHOOL OF ADVANCED STUDY UNIVERSITY OF LONDON

Institute of Germanic & Romance Studies

2012

Published by the

Institute of Germanic & Romance Studies
School of Advanced Study, University of London
Senate House, Malet Street, London WC1E 7HU
http://igrs.sas.ac.uk

© Christine Anzieu-Premmereur, Julia Borossa, Lesley Caldwell, William Cobbing, Juan Cruz, Sander L. Gilman, Jaspar Joseph-Lester, Ahuvia Kahane, Sharon Kivland, Herbert Lachmayer, Zoe Laughlin, Stéphane Le Mercier, Martin Liebscher, Claudio Magris, Juliet Mitchell, Mark Nash, Uriel Orlow, Mariano Ben Plotkin, Malcolm Quinn, Naomi Segal, Alison Sinclair, Marcella Vanzo, Hugo Vezzetti, Andrew Webber, Amy Wygant, 2012

The authors have asserted their right under the Copyright, Designs and Patents Act 1988 to be identified as the authors of this work.

All rights reserved. No part of this publication may be reproduced, stored in a retrieval system, or transmitted, in any form or by any means, electronic, mechanical, photocopying, recording or otherwise, without the prior permission of the author and the publisher.

Cover image
Sharon Kivland, from the series *L'esprit d'escalier*, 2009

First published 2012

ISBN 978 0 85457 234 2

Contents

Introduction   11
Naomi Segal and Sharon Kivland

PSYCHOANALYSIS AND THE ARTS

1. Art and Psychoanalysis (Among Other Discourses)   19
   Malcolm Quinn
2. Between Two Worlds   27
   Mark Nash
3. Transcript   39
   Sharon Kivland

PSYCHOANALYSIS IN THE FRENCH-SPEAKING WORLD

4. Freedom to Roam   55
   Julia Borossa
5. How a Child Develops a Sense of Humour During Psychoanalysis   63
   Christine Anzieu-Premmereur
6. La reproduction   77
   Stéphane Le Mercier

PEDAGOGY AND PRACTICE

7. Pedagogy and Practice   93
   Amy Wygant

8. Psychoanalysis in the University: The Clinical
   Dimension   99
   Sander L. Gilman

9. Materials for the Advancement of Conceptualization:
   An Introduction to Materials Library   109
   Zoe Laughlin

PSYCHOANALYSIS IN THE SPANISH- AND PORTUGUESE-SPEAKING WORLD

10. Speaking Experience   125
    Alison Sinclair

11. Psychoanalysis in Argentine Culture: A Social and
    Political Interpretation   131
    Hugo Vezzetti

12. Earnest Abnegation in Perpetuity   145
    Juan Cruz

PSYCHOANALYSIS AND POLITICS

13. Accidental Pasts and the Truth of History   159
    Ahuvia Kahane

14. The 'Sibling Trauma' and the Case of Judge Daniel
    Paul Schreber   167
    Juliet Mitchell

15. Spirit   189
    Jaspar Joseph-Lester

PSYCHOANALYSIS IN THE GERMAN-SPEAKING WORLD

16. Constructions in the Humanities: The German-field
    Seminars   203
    Martin Liebscher

17. Staging Freud: Reflections on Gradiva, the Muse of
    Psychoanalysis   209
    Herbert Lachmayer

18.	Gradiva Project *William Cobbing*	225

PSYCHOANALYSIS AND TRANSMISSION

19.	Transmission Impossible? *Andrew Webber*	241
20.	On Psychoanalysis and its History: Some Reflections from the South *Mariano Ben Plotkin*	249
21.	In Praise of Ghosts *Uriel Orlow*	263

PSYCHOANALYSIS IN THE ITALIAN-SPEAKING WORLD

22.	Family Matters *Lesley Caldwell*	281
23.	Identity, Writing and Uncertainty *Claudio Magris*	289
24.	On the World of Interiors *Marcella Vanzo*	303

List of Contributors	317
Bibliography	327
Index	343

Introduction

Naomi Segal and Sharon Kivland

The Institute of Germanic & Romance Studies (IGRS) was founded in 2004 out of the merger of two pre-existing University of London research institutes: the Institute of Germanic Studies (founded 1950) and the Institute of Romance Studies (founded 1989). Its role was to foster and create national and international research in French, German, Italian, Portuguese and Spanish studies by means of seminars, lectures, workshops, colloquia, conferences, publications, research training, postgraduate degrees, Research Centres and a fellowship programme.

Under its founding director, Naomi Segal, the IGRS aimed to combine the success of the IGS and IRS by creating and supporting activities both within and across individual language-fields, opening up its activities to the full spectrum of collaborative, cross-disciplinary and cross-cultural work. Thus, in addition to regular courses and events, the IGRS started life with two core programmes characterised by their inclusiveness and diversity. The 'Performance' programme in 2005–06 brought together, as well as several conferences, two UK playwrights, a German TV star reading Brecht, three Italian theatre directors, the second-year drama cohort of the Guildhall School of Music and Drama, an evening of Mozart music and letters with a Viennese string quartet and pianist, and a workshop run by a Venetian harlequin. The next, 'Psychoanalysis and the arts and humanities: a multilingual perspective', which took place in 2006–08, continued this link of the academic with the artistic. It was run under the Arts and Humanities Research Council (AHRC) Research Networks Scheme, with additional funding from the British Academy, the Modern Humanities Research Association (MHRA), the UK subject associations of French and Italian studies,

GERMAN	ENGLISH	FRENCH	ITALIAN	SPANISH
Besetzung	cathexis	investissement	carica/investimento	carga
das Unheimliche	the uncanny	l'inquiétante étrangeté	il perturbante	lo siniestro
Ich, Es	ego, id	moi, ça	io, es	yo, ello
nachträglich	deferred	après-coup	posteriore	posterior
seelisch/psychisch	psychic	psychique	psichico/mentale	psíquico
Trieb	instinct/drive	pulsion	istinto	instinto
Übertragung	transference	transfert	transfert/traslazione	trasferencia
Verdrängung	repression	refoulement	rimozione	represión

Freudian key-words, translated into English, French, Italian and Spanish

and the embassies of Austria, France, Italy and the Netherlands. This book is the result of the latter year of the programme, including the debates in its eight-seminar series and the closing conference entitled 'Vicissitudes: histories and destinies of psychoanalysis'.

What motivated this project? In this country we often hear the argument that psychoanalysis, now well over a century old and widely diffused in popularized forms in the contemporary 'therapy society', has run its course as a source of theoretical debate. Within the UK academy, it has had difficulty achieving recognition, since its claims to scientific validity are often disputed, and it is institutionally recognized only in a few departments, poised between social sciences and pure theory. At the same time, as a way of asking questions, psychoanalysis is actually thriving as never before in psychoanalytic bodies, at least 20 in London alone, where, in addition to training and supporting practitioners, full programmes of seminars or conferences are run. These take place in countries outside the UK, such as Argentina or France, in which psychoanalysis continues to play a marked role in intellectual life; and in UK research practice in the arts and humanities. It is this conjuncture of continuing debate that the network aimed to map and develop. The specific goal was to explore what issues were being aired – at the beginning of the 21st century in three continents – by people speaking English, French, German, Italian, Portuguese and Spanish.

Introduction

The programme opened in November 2006 with a conference entitled 'Freud in translation, Freud in transition'. As well as being a launch event, it was designed to get the multilingual issues of psychoanalysis onto the table. Bringing together speakers from seven language backgrounds and with an even spread of academics, analysts and artists, the two-day event began with a workshop looking at translations of the opening of Freud's *Der Dichter and das Phantasieren* (1908) into French, Italian, Spanish and English, and a plenary discussion of recent adventures in Freud translation, followed by a debate on a set of key words and their trajectories, which is shown opposite.

Ernest Jones had already warned in 1920, in the first number of the *International Journal of Psycho-Analysis*, of the dangers of allowing misinterpretations of psychoanalysis to develop through 'dilution of the meanings of its new ideas until they may be regarded as harmless'.[1] He then referred to the way opposition to psychoanalysis had developed in the USA:

> under all sorts of specious guises and by the aid of various seductive catchwords [...] A notable, and perhaps unique feature of this [...] defence against Psycho-analysis is that it conceals its negative antagonistic nature by pretending to develop a more positive attitude towards Psycho-analysis; it makes use of its technical terms, *Libido*, 'repression', etc., but in such a way as to rob them of their intrinsic meaning.

By comparing the fates of such 'seductive catchwords' in the opening conference, we examined not just where they went to but where they had come from in the original German, via the vicissitudes of repeated translation into so many other languages. And we did this on the basis of the demands that Freud's writing (in any language) makes of his readers:

> Freud assumes a reader who is ready to get involved, who can enjoy several irreconcilable senses and read between the lines. Freud seems to trust his reader and this is why he often relies on the engaging language of everyday experience [...] And he said quite explicitly that this was his scientific strategy, that we can only describe with the help of comparisons and that we have to keep on changing our

---

1 Cited by Riccardo Steiner in '"Die Weltmachstellung des Britischen Reichs": notes on the term "standard" in the first translations of Freud', in *Freud in Exile: Psychoanalysis and its Vicissitudes*, ed. Edward Timms and Naomi Segal (New Haven and London: Yale University Press, 1988), 186.

descriptions of our own conceptions because none of them will do for very long.[2]

The afternoon and evening of the first day was dedicated to an arts event run by Malcolm Quinn and Sharon Kivland and bringing together installations, activities and presentations by David Bate, Márta Csabai, Bill Furlong, Polly Gould, Lucy Harrison, Frances Hegarty, Jaspar Joseph-Lester, Sharon Kivland, Mark Lewis, Forbes Morlock, Simon Morris, Liz Pavey, Phoebe von Held and Sarah Wood in the rooms and corridors of Stewart House. Works included the artful acts of hysterics; a woman telling her life story until her words choke her; lift doors endlessly opening and closing upon scenes of consumption; the credits of a film never made followed by a new version of *Capital*; a film script of a conversation that never happened; a sound installation of non-speech; a slide work of discourse markers; a text work of translation; a machine that endlessly rewrote Freud's *The Interpretation of Dreams*; a dance-work of memory and childhood images; a series of photographs of broken objects as parapraxes; a performance combining narrative and objects; and a reading group (bookings taken). There was a certain shared address to agency and voice – or the loss of both. While the intention had been to provoke immediate discussion of the event and its theme and content, this was only partially realised, and we began to consider ways in which works of art (in their broadest sense) could be integrated into a conference as more than adjuncts to scholarly papers. The result of that consideration can be seen in the present volume.

The second-day plenaries set up the fields of discussion that would develop into the four areas of the seminar series which this book presents; each panel combined academics, analysts and artists offering their perspectives on 'Psychoanalysis and the arts', 'Pedagogy and practice', 'Psychoanalysis and politics' and 'Histories and transmissions'. The conference ended with discussion about future plans and with an invitation to a psychoanalytic discussion of Steven Spielberg's *Duel* (1971) the following day at London's Institute of Contemporary Arts.

Two months after that conference, in January 2007, an international workshop heralded the other four seminar fields – debates in psychoanalysis and the arts and humanities in areas speaking French, German, Italian and Hispanic (Spanish and Portuguese – sometimes called 'Portunhol' locally). In this second event, a multilingual group

---

2   Darius Gray Ornston, Jr., 'How standard is the *Standard Edition*?', in Timms and Segal (eds.), 197–98.

of speakers and delegates from all over Europe broached discussions on such questions as what psychoanalysis is doing for the humanities; what the humanities are doing for psychoanalysis; the cultural memory traditions in which the varieties of psychoanalysis have taken root; the tensions between the clinical and intellectual uses of psychoanalysis; and the range and variety of psychoanalytic theories, and why and how different ones predominate in different places – how, for example, the French Lacan (and his Freud) differs from the Argentine Lacan and his.

Four speakers in each language-field introduced what they felt were the main current preoccupations of their tradition, and a glimpse at the questions they raised gives a flavour of the range of debates that were pursued in the following year. For example, Céline Surprenant, an academic working in French cultural studies, highlighted what she termed 'a key problem in the philosophical reception of Freudian psychoanalysis in France (and beyond): the fact that Lacan's "return to Freud" has encouraged a selective attitude to Freud's thinking by excluding its scientific aspects'. In response to this problem, she raised two issues of particular concern: first, the biological foundation of the drive and the notion of intentionality, and second, the aesthetic role of quantity and measurement in *Jokes and Their Relation to the Unconscious*. Something similar preoccupied Patrizia Giampieri-Deutsch, a Viennese analyst and historian of psychoanalysis, who argued that 'it is crucial to find descriptions of the human in terms that are satisfying to both the disciplines of the mind and the sciences of the brain: psychoanalysis can succeed in making a decisive breakthrough regarding the traditional dualistic classification of the sciences'. Speakers from the Spanish and Italian fields directed their psychoanalytic attention more at political problems. Paola di Cori, a lecturer in gender studies at the University of Urbino who was born in Buenos Aires, showed how, in 1980s Argentina, a number of psychoanalysts turned to the study of trauma and torture, some of them treating patients who had been arrested and tortured, or relatives of *desaparecidos*. He also demonstrated that, since 2001, key issues in both therapeutic and intellectual debates, have been poverty and social catastrophe, memory and intergenerational transmission. Alessandra Cavalli, a Jungian psychoanalyst practising in London, cited Giorgio Agamben and Wilfred Bion in arguing that both psychoanalysis and the humanities must 'face the alienation of the *Homo linguisticus* who is exiled in silence in a noisy space where the media are in charge of the truth (words). Where politicians and the media have appropriated the empty space, is it possible for psychoanalysis and the arts to find a meaningful silence where meaningful (truthful) words can emerge?'

This book takes up the questions put forward at the two opening events and resumes the debates of the eight-seminar series that followed, running throughout 2007 in London, Cambridge, Edinburgh and Glasgow. It also imitates the structure and aims of the concluding conference of the project, which was held in January 2008 under the same name of 'Vicissitudes: histories and destinies of psychoanalysis'. Each section of the conference consisted of three papers: an introduction by the seminar series leader, a guest lecture by a visiting speaker and a presentation by an artist. Following our experience of the inclusion of works of art (or other forms of engagement) at the opening conference, we invited an artist to take part in each panel, with the remit to discuss her or his *praxis*. The contributions were exciting, even provocative, providing challenging and, at times, enigmatic interventions. Many of the artists' presentations were not explicitly concerned with psychoanalysis, yet there was a profound engagement with it in the discussions, both formal and informal, that followed each panel. Once again, the line-up was multidisciplinary and multinational. The eight sections of this book follow the same pattern, and reproduce the contributions, although they have also often been revised or extended.

The adventures of psychoanalysis with the arts and humanities across a five-language spectrum, and the many nations it represents, continue to thrive with the same argumentative energy as they had when this project began. We are grateful to our funders and all our speakers and writers for joining us in thinking aloud about this dynamic field and its histories and destinies.

Psychoanalysis and the Arts

1. Art and Psychoanalysis (Among Other Discourses)

Malcolm Quinn

In her essay on the art works made as part of her visiting fellowship at the Institute of Germanic & Romance Studies (IGRS), Sharon Kivland reminds us of Freud's assertion that it is impossible to translate a dream into a foreign language. Kivland's translated texts, including

> der Traum ist die Erfüllung eines Wunsches
> a dream is the fulfilment of a wish
> le rêve est un accomplissement de souhait

draw attention to this impossibility. It is crucial to note that this is an *impossibility* — rather than a 'difficulty' — of translation, produced by the triangular relation between the manifest dream-text, the latent dream-content and the unconscious wish that *insinuates* itself between these two elements. In Freud's view, a dream is an artefact produced by an unconscious wish. The structure of the dream is determined by the way that the unconscious wish has smuggled itself between the latent dream-thought and the manifest dream-content. The analysis of the dream must pay attention to how the dream has developed from latent thought to manifest content. It also requires the specific distinctions between the analyst and analysand mentioned by Freud in his *Introductory Lectures in Psychoanalysis*. Here he emphasises two positions: one in which the analyst knows nothing and another in which the analysand knows something (unconscious knowledge) but does not know that he knows it. The analyst is thereby distinguished from the analysand by a negative set of attributes. First, s/he is ignorant of something (the analysand's unconscious knowledge);

as an added bonus, s/he has also renounced her/his belief in the condition of psychic freedom:

> But in general if the dreamer asserts that nothing occurs to him we contradict him; we bring urgent pressure to bear on him — and we turn out to be right [...] Once before, I ventured to tell you that you nourish a deeply rooted faith in undetermined psychical events and in free will, but that this is quite unscientific and must yield to the demand of a determinism whose rule extends over mental life.[1]

This determinism of mental life is approached at the level of the utterance, as an analysis of the activity of the dream-work, which is made manifest in the dream as the 'accomplishment' (the finished artefact) of an unconscious wish. The work of the analyst is not a work of interpretation; rather, it is an inventory or catalogue of the analysand's interpretations, with the aim of discovering why a particular wish has assumed a specific form for the analysand. Translation is ruled out, because it assumes a knowledge other than that which the analysand holds, and also because it prevents access to the work of the unconscious at the material level of the utterance. The impossibility of translation is the possibility of psychoanalysis, as it moves from hermeneutic solutions to language problems, to an analysis of language at the level of the forms and mechanisms of signification. Sharon Kivland's works for the IGRS draw our attention to this divide between interpretation and form; as she suggests: 'Perhaps something unstable arises when a text, open to interpretation and to reading, becomes an image and reading, interpretation, strangely vanishes' (this volume, p. 44).

This 'something unstable' is the acknowledgment of a desire that has assumed form. The instability that Kivland mentions is produced as a consequence of the fact that we now encounter the text as something not situated between meanings but instead more radically positioned between forms. This instability is signalled by Kivland's references to different fonts or typefaces. She asks us to face the possibility of an unconscious causal truth which shadows the teleological truth that is sought in the act of translation. The causal truth of translation is located in a certain something (in this instance a typeface) that brings about the fall of the teleological aim of 'a good translation'. Distinct typefaces express the relation of the given form of

---

1 Sigmund Freud, *Introductory Lectures on Psycho-Analysis* [*Vorlesungen zur Einführung in die Psychoanalyse* [1915]], in *The Standard Edition of the Complete Psychological Works of Sigmund Freud*, 24 vols., ed. and trans. by James Strachey et al. (London: The Hogarth Press and the Institute of Psycho-analysis, 1953–74), vol. 15, 105–06. Hereafter abbreviated SE, followed by volume number.

a text to other possible forms and to new constructions of knowledge, rather than the relation of a text to its faithfully translated meaning. The causal truth that is sought in psychoanalysis also establishes a particular form of rigour, which can clear a path through the thickets of applied psychoanalysis discussed by Mark Nash in his essay:

> This form of literary or rather filmic exegesis was totally appropriate to the time, but I would not want to argue for its return. The arguments deployed were too strong, too convincing and there was rarely pause to ask the key question from the point of view of a scientific methodology – how could this be disproved, what counter arguments could one make? Psychoanalytic ideas had, so to speak, become part of a belief system (this volume, p. 31)

Here one can return to Freud's reference to 'a deeply-rooted belief in psychic freedom and choice', which is 'unscientific' and which must give ground in the face of the determinism of mental life. The word 'science' here requires a specific definition. Psychoanalysis does not belong to social science or humanities research, because it is not founded on the idea of social actors in the context of a life-nexus. It is not part of natural science research because of its claim that the statement or utterance itself is the preferred object of study rather than the content of the utterance, such as a scientific formula or equation. Furthermore, the view from psychoanalysis is not the view from a theory but, rather, the view from the subject-position of the analyst, who has initiated an investigation into the unconscious of the analysand. The analysand is accounted for as a knowledge construction existing precariously between forms, rather than as a set of inner experiences fitted snugly in a life-nexus.

Too much applied psychoanalysis, even at the highest levels, demonstrates both a naïve attachment to the 'good tools' of the scientific method, and an insufficient commitment to the epistemological renunciations that are required for analytic rigour, which is often ceded to the temptations of a scholarly interpretation. An example of this position is provided in a recent interview with the critic Hal Foster, one of the legatees of the growth in applied psychoanalysis in the arts and humanities mentioned by Nash. In this interview, Foster expresses his disenchantment with psychoanalysis, a youthful enthusiasm that he now approaches with a degree of wariness:

> I have to admit that I find it [psychoanalysis] less active as my work goes on. Perhaps I'm affected by the insistent abuse of psychoanalysis in the culture at large. I think there is a real difference between the situation in the States, and the situation here and in mainland Europe. In the States, psychoanalysis fled to the academy and died there! But

for all its abuses, intellectual and cultural, as with Marxism, it's a rich set of tools if they are used effectively, properly [...] I tend to think about 'the right tool for the job' – there is a pragmatics of theory [...] I'm not a member of a sect.[2]

Foster's 'pragmatics of theory', as well as his statement that he is 'not a member of a sect', indicates his interest in using psychoanalysis as a tool for interpretation along with other possible tools, rather than in a properly psychoanalytic orientation. In this regard, it is worth noting that, while Nash also takes a distance from 'my much-younger self' in his quotation from his essay on Carl Dreyer, he then goes on to explain how he has subsequently addressed these problems of interpretation through practice, in the films *Between Two Worlds* (1993) and *Frantz Fanon: Black Skin White Masks* (1996), both of which were directly concerned with the constitution of the psychoanalytic clinic and the relationship of the analyst and the analysand. Nash also mentions Kivland's psychoanalytically-informed work in the visual field, which he identifies as an activity of working through the forms of the gallery and curatorship, while addressing the problems of interpretation in applied psychoanalysis. This wider issue of the use of applied psychoanalysis in the arts and humanities is implicitly addressed by Kivland in her IGRS visiting fellowship work, by means of her critique of the 'good translation'. This critique locates rigour in a properly psychoanalytic way, as the fall of knowledge, rather than in its accomplishment:

> psychoanalysis can only operate by virtue of a knowledge 'in failure' or 'in check' (*savoir en échec*). In other words, psychoanalysis incorporates a 'checked knowledge', a knowledge traversed by a rigorous hole, whose constitutive function needs to be acknowledged and conceptualised in view of the possible emergence of a new beginning.[3]

The seminars that Sharon Kivland and I constructed for the IGRS programme were informed by the position that Dany Nobus and I had developed in the text quoted above, and by Kivland's engagement with psychoanalysis in her own writing and works of art. The seminars were heralded by an 'exhibition' of the work of David Bate, Márta Csabai, Bill Furlong, Polly Gould, Lucy Harrison, Frances Hegarty, Jaspar Joseph-Lester, Mark Lewis, Forbes Morlock,

---

2 Catherine Grant, 'Hal Foster in conversation with Catherine Grant', *Immediations*, 2: 1 (2008), 105.

3 Dany Nobus and Malcolm Quinn, *Knowing Nothing, Staying Stupid: Elements for a Psychoanalytic Epistemology* (London: Routledge, 2005), 209.

Simon Morris, Liz Pavey, Phoebe von Held, and Sarah Wood, held at the IGRS for one night on 24 November 2006 as part of the opening conference of the Psychoanalysis and the Arts and Humanities Network, entitled 'Freud in translation, Freud in transition'. The direction that individual seminars took was determined by the artists, analysts and academics who elected to take part in them. However, throughout the series of seminars, our choice of speakers and themes was shaped by an initial decision to address Lacan's seminar XVII *The Other Side of Psychoanalysis* which, until the publication of Russell Grigg's translation in 2007,[4] was only available in samizdat English versions. *The Other Side of Psychoanalysis* is in fact the title given to it by Jacques-Alain Miller, Lacan having stated in his first lecture that he intended to call that seminar *La Psychanalyse à l'envers* [*Psychoanalysis Upside-Down*].

Seminar XVII is best known for its presentation of Lacan's four discourses of the master, the university, the hysteric and the analyst. The discourses are four forms of social bond. In Lacanian psychoanalysis, they stand between language, from which discourse is built, and speech, in which discourse is expressed. I would argue, however, that the single most important element of Seminar XVII is not the four discourses, but the manner in which Seminar XVII affirms the idea of psychoanalysis as a social bond forged by the desire of the analyst.

It was this affirmation of psychoanalysis as a social bond that enabled Sharon Kivland and I to begin addressing the relation between art practice, psychoanalysis and academia taken up by the IGRS network. Recent debates on art and the social bond, some with their roots in the time of Seminar XVII, could then be examined alongside the social link established between the analyst and the analysand. On several occasions we staged this 'side-by-sideness' of the artist and the analyst quite literally in the social space of an academic seminar. It should be emphasised that our intention in doing this was not, to paraphrase a recent publication, to provide art and psychoanalysis with an 'academic face'.[5] We realised that beginning with Seminar XVII would necessarily leave out much of what passes for psychoanalytically informed commentary on art, and we would

---

4 Jacques Lacan, *The Other Side of Psychoanalysis: The Seminar of Jacques Lacan Book XVII* [*Le Séminaire. Livre XVII. L'envers de la psychanalyse, 1969–1970* [1998]], ed. Jacques-Alain Miller, trans. with notes by Russell Grigg (New York and London: W. W. Norton 2007).

5 Louise Braddock and Michael Lacewing, *The Academic Face of Psychoanalysis* (London: Routledge, 2007).

therefore have to situate the relation of art and psychoanalysis on the premise of psychoanalysis as unique social bond, taking a specific place in the four discourses.

Our first seminar, 'Art, psychoanalysis and the four discourses', held on 15 January 2007, introduced the four discourses of the master, the university, the hysteric and the analyst as a framework for discussion, using the example of an experiment undertaken at Central Saint Martin's College of Art in London in the late Sixties, which was concurrent with Seminar XVII. In this experiment, known as 'The A Course', art students were introduced to a bit of 'bare life' under conditions of dissimulated mastery, by being locked in a room with a few bits and pieces and instructed to produce something — in other words, to become the agents of freedom and knowledge.

On 30 March 2007, Phoebe von Held introduced the issue of dreams, dreaming and dream interpretation, in relation to our reading of Freud's Lecture 29 'Revision of the theory of dreams' in his *New Introductory Lectures* of 1932.[6] She went on to discuss this in relation to Diderot's fictional dialogue *Le Rêve de d'Alembert* [*D'Alembert's Dream*] (written in 1796), which seems to prophetically prefigure many later 'scientific' findings. Von Held took up the emotional and physiological basis of dreaming in relation to neurology and psychoanalysis, with reference to the work of the psychoanalytically oriented neuropsychologist Mark Solms, whom she had interviewed regarding Diderot's text. She introduced us to a section of an animated film script she was in the process of preparing. We then took part in a reading of an imaginary conversation incorporating Diderot's fictive conversation between *philosophe* D'Alembert, *salonnière* Julie Lespinasse, and the doctor Bordeu, incorporating sections of her interview with Mark Solms. Finally we viewed a short animated extract from this project.

On 30 April 2007, the artist Lucy Harrison and the architectural historian Tim Martin spoke on recent projects: the first was an unusual community/public realm art work; the second was a reflection on the subjective relation between viewer and work of art in the work of Robert Smithson. Harrison described her work with residents on Canvey Island, the establishing of a social club, founded on the presence of the artist, yet continuing in her absence. Martin

6 Sigmund Freud, 'New introductory lectures on psycho-analysis', SE 22 (1933 [1932]).

emphasised the retrospective reading of Smithson's later work in the light of drawings Smithson had made as a young artist.

On 4 June 2007, we continued our discussion of the social bond, considering the gift as a tie that binds in demanding reciprocity, placing giver and receiver within a circuit of exchange. The gift produces obligations, according to Marcel Mauss,[7] and a gift is seldom extended without implying a demand for something in return. The gift is more than the object offered, and what is given — its value — is calculated by both parties in the exchange. In an analysis, as Lacan argues, the analysand may offer the analyst a gift of words; in love, one offers the other what one does not have. Forbes Morlock presented 'Freud and the gift of flowers', a reflection on some Freudian themes in which, for a while, dreams and flowers seemed indistinguishable. Becky Shaw contributed to the analysis of the place of the artist in forms of consensus and general will. Following the award of an international art prize, she was commissioned to make a new work for a centre for people with physical disabilities. The difficult circumstances that unfolded presented an extraordinary opportunity to explore the contemporary expectation for artists to deliver public good. Drawing on Jacques Derrida's *Given Time*,[8] the work, in lecture form, explored the impossibility of the artistic gift in the context of the use of art to ameliorate social ills. At the same time, the work questioned the artist's role as social critic.

On 15 October 2007, psychoanalyst and writer Vincent Dachy and artist John Timberlake led the discussion, under the title 'Figured landscapes: positionality, picturing and the social bond', which introduced the four discourses from an analyst's point of view, alongside an artistic engagement with landscape and the sublime. In this seminar, the divide between the use of psychoanalytic terms within a general interpretative scheme in the arts and humanities, on the one hand, and a Lacanian psychoanalytic ethic on the other, became clearly marked, generating an important discussion that was developed further in the final seminar.

On 19 November 2007, in our final seminar, Polly Gould described the use of the spoken word in her work as an enactment of a 'talking cure' and a testing of the social situation. Gould is an artist whose work engages with the speaking subject, voice, power and desire,

---

7 Marcel Mauss, *The Gift: Form and Reason for Exchange in Archaic Societies* [*Essai sur le don. Forme et raison de l'échange dans les sociétés archaïques* [1950]], trans. by W. D. Halls, (London: Routledge, 2001).

8 Jacques Derrida, *Given Time I: Counterfeit Money* [*Donner le temps* [1991]], trans. by Peggy Kamuf (Chicago: Chicago University Press, 1994).

presented as performance lectures or performance video works. In the seminar, she discussed Hannah Arendt's shyness at speaking in public, as the central motif of a subtle and multi-faceted address to these concepts. The psychoanalyst Michael Kennedy then made a presentation dealing with the characteristics of the desire of the analyst. Kennedy's rigorous account of the analyst's discourse made a fitting end to our seminar series because he stressed the importance of the analyst's discourse as a unique form of social bond. In *Television*, Jacques Lacan states that 'what I call the analytic discourse is the social bond determined by the practice of an analysis. It derives its value from its being placed amongst the most fundamental of the bonds which remain viable for us.'[9] Crucially here, Lacan is arguing that the value of psychoanalysis derives from being placed among other discourses. Its uniqueness stems from its value being derived precisely in this way and not according to criteria of intellectual tradition, conceptual innovation or discursive cohesion. It is not the function of psychoanalysis to translate other discourses, so much as to disclose the possibilities and terrors that follow from being 'placed amongst' discourse, as Lacan puts it. This means proceeding to the point where all the possibilities of intellectual mastery have been ceded within a situation where the analyst knows nothing, thus allowing another discourse — that of the analysand — to be fully present. Throughout this seminar series, we have sought to reproduce the characteristics of being 'placed amongst' discourse. We did this by staging a series of encounters in which the participants were invited to be faithful to a psychoanalytic ethic that discloses a point of impossibility in the supposed 'difficulty' of translation.

---

9   Jacques Lacan, *Television* [*Télévision* [1974]], ed. Joan Copjec, trans. by Denis Hollier, Rosalind Krauss, Annette Michelson (New York: W. W. Norton, 1990), 14.

2. Between Two Worlds[1]

Mark Nash

In this chapter I will set some pointers for this book's section on psychoanalysis and the arts — inevitably my remarks will extend to cover the humanities more generally. I am a curator and an academic. I run a department for curating contemporary art at the Royal College of Art, London.[2] Previously, I was more involved in film history, theory and production (and I have recently published a collection of essays dating mainly from that time).[3] There are three aspects of this relationship between the arts and psychoanalysis to discuss: cultural, academic/intellectual and personal/clinical.

We are all aware of the wide-ranging influence of psychoanalysis on Western art and culture in the 20th century. The earliest element of this was Freud's work on dreams and the notion of the unconscious,

---

1   This essay is developed from a conference paper which included an extract from a film that gives this chapter its title, the implied ambivalence of which is extended here to the relationship of art and psychoanalysis, and the difficulties attendant in attempting to position oneself in relation to that dyad.

2   As the director of a curating course I am occasionally asked — usually by parents whose children have elected to this relatively obscure profession — what exactly is a curator? Curating is essential to the presentation and circulation of contemporary art, while not itself being regarded as an art practice, except of course when undertaken by artists! This is a rather paradoxical state of affairs. I mutter something about the origin of the term in the word *curare* [to care for] as well as the overtones of incarceration in the older term 'keeper'. There is a semantic parallel between caring for objects within an institution, but at the same time keeping them prisoner, and the duty of care one has for one's students despite their adult status. This is leading us at CCA (Curating Contemporary Art Department at the RCA) to reflections on the psychodynamics of curatorial practice.

3   Mark Nash, *Screen Theory Culture* (London: Palgrave, 2008); hereafter STC.

which found its way into surrealist art, mainstream cinema and popular culture. Some people, like my then younger self, discovered modern art through the work of Salvador Dalí, Max Ernst and (in my own case at least) British surrealists such as Dorothea Tanning. In one way or another this art attempted to represent unconscious processes, presenting erotically charged scenarios, without incurring the censorship that would be applied to more realistic representations. The clinic was represented in Alfred Hitchcock's emblematic *Spellbound* (1945), with a dream sequence choreographed by Dalí himself, and this fascination with the figure of the analyst continued in post-war cinema, including the avant-garde experiment of Yvonne Rainer's *Journeys from Berlin/1971* (1980) with film theorist Annette Michelson playing the roles of both analyst and interrogator.

My sense is that this interest on the part of artists and filmmakers has declined somewhat over the years, partly no doubt as psychoanalytic ideas themselves became part of popular culture, and because more recent developments — such as the Lacanian school — did not lend themselves to such graphic visual representations. One might argue that this is in general a good thing and analysts can just get on with professional matters outside the public eye and intellectual fashion.

The second issue I shall discuss is the intellectual and academic aspect, by which I am referring to the post-1968 explosion of structuralist theory in the UK. Structuralism, semiotics, psychoanalysis and Althusserian Marxism began to enter the vocabulary of the arts and humanities during this period and within ten years they had transformed critical and academic study. This was — as Perry Anderson pointed out in his 1968 *New Left Review* essay 'Components of the national culture'[4] — part of the process by which the UK 'caught up' with developments in philosophy and critical theory on what we used to call 'the continent'. The first wave of translation and publication happened on the fringes of academia — Stephen Heath, Colin MacCabe and Christopher Prendergast's *Signs of the Times* from 1971,[5] Stephen Bann's translations of Barthes

---

4 Perry Anderson, 'Components of a national culture', *New Left Review* no. 50 (July–August 1968), 3–57.

5 Colin MacCabe, Stephen Heath and Christopher Prendergast (eds.), *Signs of the Times: Introductory Readings in Textual Semiotics* (Cambridge: Granta, 1971). Structuralism is widely thought to have entered Anglophone academia through a 1966 conference at Johns Hopkins University, Baltimore, to which Lacan, Derrida and other French intellectuals were invited, and where Derrida delivered a lecture, 'Structure, sign, and play in the discourse of the human sciences' (subsequently included in *Writing and Difference*), which established him in the English-speaking world.

and Russian formalism,⁶ or the film journal *Screen*, with which I was associated from the early 1970s. Film was, so to speak, a Trojan horse through which these developments could enter the UK. Film studies did not really exist yet as a discipline of academic study at the level of higher education, so there were no orthodoxies to be challenged there. The visual arts followed somewhat later — it took a while for them to challenge their protective academies. This is also a relatively familiar history; the main point to note is the uneven development in the way different disciplines embraced this structuralist revolution, with the visual arts putting up particular resistance. With the help of Mary Kelly and Victor Burgin, however, we produced an issue of *Screen* concerned with extending film theory to the visual arts.⁷

It was also a very muddled and confusing time, theoretically and philosophically, at least in the Anglophone world. Twenty years of a thinker's life would be published in translation simultaneously, making it a challenge to tease out the chronological development in their thinking. Lacan, for example, was initially only present in English in the form of the mirror stage article and 'The function of language in psychoanalysis', which were included in Anthony Wilden's *System and Structure*.⁸ Freud was a different matter, given the availability of Strachey's Standard Edition translation. Over the years, what started as a ferment of disorientating new ideas became incorporated into the academy, and formed a new orthodoxy right across the humanities. It is one of the challenges of collections like this, therefore, to examine this history and the present 'conjuncture' — as we used to call it.

I will now turn my attention to the third area, that of the personal/clinical. As someone who was in analysis in the 1970s and again in the 1990s, my experience of this period is inevitably coloured by my experience as an analysand. Being in analysis, one was acutely aware

---

6   For instance, Stephen Bann and J. E. Bowlt (eds.), *Russian Formalism: A Collection of Articles and Texts in Translation* (Edinburgh: Scottish Academic Press, 1973).

7   *Screen*, vol. 21 no. 1 (Spring 1980). Alas, there was no great enthusiasm amongst the core *Screen* readership for this project to be continued within its pages.

8   Jacques Lacan, 'The Mirror Stage as formative of the function of the I as revealed in psychoanalytic experience' ['Le stade du miroir. Théorie d'un moment structurant et génétique de la constitution de la réalité, conçu en relation avec l'expérience et la doctrine psychanalytique'], communication au 14e Congrès psychanalytique international, Marienbad, *International Journal of Psychoanalysis* [1937], trans. by Alan Sheridan in *Écrits: A Selection* (W. W. Norton: New York, 1977); Anthony Wilden, *System and Structure – Essays in Communication and Exchange* (London: Tavistock), 1972.

that most of the people making arguments about psychoanalysis were not concerned with the area of clinical practice. What was being developed instead was a domain of theory and criticism that adopted a psychoanalytic vocabulary and often treated art objects — film, visual arts — as though they were patients. The critics placed themselves in what they imagined was the place of the analyst and put the text or work of art on the couch. Here is my much-younger self in an essay on the work of the Danish film director Carl Dreyer:

> Some representation of absence always circulates in the Dreyer-text, within the frame there is always some kind of barrier, something which bars access to the fictional world, whether it is a reduplication of framing as in *Michael*, a dark halo surrounding the lit scene, or the 'barred' image as in *Day of Wrath* [...] or some articulation of the two as in *Gertrud*.[9]

It was relatively easy to deploy some basic Lacanian concepts in a seductive demonstration of the ceaseless circulation of signification. And it was equally easy to demonstrate, before queer theory, that 'it is bisexuality which constitutes the trouble of the text and generates and organises its complete set of displacements and exchanges' (STC, 82).

If one looks back again at these arguments (and I am very grateful for Naomi Segal's insistence on this point), one is reminded that the operation was intended to be developed in the opposite direction, where the text took the place of the analyst and the reader the analysand. To take one example from Fredric Jameson's essay 'Imaginary and symbolic in Lacan':

> What is wanted is not only an instrument of analysis which will maintain the incommensurability of the subject with its narrative representations — or in other words between the Imaginary and the Symbolic in general — but also one which will articulate the discontinuities within the various 'representatives' themselves, not only those that Benveniste has taught us to observe between the first and second pronouns on the one hand and the third on the other, but also, and above all, that, stressed by Lacan, between the nominative and accusative forms of the first person itself.[10]

---

9   Mark Nash, 'Notes on the Dreyer text', first published in *Dreyer* (London: BFI, 1975), reprinted in STC, 80.

10 Frederic Jameson, 'Imaginary and symbolic in Lacan: Marxism, psychoanalytic criticism, and the problem of the subject', in *Literature and Psychoanalysis*, ed. Shoshana Felman (Baltimore: Johns Hopkins University Press, 1982), 381. This volume had originally appeared as a double issue of *Yale French Studies* nos. 55–6 (1977).

I had attempted exactly this project in my early writing on Dreyer but was not able to deal with the paradox which Jameson goes on to elaborate so elegantly:

> My own feeling is that you cannot deny the possibility of an adequate representation of the subject in narrative on the one hand, and then continue to search for a more satisfactory category for such representation on the other: if this is so, then the notion of some relationship — still to be defined — between the subject and this or that individual character or 'point of view' should be replaced by the study of those character systems into which the subject is fully inserted (Jameson, 80).

This points to the double bind that cinephiles such as myself created for themselves. On the one hand a deconstruction of the place of the subject in narrative and art cinema but on the other an attempt to 'read' that disruption in terms of an authorial code. Cinephilia involved a deep attachment to the very processes of that dissolution, an immersion in a cinematic unconscious, if you will, while at the same time it needed to submit those experiences to a secondary revision of theory and criticism in structuralist auteur theory.

This form of literary or rather filmic exegesis was totally appropriate to the time, but I would not want to argue for its return. The arguments deployed were too strong, too convincing and there was rarely pause to ask the key question from the point of view of a scientific methodology — how could this be disproved, what counter arguments could one make? Psychoanalytic ideas had, so to speak, become part of a belief system.

However, I find the relative lack of interest in psychoanalysis in contemporary curating and curatorial studies rather striking. Whereas psychoanalysis entered film studies relatively early, in art criticism and practice one might argue it never really developed such a momentum. One can of course point to analytically informed writers such as Adrian Stokes or a generation of now-established artists like Mary Kelly or Victor Burgin, who developed dialogues with Lacan or Freud in their work. And one would not necessarily want to encourage younger artists to develop psychoanalytic *content* in their work since, as Burgin and Kelly have already demonstrated, it becomes something *other* in the field of visual representation. For example, the introduction to the installation 'Post-Partum Document – The Complete Work (1973–79)' — as shown in the Generali Foundation Vienna in 1998 — comprises four framed baby-vests inscribed with geometric diagrams representing the processes of intersubjectivity according to Lacan. The viewer does not need, and indeed is not given, a Lacanian frame within which to read these diagrams; however, the language that the work establishes through the form of its installation connects it clearly with conceptual art. One could argue that it is precisely this othering of psychoanalysis that is one of the work's most important features.

Rather than consider the lessons that can be drawn from artists' engagement with the language and concepts of psychoanalysis, it might be useful to explore what lessons one can draw from the methodology of the clinic, both for the way art is taught and for the way art itself operates. There is a long history of art being used as a therapeutic activity — for instance, the 1970s London-based anti-psychiatry project of David Cooper and R. D. Laing,[11] and an equal fascination with work by untaught, *art brut* or outsider artists (recently, 'Inner Worlds Outside' at the Whitechapel Art Gallery London in 2006), some of whom might be categorised as mentally ill and therefore their art as 'therapeutic'. There has also been a shift of interest amongst artists themselves in the direction of collaborative activities, ones that are process-based and may involve community action or engagement).[12]

Slavoj Žižek refers to this split between the theory and the clinic as follows: 'Today one often mentions how the reference to psychoanalysis in cultural studies and the psychoanalytic clinic supplement each other — cultural studies lacks the real of clinic experience while the clinic lacks the broader critico-historical perspective'.[13] Each of these approaches, Žižek continues, 'should work on its limitation from within its horizon — not by relying on the other to fill up its lack'.

My experience of this split- or double-consciousness, from within the clinic and within critical and historical studies, was reflected in a couple of film productions that I was involved with either as director or producer/writer. The first, a short film (*Between Two Worlds*) which I directed in 1993, was concerned with both the content and the location of psychoanalysis. What happens in the analytic session and where does it take place: the consulting room, the extended conscious and

---

11 R. D. Laing was the subject of a film and installation by Luke Fowler at the Serpentine Gallery in 2009.

12 For example, the Park Fiction Collective which worked with a group of local residents in Hamburg St. Pauli on a proposal for a park project which they presented in the form of a resource centre at Documenta11 (2002).

13 Slavoj Žižek, 'Object a in social links', in *Jacques Lacan and the Other Side of Psychoanalysis*, ed. Justin Clemens and Russell Grigg, (Durham, NC: Duke University Press, 2006), 108.

unconscious of the analysand? The narrative concerned a series of psychoanalytic sessions, in which Graham, a young analysand played by Jason Durr (later of *Heartbeat* fame), presents his analyst with a series of desultory comments about his sexual ambivalence. These sessions are intercut with scenes which could be read as flashbacks and which have some kind of sexual charge — for example, chance meetings in London Fields, a flower shop. The film (and the analysis) reaches no conclusion — the sessions are terminated by the sudden death of the analyst.

I was also irritated by what I took to be incorrect representations of the Freudian consulting room — in dominant narrative film, the analyst and analysand are often placed in such a way that there could be an exchange of looks, registered, say, in a shot-reverse-shot, regardless of the fact that this was exactly the disposition that Freud felt impeded the transference relation.[14] In my enthusiasm to set that record straight I downplayed the role of the aesthetics of suture — the way the editing of the shots themselves creates a subject-position for the viewer. My film gives the viewer the impression that they are witness to a psychoanalytic process, despite the fact that for Freud this is not possible: 'The talk of which psychoanalytic treatment consists brooks no listener; it cannot be demonstrated [...] Nothing takes place in a psychoanalytic treatment but an interchange of words between the patient and the analyst'.[15]

The second, a film on Frantz Fanon that I made with Isaac Julien in 1996 (*Frantz Fanon – Black Skin White Mask*), was concerned amongst other things with an insistence upon Fanon's clinical work being in a tradition close to what was to become the movement we now know as anti-psychiatry (rather than any more-psychoanalytic tradition). In the film, we reference Fanon's development of institutional psychotherapy, which he had studied with François Tosquelles, the founder of the Clinique de La Borde, for the North African context.[16]

---

14   '[Freud] invites [his patients] to lie down in a comfortable attitude on a sofa, while he himself sits on a chair behind them outside their field of vision', Sigmund Freud, 'Freud's psychoanalytic procedure' ['Die Freudsche Psychoanalytische Methode' [1904]], in *The Standard Edition of the Complete Psychological Works of Sigmund Freud*, 24 vols., ed. and trans. by James Strachey et al. (London: The Hogarth Press and the Institute of Psycho-analysis, 1953–74), vol. 7 (1953), 250. Hereafter abbreviated SE, followed by volume number.

15   Sigmund Freud, 'Lecture 1 Introduction', in his *Introductory Lectures on Psychoanalysis* [*Vorlesungen zur Einführung in die Psychoanalyse* [1916]], SE vol. 15 (1961), 17.

16   For example, see the special issue of *History of Psychiatry*, vol. 7 part 4 no. 28 (December 1996): 'Unsung heroes — Frantz Fanon his life and work'; see also Mark Nash with Isaac Julien, 'Frantz Fanon as film', STC, 185–96.

Fanon established social spaces with which the patients could identify, for instance a *café maure*.

Finally, I will focus on ways of exploring this relation between the clinic and art practice. In the late 1990s, at the Centre for Freudian Analysis and Research [CFAR] offices and bookshop on Haverstock Hill in North London, Sharon Kivland, Danuza Machado and others set up a series of seminars and discussions to rethink the relation of art and psychoanalysis. A series of group shows, using the rooms of this Victorian house, presented exhibitions that would not be unfamiliar to visitors to the smaller East London galleries in Hoxton or Vyner Street today. On the other hand, the choice of location — the CFAR building — and the choice of titles, some of which point directly to Freudian or Lacanian themes, presented a theoretical and cultural frame at odds with prevailing art-world orthodoxies. Exhibition titles ranged from 'There is no sexual relation' to 'Disturbance of memory on the Acropolis' (both 1999). In the latter exhibition, artists were 'invited to respond to the themes of Freud's text, to ideas of fraternal and filial relations, deferral and anxiety, memory and its (re)constructions'.[17]

Their curatorial strategy was to present art works as a series of objects functioning 'as if' they could give meaning. The emphasis on 'as if' set them aside from some conventional approaches to curating. To risk a broad generalization, most publicly-funded galleries have carefully calibrated interpretative regimes, from the design of the exhibition to wall texts, guided tours, short guides, catalogues and so on. The aim of these interpretative regimes is to educate and inform the audience, although it can often veer into forms of discursive domination. The approach which Kivland and Machado developed could be compared with exhibitions which critique this institutional regime, for example the 2008 exhibition at the Barbican Centre in London, 'Martian Museum of Terrestrial Art. Mission: to interpret and understand contemporary art', curated by Francesco Manacorda. Here, works of art were presented 'as if' they had been collated by an alien curator concerned to make sense of the human artefacts presented!

This attempt to explore psychoanalytic ideas curatorially at CFAR was complemented by an attempt to rethink the relation to a work of art as equivalent to that of the transference relationship. The work of art took the place of the analyst, and the aesthetic encounter was about the desire of the painting, the exhibition, the curator. What

---

17 Sharon Kivland Curatorial Projects, http://pagesperso-orange.fr/lightsculpture/sharon/curatorial.html (accessed 20 September 2012).

do these images want? What is my place in their discourse? How do I connect my desire with theirs? — and so on. Such explorations have continued in arenas provided by institutions like the Freud Museum but, sadly, have made less impact in the mainstream art and curatorial world.[18]

Kivland and Machado's contribution to this network is an insistence on the difference which art practice represents, through attention to the structure of the seminar and conference form itself. The role of art in this position is to do with the *interruption* it can make in critical academic discourse. (This understanding of the function of art is completely at odds with the tendency in the academy to assimilate art practice into a process of research, a tendency that has been particularly successful in producing not very good art: by this I mean art which identifies the academic horizon — to use Žižek's term — as its own, rather than forcing a confrontation between discourses and practices.)

There are perhaps formal aspects of the process of the clinic itself, particularly the psychic interruption in the subject, facilitated by the Lacanian short session, which could be explored further in relation to this notion of art as critical interruption. We are all familiar with the notions of interruption as developed in Soviet montage cinema and Brechtian theatre — both montage and the Brechtian alienation effect foreground formal aspects of the two media, their editing and staging. They also require, or aim to produce, a different kind of spectator, one who is able to make intellectual as well as emotional judgements during the course of the play or film. Some experimental theatre and performance art, for instance the work of New York-based The Wooster Group, continues this aesthetic. Their website blurb puts it succinctly:

> Wooster Group theatre pieces are constructed as assemblages of juxtaposed elements: radical staging of both modern and classic texts, found materials, films and videos, dance and movement, multi-track scoring, and an architectonic approach to theatre design.[19]

There are several difficulties in making this more than a simple formal analogy. To the extent that the work of post-World War Two experimental theatre and avant-garde cinema against the dominance of narrative continuity, psychological realism and so on, has been superseded by a general postmodern aesthetic of quotation, it is

---

18   Danuza Machado, '"A little object": Danuza Machado interviewed by Alex Potts', AN Visual Arts, September 1997, 12.

19   www.thewoostergroup.org/twg/about2.html (accessed 20 September 2012).

difficult to argue that these works can develop a critique through such aesthetic devices which have really become the norm. Nevertheless it would be worth examining the theatrical lexicon involved in the performance of analysis itself to see whether there are pertinent connections to be made to theatre and art.

The theory and practice of curating as putting *meaning into circulation*, keeping meaning moving, might bear comparison with the work of psychoanalysis. One might give some simple examples by referencing two major retrospectives in London public galleries: Ed Ruscha at the Hayward and John Baldessari at Tate Modern.[20] Both are important artists; however, my question is whether the simple chronological method of display, whose aim is to show how an artist's work develops, is really the best approach. Why not develop exhibition strategies where this narrative is abandoned or thrown into question? Michel Foucault's essay 'What is an author?' which attempts to ask the question 'who or what is speaking?' was available in English from 1970,[21] yet exhibition practice continues to insist on the artist/author as a full subject as if those psychoanalytically-informed questions had never been put.

We now live in a society in which everything is cultural — the notion of art as relation, as process, increasingly replaces that of art as object. A mantra of a relational aesthetics is often used to describe this shift from object to process.[22] However, this is merely a formal description, obscuring the question of what that process is about or engages with. The idea of the 'work' involved in the work of art has largely been lost. Against the notion of the work of art as currency in the market or formalist procedure or process, I am thinking in the opposite sense — one Heidegger explores in his discussion of the origin of the work of art involving a complex social bond.[23] Unless

20 'Ed Ruscha: Fifty Years of Painting', Hayward Gallery, 14 October 2009–10 January 2010; 'John Baldessari: Pure Beauty', Tate Modern 14 October 2009–10 January 2010.

21 Michel Foucault, 'What is an author?' ['Qu'est-ce qu'un auteur?' [1969]] (*Screen* 20, 1, (1979), 13–34.

22 Nicolas Bourriaud, *Relational Aesthetics* [*L'Esthétique relationnelle* [1998]], trans. by Simon Pleasance and Fronza Woods with the participation of Mathieu Copeland (Dijon: Presses du réel), 2002. His more recent writing on the altermodern (for example Nicolas Bourriaud 'Altermodern – manifesto', www.tate.org.uk/whats-on/tate-britain/exhibition/altermodern/explain-altermodern/altermodern-explainedmanifesto (accessed 21 September 2012) continues this formalist project.

23 Martin Heidegger, 'The origin of the work of art' ['Der Ursprung der Kunstwerkes' [1935–6]], trans. by Albert Hofstadter, in *The Continental Aesthetics Reader*, ed. C. Cazeaux (London: Routledge, 2000), 81.

this bond can be renewed, says Heidegger, the work of art no longer exists as such — it might as well be a sack of potatoes or a bag of coal in the cellar! Heidegger's reflections pose a challenge for my 'two worlds' of psychoanalysis and art. How to explore that complex social bond, while at the same time accounting for its psychic effects and currency?

3. Transcript

Sharon Kivland

I will begin with a brief introduction to one of my works on translation, taken from *A Reader* (2003).[1] It recalled an exchange I had with several French friends on the exact translation of the word 'cocksucker', of which you will be delighted to know there are at least 19 delightful variations in French, and it is almost always feminine. The book accompanying the exhibition, a group show at DOMOBAAL Gallery in London, included the above correspondence – notes really – in which my dear friends, two art critics, an artist, a curator and a musician struggled to understand the word and what I was asking of them. Other works in my repertoire also take up the problem of slipping between languages and the curious shifts in meaning that come from translating but there is no room to discuss them here. Brought up in a German nursery, so to speak, I came to England when I attained the age of reason (seven years is usually considered to be the age at which a child has developed the capacity for reasoned judgment and to be responsible for her acts; in truth, I must admit that I was six and so possibly not reasonable at all) and I now live in France, where I must translate my thoughts into words daily and watch people's faces grimace unconsciously as they try to understand me. My son, who moves effortlessly between tongues, even in a single sentence, ceaselessly corrects me. However, I understand all his *gros mots* (or rather, I understand that he is saying something improper) and try very hard not to use them, for they have little resonance for me as improper terms. At times, I mistranslate what he is saying; I hear it incorrectly, and admonish him unfairly. When we are watching

---

1 Lucy Harrison, Sharon Kivland, Nina Papaconstantinou, *A Reader* (London: DOMOBAAL EDITIONS, 2003).

French television together, I often ask what this or that word or phrase means, and he almost always replies that he does not know.

As a visiting fellow at the IGRS, I began a series of text works on the glass walls of room 269. This chapter reflects what I said, so confidently at the opening conference of the Psychoanalysis and the Arts and Humanities Network held in November 2007. You may have read the notes I made at that time to accompany an exhibition that only lasted one evening, a collection of works that addressed a certain failure of agency, works in which language was inadequate or hysterical, or reduced to discourse markers.

In the third edition of *The Interpretation of Dreams* (1911), Freud adds the observation: 'It is impossible to translate a dream into a foreign language'.[2] And in a letter to his French translator, Samuel Jankélévitch, Freud states that his dream book appears untranslatable to him because of its dream texts, and his feeling that should a translation be done, it would probably scare French people away from further reading.[3] For Freud, one might say it was not so much a matter of finding a vocabulary in a foreign language that would be close to the original, translated with precision; rather, the question was whether interpretation as a method would work in a different tongue. In another letter to Jankélévitch, Freud writes: 'so much depends on the wording that the translator would have to be an analyst himself and replace the material I gave with new material from his own experience' (*LoC*: letter of 28 June 1920). *Transcript* is a project of impossible interpretation and translation, taking texts *à la lettre* and *avant la lettre*.

1. Walbaum, Caslon, Garamond

der Traum ist die Erfüllung eines Wunsches
a dream is the fulfilment of a wish
le rêve est un accomplissement de souhait

---

2   Sigmund Freud, *The Interpretation of Dreams* (*Die Traumdeutung* [1900]), in *The Standard Edition of the Complete Psychological Works of Sigmund Freud*, 24 vols., ed. and trans. by James Strachey *et al.* (London: The Hogarth Press and the Institute of Psycho-analysis, 1953–74), 99, n.1.

3   Freud, letter of 13 April 1911 (Freud Collection, Library of Congress); all subsequent references from this archive will be given in the text, prefixed *LoC*. These are cited in Lydia Marinelli and Andreas Mayer, *Dreaming by the Book. Freud's* The Interpretation of Dreams *and the History of the Psychoanalytic Movement* [*Träume nach Freud. Die 'Traumdeutung' und die Geschichte der psychoanalytischen Bewegung* [2002]], trans. by Susan Fairfield (New York: Other Press, 2003).

I began with the dream book, a book of interpretation, but I did not stay with it, finding instead a detour – one that was far from a sublimation, yet content or meaning disappeared, indeed were veiled by form, by colour, in reflection. I cannot explain my detour, but it may have been determined by the editions in my modest Freud library at the time. Looking back, I cannot come up with any other reason, but then, I would say that, wouldn't I? To admit the turning towards – or turning away – would carry the significance it now bears because of my insistence on the lack of meaning. Jacques Lacan writes 'the most significant dream would be the dream that has been completely forgotten, one about which the subject couldn't possibly say anything.'[4] My failure to explain draws attention to my act. In fact, I frequently cannot say why I have done something or why I have made certain decisions (about which I *am* certain), but one becomes more adept at sounding as though one knows why. It is often unconvincing to the listener, of course, who may not hesitate in taking the artist to task.

2. Bernard MT Condensed, Futura, Didot

die Objektfindung ist eigentlich eine Wiederfindung
the finding of an object is in fact a refinding of it
trouver l'objet sexuel n'est, en somme, que le retrouver

The dream book was set aside in favour of *Three Essays on the Theory of Sexuality* (1905), in which – as most of you are aware – Freud argues that 'perversion' (may I translate that as 'turning away') is present in all of us, and that our libidinal path begins in early childhood.[5] My English edition was the A. A. Brill translation, which has been criticized for its imperfections, so I took up Strachey's translation instead. Brill also translated *The Interpretation of Dreams*, somewhat to Freud's dissatisfaction, for since he did not send final proofs to Freud there were 'several small misunderstandings' (*LoC*: Freud letter to Brill of 22 January 1924). I do not know how good my French translation is. I read my English translation, stopping at what my students might call a 'good quote' (even annotating

---

4 Jacques Lacan, *The Seminar of Jacques Lacan. Book I. Freud's Papers on Technique. 1953–1954* (*Le Séminaire I* [1975]), ed. Jacques-Alain Miller, trans. by John Forrester (New York: W. W. Norton, 1991).

5 Sigmund Freud, *Three Essays on the Theory of Sexuality* (*Drei Abhandlungen zur Sexualtheorie* [1905], in *On Sexuality*, ed. and trans. by James Strachey *et al.* (The Pelican Freud Library, Harmondsworth: Penguin, 1977), 33–87. I did not have the *Standard Edition* to hand.

the margins or underlining), then switched to my French version, skimming, stopping at what seemed to be the same phrase, rendered differently in another tongue. My book, a Gallimard paperback from 1962 and translated by Dr Blanche Reverchon-Jouve, a doctor and psychoanalyst, is set in a particularly attractive version of Didot (or possibly a font from the Bodoni family). I then read through the German text, barely remembering the language of my childhood, which I stopped speaking at the age of six. If the phrase seemed more or less the same, but with a subtle variation, I would select it, and I have ended up with six, though there could be more. My 'ear' may not have been acute enough. I am uncertain if I can really hear the difference in meaning, the tiny shifts in reading and interpretation. When the lettering is in place, its look, its variation in colour, its assumption of different form, seem to perform, to *do something*, if I may make that claim.

3. Bodoni, Goudy Old Style, Elegant Garamond

die Objektwahl wird aber zunächst in der Vorstellung vollzogen
it is in the world of ideas, however, that the choice of an object is
accomplished at first
mais le choix de l'objet s'accomplit d'abord sous la forme de représentations

I then worked through a book of fonts, matching words to their representations. This was a fantasy on my part, to be sure, but nonetheless it did its work. Graphic details of font, kerning, leading and size do matter; they affect our reading (even the weight of a book in the hands or the way the binding allows a book to open entirely flat with no loss in the gutter has effects). The phrases become *blazons*, like a specialized language (in this case, the specialized language of psychoanalysis), like a formal description that is not defined by a picture, and yet constructs an image. I took my phrases, German, French, English, to Pascal, who turns them into material objects, vinyl letters. His small company, 'Super Victor', specializes in signs, making computer-cut lettering among other things, and he takes pride in his work. He does not read English or German, so we worked through many corrections and spoke a great dealt about translation and interpretation. The phrases had to correspond with what their physical location would be: there is a very long window in the middle, a smaller window to its left, with a small window to the right, where usually, but not always, the original German text is applied. The length of each glass section and of each phrase determine the height of the characters, their point size. Some of the fonts I chose he did not have, so I had to select others and was absurdly anxious about it. Sometimes it was hard to decide which font to use as a substitute for the one I had set my heart on, only to discover Pascal – even in his role as 'Super Victor' – could not meet my demand or desire.

4. Andale Mono, Modern no. 20, Hoefler

das Höchste und das Niedrigste hängen in der Sexualität überall am innigsten aneinander
the highest and the lowest are always closest to each other in the sphere of sexuality
ce qu'il y a de plus élevé et ce qu'il y a de plus bas, dans la sexualité, montrent partout les plus intimes rapports

Meanwhile, Malcolm Quinn and I planned our seminars, inviting artist and academic or artist and psychoanalyst in what we hoped would be a happy pairing. We determined we would discuss the social bond, behind which are the four discourses of Jacques Lacan, and we discovered a fifth discourse on capitalism, although in the end this did not amount to very much (except that the vector hits the truth).[6] Briefly, there are four places in the discourses, occupied by four elements. A set of letters, S1, S2, a barred S and a little *a* circulate in the places of agent, under which lies the position of truth, and other, under which lies the place of product or production. Each discourse is dynamic and one is not stuck in a single discourse or place for ever; indeed, these occupations of each position may be assumed, speaking the discourse of the master, the university (so closely aligned), the hysteric or the analyst, even if one is neither hysterical nor particularly analytical. In each there is a barrier, a vector that does not pass between truth and production, a barrier of either impotency or impossibility. Perhaps this is why I turned from dreams to sexuality – and there is a certain satisfaction in having three theories, three windows, no? Letters are in circulation in the discourses, four or even five of them, and letters, in or out of their place, mean something. Each discourse holds an address, an address to another, and it produces something close to truth while never speaking it. It is a way of organizing, but there is no final word.

5. Engraver's Old English, Formal, Lucia

die Neurose ist sozusagen das Negativ der Perversion

---

6 See Jacques Lacan, *Le Séminaire. Livre XVII. L'envers de la psychanalyse, 1969–70*, ed. Jacques-Alain Miller (Paris: Seuil, 1991).

> neuroses are, so to say, the negative of perversions
> la névrose est pour ainsi dire le négatif de la perversion

There is, of course, a difference between language and speech, just as there is a difference (we assume) between image and text. Images, in lectures and at conferences, for example, are very seldom anything but figures illustrating a text and are not expected to speak for themselves in that situation. Perhaps something unstable arises when a text, open to interpretation and to reading, becomes an image and reading, interpretation, strangely vanishes. Over the last two years, remarks made in passing to me in the corridor have addressed the look of the text, its three languages and their representation, eliding content, and mostly forgoing interpretation, though not always – for example, the French version of 'the finding of an object' emphasizing it being an *'objet sexuel'* (as indeed it is) does not escape notice. For a long time I thought my lovely phrases were unnoticed. Often when putting the phrases in their place, which is rather laborious, demanding careful measurement, a bold but steady hand and a level eye, I felt invisible to those who passed me, averting their gaze. I did experience satisfaction on completion of a set, and enjoyment at any level is a way of feeling that one exists. The last set of phrases, which follows below, remains in place, a work that I am told provokes comment, although the School of Advanced Study refuses to count it as an 'output'.

6. Windsor Light Condensed, Futura Light, Devine

> jede 'aktive' Perversion wird also hier von ihrem passiven begleitet
> every active perversion is then accompanied by its passive counterpart
> toute perversion active s'accompagnera donc d'une perversion passive

Vincent Dachy, who so kindly spoke at one of our seminars, suggests that art is in play in between positions, in the making of any discourse; that there is no discourse for art (though elsewhere, in talks, seminars and conversations, I have argued that it is the discourse of the analyst) for it operates where discourse is not yet constituted, doing its work precisely where discourse cannot, and finding its inspiration in the barrier, the point of impossibility or impotency.[7] One day, but not yet, I may rub white spirit over 'every active perversion is accompanied by its passive counterpart', then gently scrape the letters away, one by one, leaving an almost

---

7 Vincent Dachy, seminar 15 October 2007, Psychoanalysis and the Arts and Humanities Network, Institute of Germanic & Romance Studies, London.

invisible trace on the glass (this does sometimes work). I am left each time, after each erasure that is more a picking away, as at a scab or something nasty stuck up the nose (like *objet a* perhaps), with small balls of coloured plastic.

At this point, in my oral presentation, I held up those crushed, balled remains of language (German, French, English, no longer in any order) that I had remembered to retain and asked:

Is this what words are made of?

das Höchste und das Niedrigste hängen in

Sexualität überall am innigsten aneinander

...ourrait le cacher, et ce qu'il y a de plus bas, dans la sexualité, montrent par...

the highest and the lowe

Psychoanalysis in the French-Speaking World

4. Freedom to Roam

Julia Borossa

> Ce à quoi, souvent il faut répondre:
> – Que faites vous dans la vie?
> – Je relève des chutes.
> [Sometimes people ask me:
> 'What do you do for a living?'
> 'I pick up what has fallen down']
>
> Stéphane Le Mercier

The concluding lines of Stéphane Le Mercier's text, poetically addressing the phenomenology of his personal artistic practice, could well also serve as an apt portrayal of what a psychoanalyst does in his or her professional life. But equally apt is this pithy description provided by Christine Anzieu's young patient: 'Oh yes, a psychoanalyst is somebody who understands jokes' (this volume, p. 75). It is what these two understandings of psychoanalysis have in common that forms the thread linking the varied contributions to the French seminar group of the Psychoanalysis and the Arts and Humanities Research Network. The first statement – picking up what has fallen down – implies a compassionate physicality, a physicality very much at odds with classic accounts of the abstinent relations between analyst and analysand, shrouded in privacy and devoid of touch, whereas the second statement – understanding jokes – implies an intellectual complicity, one that acknowledges the linguistic play involved in unconscious processes but is nevertheless at odds with the pessimistic earnestness with which a discipline devoted to turning 'hysterical misery into common unhappiness' is usually approached.¹

The year-long discussions of the French seminar group highlighted the ability of psychoanalysis to transgress its own parameters in its response to an other – compassion, complicity, that is to say, its inherent creativity and adaptability. The two contributions included in this section of the volume are, in their different ways, perfect illustrations of its potential as discipline or discourse. Christine Anzieu-Premmereur's text shows just what a generous therapeutic engagement can achieve, as she insists on the analyst's freedom to be playful, 'maintaining the ability to think in the face of confusion and anxiety and keeping alive the capacity for being amazed, filled with wonder' (this volume, p. 71). Stéphane Le Mercier walks the streets of Marseilles, noticing what (and, by implication, who) has been overlooked, tossed aside. In a to-and-fro between the pavement and the studio, solid objects are born, a dignity bestowed on the desire and aspiration of his anonymous transient neighbours: 'petit matériel de bureau, outils, consoles de jeux, informatique, beauté, plaisirs de la maison, hygiène, activité sportive, jouets, jumelles, lunettes fantaisie' [basic office equipment, game consoles, do-it-yourself materials, computing, cosmetics, simple household luxuries, personal hygiene, sport, toys, binoculars, fancy sunglasses] (this volume, p. 79).

The French take-up of Freud's discoveries was relatively belated but, perhaps more than anywhere else in Europe, its reach was comprehensive, for it has extended to all significant areas of cultural and scientific life, from the visual arts to clinical psychology, from psychiatry to philosophy. Faced with this fertile receptiveness, Élisabeth Roudinesco has made the case for a 'French exception' in her analysis of the implantation and spread of psychoanalysis in France.² It is, perhaps, not surprising that the French seminar group tackled a particularly diverse and wide-ranging array of material, presented in different ways: films were screened, texts discussed by the group and more conventional seminar papers were presented as well. We also travelled to Paris for a workshop, itself divided into an exploration of the relationship of psychoanalysis to the three disciplines of

---

1   Sigmund Freud, *Studies on Hysteria* [*Studien über Hysterie*, with Josef Breuer [1985]], in *The Standard Edition of the Complete Psychological Works of Sigmund Freud*, 24 vols., ed. and trans. by James Strachey et al. (London: The Hogarth Press and the Institute of Psycho-analysis, 1953–74), vol. 2, 305.

2   Élisabeth Roudinesco and Michel Plon, *Dictionnaire de la psychanalyse* (Paris: Fayard, 1997), 318–26. See also Élisabeth Roudinesco, *Histoire de la psychanalyse en France* (vols. 1 and 2) (Paris: Fayard, [1982, 1986] 1994).

literature, politics and philosophy.³ The theoretical interests of the seminar were just as inclusive, since we discussed thinkers as diverse as Nicolas Abraham and Maria Torok, Didier Anzieu, Henri Bergson, Frantz Fanon, Jacques Lacan and Jean Laplanche.⁴

The common ground was that from the outset we were intent on thinking about the status of psychoanalysis as an ethical and political discourse. This we took to include, but to extend beyond, its clinical remit, so that our inquiry proposed to consider seriously the internal politics of psychoanalysis, the way it regulates its transmission, taking possession of and transforming its theoretical legacies – its professional vicissitudes. But taking such questions seriously proved inseparable from looking at the ways in which psychoanalysis interfaces with a broader political sphere, specifically in its capacity to address itself to traumatic social realities and how these may affect both the individual and the group. As put by Didier Anzieu, whose 1975 rallying-cry for the transformative potential of psychoanalysis, 'La psychanalyse, encore', formed the basis of our first discussion: 'Le problème n'est pas de répéter ce qu'a trouvé Freud face à la crise de l'ère victorienne, il est de trouver une réponse psychanalytique au malaise de l'homme dans notre civilisation présente' [The problem is not to repeat what Freud discovered in relation to the crisis of the Victorian era. It is to find a psychoanalytic answer to the discontents of modern man in our present civilization].⁵ And in order to achieve this, psychoanalysis has to show itself capable of immense adaptability, as a true and apt response to the suffering human subject within and

---

3 Organised by Anne-Marie Picard-Drillien of the American University in Paris; a volume of these and other essays will be published under the title *Le Corps de l'autre: mémoire, psychanalyse, politique* [*The Body of the Other: Memory, Psychoanalysis, Politics*], ed. Julia Borossa, Anne-Marie Picard-Drillien and Naomi Segal.

4 The following are some of the texts referred to, in order of their discussion: Didier Anzieu, 'La psychanalyse, encore', *Nouvelle Revue française de psychanalyse* XXXXIX, nos. 1–2 (1975); Didier Anzieu, *Les Enveloppes psychiques* (Paris: Dunod, [1987] 1996); Jean Laplanche, *Essays on Otherness*, ed. John Fletcher (London: Routledge, 1999); Frantz Fanon, *Peau noire, masques blancs* (Paris: Seuil, 1952), trans. by Charles Lam Markmann as *Black Skin, White Masks* (New York: Pluto Press, 1986); Jacques Lacan, *Écrits* (Paris: Seuil, 1966), trans. by Bruce Frink as *Écrits* (New York: Norton, 2002); Henri Bergson, *Le Rire* (Paris: Alcan, [1900] 1924); Nicolas Abraham and Maria Torok, *L'Écorce et le noyau*, ed. Nicholas Rand (Paris: Flammarion, [1978, 1987] 2001); trans. by Nicholas Rand as *The Shell and the Kernel* (Chicago: University of Chicago Press, 1994).

5 Didier Anzieu, *Psychanalyser* (Paris: Dunod, 2000), 258–59, trans. by Naomi Segal, in *Consensuality: Didier Anzieu, Gender and the Sense of Touch* (Amsterdam and New York: Rodopi, 2009), 27.

outside the conventional frame of the enclosed analytic space. Anzieu continues: 'un travail de type psychanalytique a à se faire là où surgit l'inconscient: debout, assis, ou allongé, individuellement, en groupe ou dans une famille, pendant la séance, sur le pas de la porte, au pied d'un lit d'hôpital' [We need to do work of a psychoanalytic kind wherever the unconscious emerges: sitting, standing, or lying down; individually, in groups or families, during a session, on the doorstep, at the foot of a hospital bed]. To my mind, this constitutes a call for a freedom to roam, claimed for the act of psychoanalysing as much as for the unconscious itself. With this call, Anzieu challenged psychoanalysis to prove itself timely, to be of his time, of our time. It must show its currency. To define psychoanalysis as compassionate physicality (picking up what/who has fallen down) or as intellectual complicity (understanding jokes) is to take up this challenge.

This wish to confront psychoanalysis with ethico-political questions led to our screening and discussion of Michael Haneke's film *Caché* [*Hidden*] (2005), with its theme of the hidden consequences of France's colonization of Algeria. Our discussion contrasted political readings of guilt (specifically here France's forcible repression of the Algerian uprising, of the deadly force used by its security forces against Algerian demonstrators in Paris in October 1961, and the present-day consequences of these historical acts of violence) with psychoanalytic ones: oedipal relations, castration anxiety, narcissistic injury. The film also provoked reflections on the transgenerational consequences of violence and trauma. In the subsequent Paris workshop Janine Altounian expressed this latter theme more directly in her paper on the Armenian genocide and its inscription across successive generations. In this respect, we felt that reading Frantz Fanon's work would be crucial to our enquiry.

Emerging from a confrontation with the fact of the violent anti-colonial struggle in Algeria and the fact of violence perpetrated against a racialized other, Fanon's critical engagement with psychoanalysis remains timely. We approached him through *Peau noire, masques blancs* [*Black Skin, White Masks*], the book in which Fanon discusses psychoanalysis most directly, and a screening of Isaac Julien's documentary about him.[6] Fanon's work, while in some ways clinically closer to psychiatry and theoretically closer to existentialism and phenomenology, keeps faith with a belief in the universality of the human experience at the heart of the psychoanalytic enterprise, all the while looking squarely at the

---

6   Isaac Julien (dir.) *Frantz Fanon – Black Skin White Mask* (1996), produced by Mark Nash, who presented the film to the seminar group.

actual, material and psychic consequences of social (colonial and racist) violence. In these two seminars, on *Hidden* and on Fanon, the figure of the child proved central. In the first, we explored the figure of the protagonist's child-self, inhabited by guilt and a repository of social trauma; and in the second, a very similar child, the young French boy who plays a central role in one of the most famous scenes in Fanon's work, crying out 'Maman, regarde le nègre, j'ai peur!' [Mama, see the Negro, I'm frightened!],⁷ who speaks as a result of the weight of cultural fantasies that have been transmitted to him and thereby puts into play a crisis of subjectivity in the adult black male. According to Fanon, in that moment where he is seen not as a man but as a black man, he is created as other by the cultural ideas of white society.⁸ Isaac Julien's film, which also emphasises that scene and its staging, along with powerful case vignettes of either victims or perpetrators of social violence, allowed us to reflect on the many aspects and effects of social trauma.

In the Paris workshop five months later, these general themes emerged once again across seven distinct contributions: first, the idea of trauma, mourning and their psychic and social consequences; secondly (and not unrelatedly), that of filiation and social formations. As part of the proceedings, the writer and psychoanalyst Marie Darrieussecq – completely poised but visibly moved – gave readings from her latest novel *Tom est mort* [*Tom is Dead*] (2007), the narrator of which is a mother whose young son has died 15 years earlier in far-away Australia. The book explores the effects of that death on herself, her surviving children and on language.⁹ The discussion that followed inevitably opened up questions of the Real and how the death of a child can act as the limit to symbolization and thought, as well as to emotion. This may be said to capture the very essence of the traumatic. How is it possible to live while carrying a corpse around inside oneself? How can we shed that corpse without abandoning it? How might we best remember the dead? This is a particularly moving clinical question to pose, but it is also pertinent for society. Janine Altounian, whose family was profoundly marked by the Armenian genocide, made us reflect on death and transmission in an entirely different way, by directly tackling the question of the transgenerational transmission of trauma and the possibility of

---

7 Frantz Fanon, *Peau noire, masques blancs* (Paris: Seuil, 1952), 90.

8 See also Julia Borossa, 'Narcissistic wounds, race and racism: a comment on Frantz Fanon's critical engagement with psychoanalysis', in *Narcissism: A Critical Reader*, ed. Anastasios Gaitanidis and Polona Curk (London: Karnac, 2007).

9 Marie Darrieussecq, *Tom est mort* (Paris: POL, 2007).

mourning. She presented the experiences of yet another child, her father, who years later had recounted the family's losses during an enforced flight to Syria, and later France, and caused us to question what acts as a barrier to remembrance, transmission and working-through, at the level of both the individual and the group.

We had wagered that psychoanalysis did have a contribution to make, at individual and social levels, and that it was a responsive discourse, capable of stretching its own parameters, with potentially transformative effects. Also at the Paris workshop, Anne-Marie [Augustina] Bourelly gave us a detailed and fascinating Lacanian interpretation of Pedro Almodóvar's *Volver* (2006), in which she showed how a specifically female and anarchic system of social relations, functioning as an alternative to capitalism, could be put in place through the murder and hiding away of the father's body (standing in for the ritual devouring that Freud invokes in *Totem and Taboo*)[10]. The transformative power of alternative filiations were also the theme of Monique Schneider's implicit critique of patriarchal (and oedipal) systems of filiation through a virtuoso reading of Racine's plays, which uncovered the subversive power of hybrid or double filiations. It served as a timely reminder that the theoretical tools psychoanalysis gives us can be seen to function both as a shoring-up and a critique of patriarchy. Back in London, Amber Jacobs explicitly took up this critical line, uncovering another myth, another murder behind the oedipal one, that of the mother. She evoked the lost story about the murder of Metis, Athena's mother, whom Zeus devours, giving rise to the myth of male generativity – the idea that Athena sprang fully formed from Zeus' head, a myth which, according to Jacobs, was itself forbidden by a foreclosed maternal law. Psychoanalytic discourse can bear the weight of such rereadings, necessary to its timeliness.

Two further papers specifically touched on the kind of receptivity that psychoanalysis is capable of, albeit in quite different ways. Anne-Marie Picard-Drillien's presentation at the Paris workshop invited us to think about what happens when we read. Is reading in the wake of Freud a form of incorporation or a permeability to another? Is it self-sufficiency or receptivity? What is the nature of that particular enjoyment? Céline Surprenant's fascinating account of the comic of movement in Freud, depending on contrast (between large and small,

---

10   Sigmund Freud, *Totem and Taboo* [*Totem und Tabu* [1912–13]], in *The Standard Edition of the Complete Psychological Works of Sigmund Freud*, 24 vols., ed. and trans. by James Strachey *et al.* (London: The Hogarth Press and the Institute of Psycho-analysis, 1953–74), vol. 13.

for example) looks at whether it is possible to recuperate a sense of physicality in the Freudian text which is not merely reducible to positivism.

But what continues to insist is the question of the efficacy of psychoanalysis, its work. This account started off by evoking its receptivity in terms of compassion and complicity. In her chapter, Christine Anzieu-Premmereur shows us how she carefully nurtures her young patient's sense of humour by her attentive laughter and by collaborating with him in a symbolic game, thereby shoring up his subjectivity against archaic trauma:

> He took blank pages, crumpled them, and I had to guess whose disabled body it was, a girl who had an accident, a baby who had fallen down or a wounded cat. Then we had to fill those empty vulnerable forms with playdough, make creatures full of shiny colours and tied together with string and Peter chose a name for each of them. Fragile envelopes became strong characters with identity, like his own ego functioning. (this volume, p. 73)

We can see a striking analogy with Le Mercier's practice, as his work enables shiny objects to emerge from the detritus collected on street corners:

> Autre passage, du blanc mat au noir brillant, de la poussière de plâtre à la concentration minérale, diffusion/concentration. Et puis l'étendue de la main chaque jour vérifiée. Exercice de la main, danse semblable à un patin noir mordant l'épaisseur de la glace.
>
> [A second passage, from matt white to shiny black, from the dust of the plaster to mineral concentration, diffusion/concentration. And then, the expanse of the hand, ascertained each day. An exercise of the hand, a dance similar to a black skate biting into the thickness of the ice. (this volume, p. 80)

What is represented in both cases is the minutiae of labour, as it allows for a positive space for another to emerge, albeit slowly and painfully.

In this respect, I wish also to evoke the thoughts of Richard Beardsworth who gave the last paper during the Paris workshop and argued eloquently for psychoanalysis to stand as a critical and rejuvenating discourse central to political philosophy, leading to a new ethics that incorporates loss. For the inevitable human experience of loss and injury, as an individual and as part of a group, the ability to mourn and the chance to remain creative, was what the French seminar group had undoubtedly been engaging with throughout. To conclude, let us invoke Didier Anzieu once more:

Si nous savons la délivrer des idolâtries et des désuétudes toujours recommençantes et si nous persévérons à prendre avec l'intelligence du corps, du cœur et de la pensée, nous pouvons beaucoup attendre et beaucoup demander de la psychanalyse encore.

[If we are able to liberate it from the successive waves of idolatry and rejection and if we persevere in taking stock with the intelligence of the body, the heart and thought, we have much to ask of psychoanalysis and much to expect of it, still] ('La psychanalyse, encore', 146)

5. How a Child Develops a Sense of Humour During Psychoanalysis[1]

Christine Anzieu-Premmereur

According to Sigmund Freud, humour is the triumph of the ego, which pretends to be invulnerable while revealing what is painful.[2] This capacity for playing with anxieties is based on an ego that must be well enough organised to be aware of its own feelings. In young children who have suffered from early trauma, the building of an ego is connected with the capacity for playing with painful feelings. When they share their despair with the therapist, those children develop a strong sense of humour. The creative use of humour helps a child to become social, to cope with stress and anxiety, to express itself artistically and to think critically.

In traditional Navajo Indian culture, a child is viewed as the ultimate gift. An infant is constantly watched over and kept in a cradleboard until it laughs for the first time. This moment marks the child's birth as social being. The member of the family who makes the baby laugh must then provide for a celebration in honour of the child.

Babies start laughing around the age of six months and at just one year old they begin to make up their own funny actions. Early evidence of humour based on the recognition of incongruous actions occurs in seven- to eight-month-old babies, who will laugh during physical-

1 A version of this essay has appeared in the *Journal of Infant, Child, and Adolescent Psychotherapy*, vol. 8, no. 3 (2009), 137–44.

2 Sigmund Freud, *Jokes and their Relation to the Unconscious* (*Der Witz und seine Beziehung zum Unbewussten* [1905]), in *The Standard Edition of the Complete Psychological Works of Sigmund Freud*, 24 vols., ed. and trans. by James Strachey et al. (London: The Hogarth Press and the Institute of Psycho-analysis, 1953–74), vol. 8, 234. Hereafter abbreviated SE, followed by volume number.

and-social-surprise play with parents, as long as it is not too intense. Reacting to incongruity is not the same as reacting to novelty, which may lead to fear; an incongruous stimulus is mis-expected while a novel one is unexpected. A one-year-old girl laughed uproariously as she put her socks on her head and asked her mother to do the same, but she was frightened when she saw her mother wearing a new hat that she had never seen before.

Young children use preverbal symbols, deliberate finger and body movements, clowning, exaggerated gestures and vocal sounds to initiate humorous play with their parents. Toddlers' attempts at comedy include verbal humour such as mislabelling, puns and nonsense games.

Make-believe play and the expression of humour have many characteristics in common, but they differ in the sense that in serious make-believe, children replicate real-world events in ways that make sense for them, whereas in humorous make-believe, they deliberately distort the real world through incongruous actions and language, and do not act as though the pretend world were real. On the contrary, the purpose of the fiction is specifically to make others laugh. Peter, the little boy I will present in this chapter, knew he could make me laugh by pretending to eat all the things in the supermarket instead of buying them, or by threatening to eat his school and all the teachers.

Play is a necessary component of humour and, as Winnicott shows, the role of the therapist is to provide a creative space where play is made possible.[3] Humour aids social bonding and is a relief from stress and strain; humour liberates a child from the adults' expectations that it must perform and behave well. Humorous play, joking behaviour, incongruous actions and language, nonsense words — all these are the tools to help the child control and master the world despite its inferior status.

Freud reserved the German term *Humor* for actions that help a person to cope with events in which the recognition of incongruity would have aroused fear, sadness or anger.[4] The use of humour as a coping mechanism enables the child to gain an altered perception of the situation and to reduce its threat.

Freud proposed three stages of the development of humour, beginning with *Spiel* [play] at the age of two or three, followed by *Scherzen* [jesting], at four to six, and finally true *Witz* [joking], which begins around the age of seven. Jesting may be the originating point for nonsense or comical expression because it is not intended to

---

3   D. W. Winnicott, *Playing and Reality* (New York: Routledge [1971] 2002), 40.
4   Sigmund Freud, *Humour* [*Der Humor* (1927)], SE 21, 120.

convey meaning, while joking provides socially acceptable ways of expressing feelings or conveying hostile or sexual meanings. Jesting requires an audience and results from the discovery that adults prefer reasonableness to absurdity. Joking allows the expression of feelings that are normally repressed.

The youngest children express their humour through mastery play, while somewhat older children use jesting to convey absurdities, and only the oldest child uses the joking method, still in a quite crude form, to convey feelings that cannot be expressed in polite society. The bathroom humour of young children seems to be a precursor of the joking stage.

In therapy, the language of children is play: when they are able to play, they can convey what has happened to them, what they felt about it, what they want and what they need, and they can tell their jokes over and over again. A child will use jokes to go back to life experiences that have confounded its ability to cope.

It takes two people to tell a joke, and the one who hears it has to react immediately and show the right emotion. When Peter, bilingual in French and English, was four-and-a-half, he had just begun to talk after a long depression that had delayed his development, and to play at creating soft transitional objects that could help him deal with a severe separation issue. He told me this joke: 'Which side of the dog has the most hair?' Of course, I couldn't answer, which made him very happy, feeling he had got some mastery over me. Then he said: 'The outside', and I laughed a lot. At the same time, I realised that he was talking about his own inside being wounded and painful.

Peter was facing a number of challenges — fear of object loss, fear of rejection and abandonment, fear of inadequacy and failure — while also having to learn how to regulate his infantile omnipotence. Humour as an ego defence became available for him when a well-integrated ego was in place.

In *Project for a Scientific Psychology*, Freud posits the baby's original helplessness as the prototype of all traumatic situations.[5] The state of helplessness is linked to the infant's initial powerlessness in the face of its needs. With a vulnerable and immature self, and a fragile object-relation, the beginning of psychic life is a struggle to keep the link with the object and to deal with the high quantity of internal arousal, which can disorganise the premature ego.

If an infant does not have the experience of a mother or caregiver who is able to merge with its experience and protect it from the

---

5 Sigmund Freud, *Project for a Scientific Psychology* [*Entwurf einer Psychologie* (1895)], SE 3, 120.

consequences of its helplessness, it will experience what Donald Winnicott refers to as 'unthinkable anxiety, primitive agonies and annihilation'.[6] When the caregiver cannot hold the baby in a reliable way, the sense of 'continuity of being' is damaged; the baby receives a traumatic communication, which produces archaic anxiety.

Such a failure of the caring environment is traumatic for a baby, who is totally dependent. In a psychoanalytic treatment, if its ego is structured enough, a child can reproduce in the transference what it had experienced in babyhood. The psychotic anxieties it experiences in relation to those past agonies include a sense of going to pieces, falling into space, having no relation to the body, having no orientation, and being completely isolated because it has no means of communication. This threat of annihilation is traumatic.

When a developmentally-delayed child is in psychoanalytic psychotherapy, it can repeat those traumatic feelings through the transference, as well as through playing and the experience of being held within a strict and secure psychoanalytic frame. Then, when a sense of humour occurs, it is always in relation to a defence against those fears. These young patients use humour as a counter-phobic mechanism, which gives them the sadistic pleasure of putting the therapist in the position of the passive one while they feel invulnerable. It also allows the child to feel pleasure at expressing fantasies of destruction and ambiguous feelings towards the object.

Peter suffered from severe anorexia as a baby and was abused by a sadistic childminder; he discovered a sense of humour one day when he was playing at feeding me with a spoon and I was making noises of pleasure. He pulled the spoon away just at the moment I was supposed to enjoy the pretended food and started laughing irresistibly, and the more I played at being frustrated, the more delighted he was. Playing and humour here allowed an interesting condensation of aggression, frustration, bad-object relations and overcoming the depression.

When showing a sense of humour, a damaged child is able to tolerate the anxiety caused by traumatic events. Humour allows one to play with limits, the limits of what is socially acceptable, the limits of the body, the limits between reality and fantasy, between the self and others. All the steps in childhood anxiety are associated with a specific humour: stranger anxiety, the issue of separation, the body and its erogenous zones.

---

6 D. W. Winnicott, 'The fear of breakdown', in *Psycho-Analytic Explorations* (London: Karnac [1963] 1989), 90.

This is very different from dramatic laughter and the arousal of the manic defence. Humour comes from the association between pleasure and control, primary and secondary processes. Young children play with unusual and amazing situations, clowning, faking cruelty and sadism, joking about differences or making faces, playing with gender difference, anal excitement and genital exhibitionism, all this while contriving, with the arbitrary organisation of language, to be nasty and charming at the same time.

In his theory of the skin-ego, Didier Anzieu explores how the earliest experiences of being touched by the mother organise a container for psychic functioning that may form a kind of mental space in which representations and fantasies are held. If this maternal container is stable and flexible enough, then the early fears, anxieties and violent experiences can be transformed and eventually associated with the sense of humour.[7]

'The term "skin-ego" designates a mental representation that the child forms on the basis of its experience of the surface of its body and uses to picture itself as the vessel of mental contents' (ASE p. 40). The skin-ego belongs to the stage in development when the psychic ego becomes differentiated from the body ego on the practical level while remaining indistinguishable from it in the imagination.

This theory returns to Freud's concept of the body ego and the topographic model, and shows how the skin can be imagined to separate, bind, and layer various parts of the mental apparatus: conscious, preconscious and perception. Anzieu argues that these three regions of the mind are analogous to the layers of the skin. What the skin-ego contains or separates can be designated as various levels of consciousness. The concept of 'psychic envelope' or container relates to the different layers of the skin or body image.[8] The skin's capacity to contain is related to the idea of the skin-ego *containing* contents of the unconscious. Anzieu sees problems or defects in the skin-ego relating to predominantly borderline and narcissistic conditions.

John Bowlby's research on attachment and loss and that of Winnicott on 'good-enough mothering' stress the way in which

---

7 See Didier Anzieu, *Le Moi-peau* (Paris: Dunod [1985]), trans. by Chris Turner as *The Skin Ego* (New Haven, CT: Yale University Press, 1989), 55. Hereafter abbreviated ASE.

8 See Didier Anzieu, *Les Enveloppes psychiques* (Paris: Dunod, [1987] 2000), trans. by Daphne Briggs as *Psychic Envelopes* (London: Karnac Books, 1990), 43. Hereafter abbreviated APE.

the infant needs and uses the early relationship with the mother to establish not only security but also the ability to learn to play independently.⁹ The pleasure of contact with the mother's body and the faculty of clinging are thus at the basis of both attachment and separation.

Under the care of its mother (or her substitute), an infant receives both stimulation and communication. If this is successful, the skin-ego is established, responding to the need for a narcissistic envelope, which gives the psychic apparatus the assurance of a constant, secure basic well-being. Ultimately, growing out of this first configuration, the skin-ego is the foundation for the possibility of thinking.

The skin-ego is an envelope which contains thoughts and provides the activity of thinking with limits, continuity and a protection against the instincts. In the case of those suffering from borderline disorders, by contrast, the whole structure of the skin-ego is threatened: they cannot tell if a perception is coming from inside or outside the psyche. It is difficult for such patients to contain their feelings; the self becomes an empty place, causing severe anxiety. The psychoanalytic process can help to reconstruct the skin-ego with its functions: container, support, excitation-screen and libidinal recharging.

Since the skin-ego gives the psyche a secure feeling of well-being, it acquires two abilities. First, it sets up barriers protecting the internal world; these barriers later become defence mechanisms. Second, it is able to screen exchanges with the id, the superego and the outside world. As a consequence, the skin-ego sets up the ability to think.

In *Les Enveloppes psychiques* [*Psychic Envelopes*], Anzieu develops the concept of the *signifiant formel* [formal signifier] (APE, 15) These signifiers are characterised by their dynamic nature: they are concerned with changes of form; they are spatial, capturing the psychic properties of space; and they represent not psychic contents but psychic containers. They are impressions, sensations and ordeals that are intense and experienced too early for them to be put into words. They are representations of bodily states, and identifying them is useful to the psychoanalyst who wants to identify and interpret damage to the construction of the ego.

If their mother has been able to give meaning to their experiences, children can go on to give meaning to their bodily feelings. Babies and toddlers communicate through gestures and expressions what they feel with pleasure or displeasure, things that put them at risk of disorganisation and chaos. Psychoanalysts who work with babies

---

9 D. W. Winnicott, *Playing and Reality* (New York: Routledge, 1971), 112.

and children try to communicate these threatening experiences by following Winnicott's suggestions about archaic anxieties and Anzieu's representations of archaic signifiers: falling into space, shrinking, twisting, tearing apart, piercing, exploding, being empty or fragmented.

> Each individual's fundamental formal signifier derives from a time when they were not yet capable of repression, still tied in psychically to the closeness to the mother that Anzieu calls the 'common skin'. Its structure is different from that of phantasy. It takes the form of a sentence that has a subject and a verb but no object-complement; often the verb (in French) is reflexive; and the subject is a part of the body or an isolated physical form, never a whole person. It is not a scene or an enactment but 'the geometrical or physical transformation of a body (in the general sense of a portion of space) which entails a deformation or destruction of form' (15); the space in which it appears is two-dimensional, and the patient senses it as external to himself or herself. Anzieu gives examples: 'a vertical axis is reversed; a support collapses; a hole sucks in [...] a solid body is crossed; a gaseous body explodes; [...] an orifice opens and closes; [...] a limit interposes; different perspectives are juxtaposed; [...] my double leaves or controls me; [...] an object abandons me' (15-16). In the second part of this book, I will be looking, in cultural figures and artefacts, for a series of formal signifiers and how to compare and explore them. The characteristic formal signifier of Gide's desire, for instance, is twofold: 'a compulsion to empty the body of its fluid content', and 'a straight line that ends in a swerve' [...], that of the public figure of Princess Diana 'a circle around, into and out of, the surface-point of the skin', that of the mode of love in *The Piano* 'the caress of the back of the hand', that of certain recent films 'desiring from inside the body of another'. What Anzieu's theory offers to such cultural readings is a structure and vocabulary that may be able, consensually, to contain them without pre-empting them.[10]

A patient who cannot express in words the neglects or failures of their early environment will signify the defect and its consequences through their body and their sensations. It is a mistake to understand this solicitation as sexual, and the therapist must not give the patient what the mother failed to give, must not touch their body. It is by an active but purely verbal response that the analyst transforms the patient's body-signals into symbolic communication. This work allows the patient not only to communicate about their immediate

---

10 Naomi Segal, *Consensuality: Didier Anzieu, Gender and the Sense of Touch* (Amsterdam and New York: Rodopi, 2009), 31. The examples are taken from Anzieu, *Les Enveloppes psychiques*, 15–16, translation Segal's.

sensations and bodily experiences but to think and talk about them. If the mother was unable to echo the baby's experiences, no meaning could appear; the ability to experience oneself as feeling is connected to the mirror the mother offers her child by herself feeling what it experiences. The analyst holds the patient with his or her attention, preoccupation and active interventions, maintaining the patient's experience of being contained. By echoing the patient's archaic experiences, the analyst provides a circular relation where the perceptions and sensations are shared, contained and expressed through words. [Psychoanalysis is] 'une peau vivante pour les pensées' [a living skin for thoughts], writes Evelyne Séchaud in her comments on the skin-ego.[11]

Wilfred Bion refers to a 'mental skin' that will allow the introjection of thinkable elements.[12] But if the patient's archaic fears were too intense, they will interfere with this process and forbid the access to representations and symbolisations. The acquisition of language will be delayed, and no sense of humour will appear.

In his 1905 study *Jokes and Their Relation to the Unconscious*, Freud makes an association between humour and the ego, in the sense that both claim to be invincible, enabling the victory of the pleasure principle, the triumph of narcissism. As he summarised over 20 years later:

> The main thing is the intention which humour carries out, whether it is acting in relation to the self or other people. It means: 'Look! Here is the world, which seems so dangerous! It is nothing but a game for children — just worth making a jest about!' If it is really the superego which, in humour, speaks such kindly words of comfort to the intimidated ego, this will teach us that we have still a great deal to learn about the nature of superego. [...] If the superego tries, by means of humour, to console the ego and protect it from suffering, this does not contradict its origin in the parental agency. (SE 21, 166)

Depressive issues are a major point in the appearance of the sense of humour: the terror at losing the love of the object and thus all meaning. Freud saw the roots of the sense of humour in the baby at the breast, smiling at its mother; this is why Janine Chasseguet-

---

11 Evelyne Séchaud, 'Didier Anzieu: penser les pensées', in *Didier Anzieu: le Moi-peau et la psychanalyse des limites* (Paris: Eres, 2007), 30.
12 Wilfred Bion, *Second Thoughts: Selected Papers on Psycho-analysis* (London: Karnac, 1967), 39.

Smirgel writes that the person who has a sense of humour is trying to be their own loving mother.[13]

Humour is an interpersonal affair; it is about playing with the pain of the subject who loves the object and it is funny only if there is a partner, real or imaginary. The goal is to make the other laugh at one's weakness or forbidden desire. The emotional involvement of a spectator is essential: the one who is displaying humour obtains the pleasure of success, a narcissistic value, and is no longer alone in suffering; they even sometimes get the joyful feeling that they are really alive. Think of the plays of Samuel Beckett, full of a despair that is made to be laughed at.

The psychoanalyst's sense of humour, the 'as-if' quality of their interpretations, their responsiveness to the patient's jokes, all add to the transitional quality of the setting. The analyst gives the child an active support and container for its painful experiences of distress or emptiness.

Child analysis is no laughing matter. The analyst must face the frustrations of not understanding, not knowing, encountering ambiguity and contradictions, all the more if the child is not yet able to speak. But these are the very same capacities that are needed in the acquisition of a sense of humour: maintaining the ability to think in the face of confusion and anxiety, and keeping alive the capacity for being amazed, filled with wonder. It is part of the analyst's floating attention and freedom to be playful. Equally, it is essential for the analyst to be able to play the role of the third party, not only as the witness of the child's jokes, but also as the implicit object of criticism as a parental imago.

During psychoanalysis, some children discover this joy at being creative and funny, at playing with misfortune and remaining optimistic in the face of adversity: these changes signal the recovery of their skin-ego!

When I met him for the first time, at the age of three, Peter was a sad, skinny little boy who was uneasy with his body and did not speak. He had spent long, boring days in the company of a depressed childminder while his parents were fully occupied by their professions. They came for consultation because they had been told their son might be too behind to start nursery school. Peter was

---

13 Janine Chasseguet-Smirgel, 'The triumph of humor', in *Fantasy, Myth and Reality, Essays in Honor of Jacob Harlow*, ed. H. P. Blum (New York: International Universities Press, 1988).

anorexic, had no language and did not smile or play. But his gaze was very attentive and I had no problem in making a connection with him.

I saw him with his mother in a dyadic twice-a-week psychotherapy for six months, then alone in a psychoanalytic setting for three years. It was a difficult treatment, which ended up going very successfully. He is now a well-developed, strong boy who plays football and is good at school. He writes a lot of poetry.

What was striking was the appearance of his sense of humour as soon as he was able to talk. We started therapy by throwing and catching a ball and I expressed to him his despair when his parents were absent and he was facing the depressed childminder. Peter had been a particularly passive, silent baby who was not interested in eating and did not play with his mouth. During the sessions, he followed my own play while looking at me intensely, and I felt that he was glued to my gaze.

When he was three-and-a-half, he went away for a week's holiday, and came back to the sessions full of anxiety; he was shy, afraid of me. He found a piece of paper that he had left in his file and was surprised. I told him that I kept everything we made together and was thinking of him while he was away. The same day, he discovered in a cupboard a train with the carriages stuck together by magnets. He was greatly interested and we played at putting a long train together; I told him that they were 'attached' as he was to his mother, as we were even after a separation. The next session he said his first word — 'attach' — asking me to open the cupboard to play with the train. His mother cried with joy. The word 'attached' became a ritual to start every session. From that moment his language developed very well.

After this, most of the playing was about being contained, enveloped or firmly held. The first smiles and, soon after, laughs occurred when Peter chose to pretend to feed me with a spoon. This phase of cruelty was followed by a period of hide-and-seek and separation issues. Peter showed obvious separation anxiety, anger at being left alone and pain at saying goodbye. Together we found a solution to deal with this painful situation: we made some cats out of paper and soft cloth which would stay in my office when he left, or could be taken home. One of them became his first transitional object. Now time began to exist: we could count the number of nights between two sessions and Peter decided that when he grew up he wanted to be a 'blanket-maker'.

This was an exceptionally creative time for him. Along with the transitional space, he acquired a new libidinal life that made him a particularly lively child, no longer passive or sad, suffering from excessive anxiety, and no longer depressed.

The next new game was feeling empty envelopes: a kind of squiggle game in 3D.[14] He took blank pages, crumpled them, and I had to guess whose disabled body it was, a girl who had had an accident, a baby who had fallen down or a wounded cat. Then we had to fill those empty vulnerable forms with playdough, make creatures full of shiny colours and tied together with string, and Peter chose a name for each of them. Fragile envelopes became strong characters with identity, like his own ego functioning. At that time, he was able to begin a sentence by saying: 'Moi veux' ['I want'] or 'Moi pense' ['Me think'].

When I interpreted his need for the protection of a solid container, he answered: 'Oui, c'est contre les trous qui risquent de tout vider de dedans, tu comprends?' ['Yes, against the holes that might make everything empty from the inside, d'you understand?']. And we both remembered the terror he had felt at the swimming pool, when he thought his body might dissolve into the water.

At that time Peter started to play with language and tell stories that made him laugh uproariously, an experience he wanted to share with me. The first jokes were about the body and its failures:

> What do little ghosts drink?
> Evaporated milk.
> What did the teddy bear say when he was offered dessert?
> No thanks, I'm stuffed!
> Why couldn't the skeleton go to the dance?
> He had no body to go with!

In the waiting room, he called me Mrs Poo-poo, which horrified his parents. All his troubles in relation to eating, with the sadistic childminder and in relation to the very strict, early toilet training he had endured became the source of jokes and tricks. Infantile sexuality recovered its role when he was able to form a strong skin-ego and a secure libidinal cathexis towards his love objects. Then he greeted me at the beginning of every session with a joyful: 'What's up? ... The sky!'

---

14 See D. W. Winnicott 'The squiggle game' [1968], reproduced in *Psycho-Analytic Explorations*, ed. Clare Winnicott, Ray Shepherd and Madeleine Davis (London: Karnac, 1989), 299.

Peter started primary school at the normal age of six. At that time he became more obsessive, highly anxious about what the adults would expect of him. His ability to make jokes and make fun of both himself and his parents and the teachers was particularly helpful. He felt that he was different from the others, being very shy and disconnected, and he was especially afraid of failing and disappointing his parents, who desperately wanted him to be a gifted child. His father had been so wounded to have a son who had been diagnosed early on as autistic that he wanted him to become a genius.

At school he learned some riddles about 'the moron', which became a way of expressing his own suffering. The moron does crazy things and is defective, but he is also the clever fool who surprises us by turning out to have a reason for the unintelligible things he does; and the one who asks the riddle triumphs over both the moron and everyone else. The moron survives every catastrophe and thus he is a symbol of invulnerability. One of Peter's favourites was a classic one, which he could use to report on his own depression: 'Why did the moron jump off the Empire State Building? Because he wanted to make a smash hit on Broadway'.

Peter was angry with his parents and transferred his aggression to his teachers. Afraid of losing control, he would write jokes about the adults, which he brought to me during our sessions, as secrets that we could share. Understanding how important taboos and norms are to others gave him the power to make his schoolmates laugh. This secret exchange with me had an incestuous quality, by attacking father figures. Peter's parents have no sense of humour and it was easy to upset them with playful sayings, for example, about grammar or language or the world of adults:

'In the sentence, "the thief has stolen the apples", where is the subject? In prison!'

'Why are fish so smart? Because they live in schools.'

'Why did the scientist put a knocker on his door? He wanted to win the No-bell prize.'

And the last one:

'The geography teacher was lecturing on map reading. After explaining about latitude, longitude, degrees and minutes, the teacher asked: "Suppose I asked you to meet me for lunch at latitude 23 degrees, 4 minutes north and longitude 45 degrees, 15 minutes east...?" After a confused silence, a voice volunteered: "I guess you'd be eating alone".'

Other jokes were directly about his transference towards me: 'What did the ground say to the earthquake? You crack me up!' Or, when he discovered how to pretend to take idiomatic expressions literally, he played with the expression 'falling in love' by lying on the floor at my feet.

His love affair with me was intense at that time, and then it decreased with the latency period. At this point he made his last joke: 'A piece of sugar is in love with a spoon, and asks could we meet? Yes, she says, in a coffee.'

Peter's humour was a narcissistic affirmation and at the same time an obsession with being able to control language. It was a defence against his autistic and depressive anxieties, and also a good way of being able to think. Later on, he became more interested in writing poetry.

Freud insisted on keeping the word humour only for actions or expressions that allow the integration of experiences of fear, sadness or anger. Following this, I can say that Peter acquired a real sense of humour!

A few years after the end of the psychotherapy, Peter came back with his parents to report on his progress at school. His mother asked him if he remembered when they came together and if he knew that I was a psychoanalyst. He answered: 'Oh yes, a psychoanalyst is somebody who understands jokes.'

I have chosen this topic, the sense of humour, because it was one of the qualities of my father, Didier Anzieu: to play with language, to make fun of himself, to decrease the distress in critical moments of life, and to share the laughter with others.

6. La reproduction

Stéphane Le Mercier

1

Marseille. Je sors et je marche sans autre but que de collecter blisters et emballages thermoformés, abandonnés sur les trottoirs de la ville. Ma déambulation est un récit sans cesse différé, régulièrement interrompu par mes retours à l'atelier. Allées et venues à la manière d'un demandeur d'asile, d'un ouvrier en mal de chantiers. BIS REPETITA. Marseille. Je sors et je marche sans autre but que de collecter blisters et emballages thermoformés, abandonnés sur les trottoirs de la ville. Ma déambulation est un récit sans cesse différé, régulièrement interrompu par mes retours à l'atelier. Allées et venues à la manière d'un demandeur d'asile, d'un ouvrier en mal de chantiers.

[Marseille. I go out and walk with no other aim than to pick up blisterpacks and other vacuum-formed wrappings that people have dumped on the town's pavements. My wandering is an endlessly deferred narrative, interrupted every so often by returns to my studio. Going back and forth like an asylum-seeker or a workman looking for a building site. REPEAT. Marseille. I go out and walk with no other aim than to pick up blisterpacks and other vacuum-formed wrappings that people have dumped on the town's pavements. My wandering is an endlessly deferred narrative, interrupted every so often by returns to my studio. Going back and forth like an asylum-seeker or a workman looking for a building site.]

2

Shawn Wilbur writes:

> Some of this population was composed of what Virilio will term 'dromomaniacs', a lumpen class which rules the roads, in the absence of any centralized 'highway patrols'. These highwaymen will play an important role in the conflict between urban centers. They are, as Virilio sees them, speed and motion, only in need of more or less precise targeting. The term 'dromomaniac' is particularly significant, since it refers both to a particular historical social group and to a medical condition characterized by 'compulsive walking'. What Virilio is describing is a 'dromocratic revolution' in which speed becomes a dominant factor in Western societies. He describes 'dromocrats' and 'dromomaniacs' – something like his version of the bourgeoisie and the proletariat – and we are left to wonder where we stand, or where we walk.[1]

3

Plus tard, le mouvement qui consiste à couler du plâtre dans ces formes collectées définira l'essence même de ma pratique. Soit un geste sculptural, dit de première urgence, un geste vite, d'origine manuelle et porté à l'endroit d'un objet unique. En tant que tel, dans sa vitesse et sa détermination, il est apte à reproduire le sens ancien de la pharmacopée et l'éventualité possible d'une guérison perdue. Transvasement, passage.

[Later on, the essence of my practice will be defined as the movement that consists of pouring plaster into the forms I have picked up. This might be a sculptural gesture, of the utmost urgency, a quick gesture, originally of the hand, directed towards a unique object. As such, in its speed and specificity, it could be said to be reproducing the old meaning of pharmocopia and the possibility of a lost cure. Decanting, passing.]

4

Dans mon souvenir, Marseille, plus que tout autre ville, produit ces fantômes de formes, ces emballages transparents et secs. Est-ce dû à la topographie de la ville? Une succession de villages, de quartiers populaires. Multitude de bazars, de solderies, de marchés aux puces

---

1 Shawn Wilbur, 'Paul Virilio: speed, cinema, and the end of the political state', *Speed* (electronic journal), 1997, 1 (4), 1–10 (originally posted on the internet in 1994).

improvisés où échouent les reliefs d'une autre société, nantie et périphérique celle-là, mêlés aux contrefaçons asiatiques.

Ces objets sans qualité et dont le prix d'achat dépasse rarement quelques euros sont visibles sous leur coque transparente. Au contraire des vitrines des boutiques de luxe et des grands magasins, ces protections sont aisément fracturables. Aussitôt vus, aussitôt acquis. En cela, ils poursuivent l'exposition systématique des tuyaux à travers le bitume percé, des sacs-poubelles éventrées, des boîtes à lettres branlantes. Ils prolongent exagérément la visibilité de chaque rue, de chaque façade. Et s'ils miment les figures dominantes de la culture marchande, ils le font sur un mode burlesque, un rien pathétique. Formes exagérées, couleurs inadéquates, résistance nulle.

[In my recollection, more than any other town, Marseille produces these phantoms of forms, these dry, transparent wrappings. Is this something to do with its topography? There's a succession of villages and working-class districts. Masses of corner stores, discount shops, improvised flea-markets where the leftovers of another society have ended up, a society that's well-heeled and suburban – all this mixed in with Asiatic forgeries.

These objects, which are worthless in themselves, none costing more than a few euros, are visible within their transparent shell. Unlike the windows of smart shops and department stores, these protective coverings are easy to crack. No sooner seen than acquired. In this sense, they follow the systematic exposure of pipes seen through holes in the tarmac, disembowelled dustbins, letter-boxes hanging open. They prolong in an exaggerated way the extreme visibility of each street, of each façade. And if they mimic the dominant images of the commercial culture, they do it in a burlesque mode, just a bit touching. Exaggerated forms, feeble colours, absolutely no resistance.]

5

Énumération : petit matériel de bureau, outils, consoles de jeux, matériel de bricolage, informatique, beauté, plaisirs de la maison, activité sportive, jouets, jumelles, lunettes fantaisie. Un monde complet. Une caverne reconstituée, avec ou sans projection.

[List: basic office equipment, tools, game consoles, do-it-yourself materials, computing, cosmetics, simple household luxuries, sport, toys, binoculars, fancy sunglasses. A total world. A reconstituted cave, with or without projection.]

6

En fait, les objets de consommation m'importent peu et, s'ils me retiennent, c'est pour leur capacité à être reproduits encore une fois, pour cette manière sinueuse qu'ils ont de s'imposer à moi. Forme fantomatique, je le répète, enveloppe de forme, stade ultime de la matière marchande. Ce qui retient mon regard? Un ensemble de membranes décollées, équivalent du processus photographique issu de la pensée spiritualiste du XIXème siècle. Photographe sans appareil, matérialité nimbée de mystères. La photographie, elle aussi, est un moulage. Il faudra donc s'inscrire dans ces espaces secrets à jamais délaissés. Ceux de l'abandon, du mystère de l'abandon et de leur reconstitution méticuleuse. En somme, il s'agit toujours de prélèvements et comme la photographie spirite fut systématiquement refoulée des manuels d'histoire, il est fort à parier que ces reliefs sculpturaux bénéficieront d'une réputation douteuse.

[In fact I am not interested in consumer objects; the reason I stop to collect them, that I am drawn to them, is because they are things that are capable of being reproduced over again, and because of the insinuating way they make their demands on me. Ghost-forms, let me say again, the wrappings of form, the final stage of commercial material. What is it that attracts my eye? A collection of unstuck membranes, similar to the photographic processes that emerged from the spiritualism of the 19th century. A photographer without a camera, a materiality haloed with mysteries. Photography too is a kind of plaster-cast. We must sign up to these secret, neglected spaces: spaces of abandonment, of the mystery of abandonment, and of the meticulous reconstitution of the object. In other words, it's always a matter of sampling and, just as spirit photography was systematically repressed from the history books, so it's a fair bet that these sculptural reliefs can look forward to a dubious reputation.]

7

Rapide collecte, là, près du carton, au coin de la rue sur le bitume jaune poussière. Rapide moulage que le recouvrement à la mine de plomb complètera lentement, excédera à force de lenteur. Autre déambulation, sur le motif cette fois et crayon à la main. Autre passage, du blanc mat au noir brillant, de la poussière de plâtre à la concentration minérale, diffusion/concentration. Et puis, l'étendue de la main chaque jour vérifiée. Exercice de la main, danse semblable à un patin noir mordant l'épaisseur de la glace.

[A quick collection, here, right next to a cardboard box, on the street corner, on the dust-yellow tarmac. A quick cast, which will be completed, exceeded later by a slow process of covering it with pencil-scribbles. This will be a second wandering, this time in situ, pencil in hand. A second passage, from matt white to shiny black, from the dust of the plaster to mineral concentration, diffusion/concentration. And then, the expanse of the hand, ascertained each day. An exercise of the hand, a dance similar to a black skate eating into the thickness of the ice.]

8

Le paysage, on n'arrête pas d'en parler. Freud à Rome, Jensen à Pompéi. Et puis, aujourd'hui, le monde vu du ciel, Google Earth, les dégâts occasionnés par le Tsunami et la pollution mondiale. 'Die Landschaft ist nicht die Lösung'.[2] Avec ou sans GPS. Carte annulée, boussole affolée. Citons Chateaubriand, chose rare, *Voyage au Mont-Blanc*: 'Tout ce que je demande, c'est qu'on ne me force pas d'admirer les longues arêtes de rochers, les fondrières, les crevasses, les trous, les entortillements des vallées des Alpes'.[3] Impossible de s'élever donc, retour à la case départ. Ce qui nous reste, ce qui restera. Au bas mot, ce qui survient là, sur les trottoirs de la ville avec l'évidence d'une bouteille brisée après une noce nocturne. Entropic-City.

Landscape. We talk about it all the time. Freud in Rome, Jensen in Pompeii. And today, the world as seen from the sky, Google Earth, the ravages of the Tsunami and world-wide pollution. 'Die Landschaft ist nicht die Lösung'.[2] With or without GPS. The map is void, the compass in a panic. To cite Chateaubriand (a rare occurrence), *Voyage au Mont-Blanc*: 'All I ask is not to be forced to admire those long ridges of rock, potholes, crevasses, holes, the tangles of the Alpine valleys'.[3] No way to go further up, then: back to square one. Whatever is left, whatever will remain. At least what turns up on city pavements is as certain as a broken bottle after an all-night rave. Entropic City.

---

2 *Die Landschaft ist nicht die Lösung* (*Landscape is not the Solution*) is the title of a catalogue on the work of German artist Claude Horstmann (Nürtingen: Stiftung Domnic, 2004). Horstmann collects words from newspapers and magazines found when travelling and from overheard conversations, constructing new texts from them, represented as drawings. She also works in performance, sound and photography.

3 François-René de Chateaubriand, 'Voyage au Mont-Blanc; *paysages de montagnes*', in *Œuvres complètes de M. le vicomte de Chateaubriand* (Paris: Pourrat Frères [1806] 1836), vol. 13, 142.

9

Le signe est de mise partout et décline ses poses avec facétie. Ce qu'il faut bannir? La trace et sa conscience aiguë du réel. L'objectif de l'époque? Produire des formes reconnaissables. Ce qu'il faut bannir? La trace, l'informe et leur conscience aigue du réel. Mais n'est-ce pas le projet réel de l'activité artistique comme déambulation que de s'accaparer ce que la marchandise et le profit ont toujours méprisé? Ce droit de privilégier l'expérience à la règle et de faire de ces « non-choses » des laboratoires du sensible?

[Signs are everywhere and they enumerate their poses facetiously. What must we banish? The trace and its acute awareness of the real. What is the objective of our times? To produce recognizable forms. What must we banish? The trace and the shapeless thing, their acute awareness of the real. But surely the real aim of wandering as an artistic activity is to hoard the things that commerce and profit have always despised. It is the right to privilege experience over measurement and to make these 'non-objects' into laboratories of the perceptible.]

10

Ce à quoi souvent il faut répondre:
'Que faites-vous dans la vie?
– Je relève des chutes.'

[Something people often ask me:
'What do you do for a living?'
'I pick up what has fallen down.']

IMAGES:

La reproduction, 2005–09
variable dimensions, graphite on plaster
exhibition view: *Ultimos Dias*, 2009, Sepa-Rennes
photographs: Stéphane Le Mercier

La reproduction, Ghost writer, 2008
(35 x 35 x 17 cm), graphite on plaster and wood
private collection
photograph: Hervé Beurel

Pedagogy and Practice

7. Pedagogy and Practice

Amy Wygant

In the early pages of his 1670 *Traité de l'origine des romans* (*Treatise on the Origin of the Novel*), the French Jesuit-educated humanist scholar, bishop, polymath, tutor to royalty and man-about-town, Pierre-Daniel Huet, had this to say about pedagogy:

> Comme l'esprit de l'homme est naturellement ennemi des enseignemens, et son amour-propre le révolte contre les instructions, il le faut tromper par l'appas du plaisir et adoucir la sévérité des préceptes par l'agrément des exemples, et corriger ses défauts en les condamnant dans un autre.[1]

> [Since the natural inclination of the human spirit is to resist whatever is being taught, and its narcissism sets it against instruction, it has to be fooled by the lure of pleasure, and the severity of principle has to be lightened up by means of interesting examples, so correcting our own faults by condemning them in someone else.]

Huet's observation is rich in references to his own background as a product of Jesuit pedagogical strategies, which included the staging of edifying school plays and the concealing of nuggets of learning in the riddling, puzzling text-image genres of the emblem and the device.[2] He is writing as well for a very particular audience: those in the midst of constructing a new kind of mixed-gender sociability, the

---

1   Pierre-Daniel Huet, *Traité de l'origine des romans* [1670] (Paris: Dessessarts, 1798–99), 4. http://gallica2.bnf.fr/ark:/12148/bpt6k650112 (accessed 20 September 2012). For one of the most recent work on Huet, see April G. Shelford, *Transforming the Republic of Letters: Pierre-Daniel Huet and European Intellectual Life* (Rochester, NY: University of Rochester Press, 2007).

2   See G. Richard Dimler, S. J., *Studies in the Jesuit Emblem* (New York: AMS Press, 2007).

mid-century salon, which had begun to redefine taste and to judge that learning should be a pleasure, not a hard slog. However, my rough, psychologizing translation of the passage above, which does a bit of violence of its own to the major specialist topics of *amour-propre* and *agrément*,[3] does not begin to do justice to the real pessimism and violence of Huet's language.

The human spirit is, he says, an enemy, a natural enemy in the predatory, food-chain sense, of 'des enseignemens'. This means that it pits itself not against some global notion of teaching, but more exactly against the manifold and multiple acts of teaching which convey things taught. It revolts, in his precise wording, against being instructed, and has to be duped into learning by the trickery of the 'appas', which can certainly be a bait or lure for pleasure in a sexual sense.[4] The English translation of Huet's text, which appeared two years later, does not mince words at this juncture: 'Tis to be deceived by the blandishments of pleasure'.[5] Huet then skirts around a very subtle and complex process wherein a severe body of precept is sweetened ('adoucir') by the ornament ('l'agrément') of example. The conceptual structure of which the body clothed in ornament is an example occurs throughout the century, from the body of the tragedy, its action, being clothed by its verse,[6] to the body of a saraband being decorated with mordents and trills.[7] But lest we dismiss this structure's application to pedagogy as merely a simple Mary Poppins-like 'spoonful of sugar', Huet's final clause intervenes to muddy waters which never were, and have never since been, particularly clear. That which was the ornament is in fact the operator of learning: the student may learn 'by example', but the actual mechanism of this 'by' is undecided: it can be either effective ('by means of') or adjacent ('while, at the same time as, in the vicinity of'). We correct our own faults, either 'en' [while] condemning them

---

3 See Kathryn Hoffmann, *Society of Pleasures: Interdisciplinary Readings in Pleasure and Power During the Reign of Louis XIV* (New York and Basingstoke: St. Martin's Press and Macmillan, 1997).

4 See Jean Racine's tragedy, *Phèdre* (1677), where the 'appas' of the young Aricie are necessarily qualified as 'innocents' (I. 1. 55).

5 Pierre-Daniel Huet, *A Treatise of Romances and their Original* (London: printed by R. Battersby for S. Heydrick, 1672), 3–4. *Early English Books Online*, http://eebo.chadwyck.com/home (accessed 20 September 2012).

6 See my *Towards a Cultural Philology:* Phèdre *and the Construction of 'Racine'* (Oxford: Legenda, 1999).

7 See Margot Martin, 'The rhetoric of *mouvement* and passionate expression in seventeenth-century French harpsichord music', *Seventeenth-Century French Studies*, 31 (2009), 137–49.

in others, so treading a fine psychological line between hypocrisy and the discontents of civilization, or 'en' [by means of] condemning them in others, judges, task-masters, pitiless subjects of the superego that we are.[8] How, then, do we learn? Either way, the opacity of 'en', a ruse of the learner to match Huet's trickery of teaching, is stunning.

The French 17th century made only the odd cameo appearance at the Glasgow and Edinburgh discussion group, 'Pedagogy and practice', part of the core programme 'Psychoanalysis and the arts and humanities' run by the Institute of Germanic & Romance Studies, University of London, throughout 2007. Yet it is a striking fact that the group's participants, both academics and teachers from the universities of Glasgow, Edinburgh and Stirling, and teachers and psychodynamic practitioners from the Scottish Institute of Human Relations, Glasgow and Edinburgh, found themselves revisiting Huet's claims about learning and teaching in the everyday terms of our contemporary experience in classroom, counselling and supervision. The group devoted three spring sessions to texts and issues that framed grand discussion questions, and three autumn sessions to case study texts that seemed to pivot around the questions we had framed.

According to Huet, students are apt to say 'no', enemies of teaching that they are. And quite right too; for Kirsty Hall, leading the group's first framing-text meeting, this 'no' from the learner is constitutive and might indeed be the saving of psychoanalysis.[9] 'No', after all, plays a role as the discriminations that recognize or create difference. As such, it is the basis of the structures that enable access to both language ('cat' is not 'bat' is not 'rat') and the unconscious. 'There is no stronger evidence that we have been successful in our effort to uncover the unconscious', wrote Freud, 'than when the patient reacts to it with the words, "I didn't think that", or "I didn't (ever) think of that"'.[10] Let learning be productively located in this border-land of 'no' and, Hall claimed, it would no longer mean the acquisition

---

8 The 1672 English translation opts for the synchronous: 'and thus our own faults may be amended while we condemn them in others' (*A Treatise of Romances*, 4).

9 Kirsty Hall, 'What happens when someone says "no"', paper delivered to the 'Pedagogy and practice' discussion group, 19 February 2007, Scottish Institute of Human Relations (SIHR), Glasgow.

10 Sigmund Freud, 'Negation' [Die Verneinung' [1925], in *The Standard Edition of the Complete Psychological Works of Sigmund Freud*, 24 vols., ed. and trans. by James Strachey *et al.* (London: The Hogarth Press and the Institute of Psychoanalysis, 1953–74), vol. 19, 239. Hereafter abbreviated SE, followed by volume number.

of and acquiescence to received knowledge, but instead the default setting of learning would be the question, and revolt would indeed be its daily chore.

After a brief flirtation with the fashionable Cartesianism of the salons, Huet became one of the most eloquent anti-Cartesians of his day, and he had at least this in common with Jacques Lacan. Eugene de Klerk, in the second of the group's meetings devoted to framing texts (see above), argued that Lacanian psychoanalysis permits itself to be read as a lesson in ethics.[11] This reading goes to the structure of the pre-ontological subject, that subject which exists prior to being, whose *cogito* begins not with 'I', but indeed with a question, 'What is it that you want me to be?'. A Lacanian pedagogy would equip itself to enter into relation with this tremendously fragile yet infinitely monstrous subject, and with its desire for knowledge that impels it to marshall all the trickery of the transference in its pursuit of meaning. The human creature will learn one thing rather than another, and in one way rather than another, as the lure of the example knocks it from pillar to post. But its 'no', the gesture of revolt, is useful not just to the analyst who might be alert to indices of the unconscious, but also to the bearer of that unconscious. If doubt, for Descartes, thinks, then doubt, for Lacan, speaks, and it uses a discourse which overwhelms it but does not succeed entirely in neutralizing its agency. Here we approach the heart of Huet's darkness, the indecision of 'en'. How, exactly does the transference make the subject more fully itself? How does the example teach? 'En', wondrously, seems not to stitch up meaning conclusively. It seems to provide a glimpse of a gap in which the learner can escape from the socio-symbolic net that the teacher is extending, and can prevaricate.

'If knowledge about the unconscious were as important for the patient as people inexperienced in psycho-analysis imagine, listening to lectures or reading books would be enough to cure him.'[12] The group's third meeting was intended to be a testing of the multiple analogies between the psychoanalytic scenario and academic teaching. Learning and therapy are surely coincidental. '"The best thing for being sad"', replies Merlin to T. H. White's once and future king, '"is to learn something. That is the only thing that never fails"'.[13]

---

11 Eugene de Klerk, 'The ethical status of the unconscious', paper delivered to the 'Pedagogy and practice' discussion group, 19 March 2007, SIHR Glasgow.

12 Sigmund Freud, '"Wild" psycho-analysis' ['Über "wilde" Psychoanalyse' [1910]] SE 11, 225.

13 T. H. White, *The Once and Future King* [1958] (New York: Ace Books, 1987), 183.

But does their relation extend beyond coincidence? Are students, for example, in need of a cure? The once-buzzy pedagogical buzzword, 'relevance', may unite the two fields of practice and pedagogy, for it is etymologically not, as we might assume, a cousin of 'relate', but instead belongs to the same family as 'relieve'. When we sense the spirit that we call 'relevance' in teaching, when its activity or content is 'meaningful', the idea is not that it reduplicates us, but instead that we have been succoured, delivered, set free from some burden or affliction – but what?[14] The 'wild' practitioner described in Freud's short paper on 'wild psycho-analysis' is the object of Freud's own 'no'. The practitioner's technical procedure is incorrect, his scientific understanding inaccurate. Yet Freud himself points out that this very defective technique may sometimes produce a cure, and it has since found a significant application in Gestalt therapy. Cure, then, cannot be the point of the 'no': the point goes instead to the establishment of the institution, in Freud's case the International Psycho-Analytical Association 'to which members declare their adherence by the publication of their names, in order to be able to repudiate responsibility for what is done by those who do not belong to us and yet call their medical procedure "psycho-analysis"' (Freud, 226–27).

Is the institution, then, an adequate response to the wildness that Freud encountered in the wild psychoanalyst? 'No', would clearly have been the response of Scotland's most important public intellectual of the 20th century, the psychiatrist and psychoanalyst R. D. Laing, whose lifelong double edge of desire and rejection with respect to the university the group considered as a case study in the course of its autumn meetings at the SIHR, Edinburgh.[15] And 'no' would equally have been the response of Cornelius Castoriadis, whose article 'Psychoanalysis and politics' takes up Freud's repeated remark that psychoanalysis, pedagogy and politics are the three impossible professions.[16] The impossible desire to replicate oneself, then, as teacher, analyst, or law, was considered by Lindy Barbour in

14 See my 'Relevance and its discontents: teaching Sofia Coppola's *Marie Antoinette*', in *Teaching the Early Modern Period*, ed. Derval Conroy (Basingstoke: Palgrave Macmillan, 2011).

15 Amy Wygant, 'R. D. Laing and psychoanalysis in the university', paper delivered to the 'Pedagogy and practice' discussion group, SIHR Edinburgh, 6 December 2007.

16 Cornelius Castoriadis, 'Psychoanalysis and politics', in *World in Fragments. Writings on Politics, Society, Psychoanalysis, and the Imagination*, ed. and trans. by David Ames Curtis (Stanford: Stanford University Press, 1997), 125–36; seminar presentation by Kirsty Hall, SIHR Edinburgh, 20 November 2007.

a discussion of the 'hauntology' of object relations. The internalization of the institution by the individual may never be anything more or less than a haunting: the teacher as ghost may be a suitably complex pedagogical emblem.[17]

With the evocation of the emblem, we return to Huet and his Jesuit-led pedagogical strategy of the hard core of teaching wrapped up in the lightness of example, and there follows here a wonderful concretization of Huet's 'en', teaching in the vicinity of, or by means of, example, put into effect by Zoe Laughlin and Materials Library. Writing now as one who has held her cube of aerogel, the world's lightest solid, 99.8 per cent air, I can recommend its ghostly translucence as instructively open, non-resistant to meaning, wondrously conducive, indeed conductive, to saying 'yes'. Sander Gilman's contribution, finally, observes another kind of materiality, the importance of place for psychoanalytic training. Can the university ever be its home? The President of the University of Chicago, Robert Maynard Hutchins, who appointed a psychoanalyst to his faculty in 1930 – an appointment that proved a disastrous failure – was also a champion of Great Books, at least in part because they were, in his opinion, 'teacher-proof'. Let us hope that this aggression strange in one charged with leading a university faculty, the desire to dispense with embodiment and the mediation of the teacher, will in retrospect seem only quaint, and that new structures and new institutions of pedagogy and practice now coming into being will prove to be lighter, more supple, more affirmative than before.

---

17 Lindy Barbour, 'Ghosts', seminar presentation to the 'Pedagogy and practice' discussion group, SIHR Edinburgh, 1 November 2007.

8. Psychoanalysis in the University: The Clinical Dimension

Sander L. Gilman

The question of how psychoanalysts are to be trained is once again a topic of discussion. During the decades of debate about content – what was to be imparted in a psychoanalytic training – the question of how and where psychoanalysts were to be trained had virtually vanished. The training institute model was taken as a given. In the 21st century the question of content seems relatively unimportant. What had been rigid and competing schools of thought has given way, in most cases, to a sense of the necessary eclecticism of psychoanalytic theory. What is now being questioned is where and how this new eclecticism is to be imparted.

After the Ninth Psycho-Analytical Congress at the beginning of September 1925 at Bad Homburg, Max Eitingon, creator of the first functioning training institute, made the following claim: psychoanalysis had to develop:

> that which Freud has created, to guard it from a premature fusion and so-called synthesis with other fields of thought and different methods of investigation and work, and ever [sic] to give clear definition to that which is specifically our own. Now the fate of our work is in the hands of our successors, and it is to them more and more that we must turn our attention. We must endeavour to meet this our most pressing need by making suitable provision.[1]

The anxiety about intellectual synthesis was indeed a demand for psychoanalysis to avoid the strains of the Humboldtian university,

---

1 'Report of the Ninth Psycho-Analytic Congress', *Bulletin of the International Psychoanalytic Association* 7 (1926), 130.

created not only to research and teach but also to test ideas across and within disciplines. The university demanded certain models of learning, certain definitions of science, which psychoanalysis seemed not to meet. (But most vitally, clinical psychiatry, neurology and psychology were by the 1920s the implacable foe of psychoanalysis for reasons well beyond debates about 'science' in the university.) Remain separate and remain pure, said Eitingon. His talk was heralded with a powerful round of applause and after a debate of over three hours the proposal to limit training to the institutes was accepted.

Hermann Nunberg of Budapest, speaking at the Fifth Psycho-Analytical Congress of 1918, was the first to propose such a training institute. But it was in Berlin, following the establishment of the free clinic, that the model for psychoanalytic training was formally developed. The training committee of the International Psychoanalytic Institute and one of the first generation of female physicians, Karen Horney, in her role as the first training director in Berlin, shaped the analytic institute as we now know it. Horney was also one of the few non-Jews to work in the training institutes.

Psychoanalytic Institutes, with required formal training analysis, were created in Berlin, then Vienna and then Budapest. All were also associated with the free clinics – *ambulatoria* – established to make psychoanalysis available to the greater public and provide a training platform for analysts.[2] Soon thereafter the institutes in London, Frankfurt am Main and New York were created. In Vienna, as Helene Deutsch noted in 1932, 'a large number of eager young people – physicians and teachers – can only be accepted on a "waiting-list" because the financial limitations of our Institute, in spite of the sacrifices of the workers there, do not make it possible to provide training for all those who desire this'.[3] That year 32 candidates were enrolled in Vienna alone.

But why had not the training of analysts taken place in the existing research university model in the 1920s? Freud's combined hesitation and desire about his relationship with the University of Vienna and his colleagues there had coloured the unfolding of psychoanalytic training.[4] Academic opposition to psychoanalysis had already risen

---

2 See Elizabeth Ann Danto, *Freud's Free Clinics: Psychoanalysis and Social Justice, 1918–1938* (New York: Columbia University Press, 2005).

3 Helene Deutsch, 'The training institute and the clinic', *International Journal of Psychoanalysis* 13 (1932), 255.

4 See George Makari, *Revolution in Mind: The Creation of Psychoanalysis* (New York: Harper/HarperCollins, 2008).

from this quarter before the turn of the century and was couched in rhetoric that was clearly anti-Semitic. Why? As the Viennese saying of the time ran: 'Who's to blame?' 'The Jew.' 'Why?' 'Because that's the way it is.'

Freud's desperate need to achieve academic respectability at the Viennese medical school is already the stuff of much historical research. His eventual adjunct professorship was important to him as a mark of recognition of his work that would also give him a much needed financial boost. It held high significance, too, in a country to this day obsessed with titles. Thus Freud would be addressed as 'Herr Professor Doktor', while his wife became 'Frau Professor Doktor'. With an edge of bitterness, Freud lamented how much more easily he would have been granted the medical school appointment if his name had been Oberhuber, a sturdily Austrian name.[5] The slot assigned to him for his weekly lecture, Saturday 5–7 pm, assured an audience of as few people as possible. Indeed if you look around Vienna today for Freud's memorials you can find the public housing project called the 'Sigmund Freud Hof' [Sigmund Freud Court], where a plaque reads: 'Dr. Sigmund Freud, Professor of Neurology at Vienna University, Founder of Psychoanalysis, 1856–1939'. Freud's status even in contemporary Vienna is keyed to his title first and only then to his role in the history of psychoanalysis.

The opposition to psychoanalysis in the departments of psychiatry at that institution, especially on the part of Julius Wagner-Jauregg, who won the Nobel Prize in 1927 for the treatment of syphilis by malaria infection, is less well documented. This was despite the fact that Freud had defended him in court after World War One against the charge that he had tortured soldiers suffering from 'shell shock' by using electrotherapy. Clinical psychiatry was in thrall to a somatic model ascribed to the Munich Professor of Psychiatry Emil Kraepelin, but well represented in the Vienna of the 1920s. The situation in Berlin was little better. While some of Freud's teachers, such as Ernst Brücke, had been trained there, the medical establishment was clearly anti-psychoanalysis from the turn of the century. Indeed Theodor Ziehen, who arrived there in 1904 as professor of psychiatry, was an advocate of association psychology. This approach was a neurological theory in which psychopathology was seen as the result of the repetitive pairing of two stimuli when the experience of one leads to the effects of another. (This is sometimes called Pavlovian association after

---

5 See letter from Freud to Karl Abraham of 23 July 1908, in *The Complete Correspondence of Sigmund Freud and Karl Abraham 1907–1925*, ed. Ernst Falzeder, trans. by Caroline Schwarzacher (London: Karnac Books, 2002), 53.

Ivan Pavlov's pioneering of classical conditioning.) Ziehen was one of the path-breakers in Germany of the dominance of Kraepelinian psychiatry, the forerunner of our contemporary clinical psychiatry rooted in brain science and genetics. Neo-Kraepelinian psychiatry competed with psychoanalysis in the 1920s; but by the 1980s it had achieved worldwide dominance. Indeed the history of American psychiatry, as mirrored in the official *Diagnostic and Statistical Manual of the American Psychiatric Association* in five different editions from 1952 to 2000, records the inexorable replacement of psychoanalytic categories with those of neo-Kraepelinian psychiatry.

In spite of this competition there was a moment in the United States where a *rapprochement* between the university and psychoanalysis might have been possible. This moment occurred following the invitation Robert Maynard Hutchins extended in 1930, to the Hungarian-born psychoanalyst Franz Alexander from the Berlin Institute, to become the first professor of psychoanalysis within a university – and indeed, as Alexander was a physician, within a medical school. As early as 1911, Ernest Jones had spoken before the Chicago Neurological Society about the radical difference between those 'violently opposed and those eager to learn and understand the "new psychology"'.[6] Jones's talk did not result in a widespread acceptance of the new psychology in the Chicago community. 'The controversy did not last long because those who tried the method were soon overwhelmed by transference reactions of love and hate from their patients' (Grinker, 159). Yet here the opposition within the university, as well as within the established psychoanalytic training elite, made this impossible. Hutchins quickly gave in to the pressure from both his medical faculty and the conservative Chicago community and felt that a sexually-based psychological treatment was not appropriate for a university:

> [Alexander] was asked to see patients in consultation, began the analyses of interested young psychiatrists, and fatefully began a seminar in the Department of Medicine attended by clinicians and basic scientists; in fact, the seminar was open to all faculty members of the university. Alexander, born in Hungary, spoke English with an accent at the time, mixed the genders of pronouns, and his extemporaneous speech was somewhat stuttering. By intention he spoke first about psychosomatic disturbances and unfortunately used the example of a woman whose constipation was cured by

---

6 Roy R. Grinker, Sr., 'The history of psychoanalysis in Chicago, 1911–1975', *Annual of Psychoanalysis*, 23 (1995), 158.

Alexander's advice to the husband to present her a bouquet of red roses!

At that point the hostility of the basic scientists erupted and a diarrhea of criticism and invective overwhelmed Alexander as never before or since. The seminar came to a standstill necessitating the dean, Dr. Franklin McLean, to circulate a memorandum ordering that discussion be reserved until the completion of the seminar, months ahead. The audience melted away, myself among them, and the seminar fell apart. (Grinker, 162)

Alexander saw the writing on the wall. At the end of 1931 he left Chicago for Boston. He was soon to return to Chicago with financial support from the Chicago businessman Alfred K. Stern. His money established the independent Chicago Institute on 25 February 1932. He founded the stand-alone Chicago Psychoanalytic Institute – the second in the United States, after New York City. Karen Horney, the Berlin Institute's director of training, who had formulated the first comprehensive curriculum for psychoanalytic training, took over the same role in Chicago.

The subsequent history in the United States and Europe following Freud's death made the analytic institutes all-powerful in the training of psychoanalysts. As powerful as they became, their hegemony was also regularly contested. As early as 1947, Michael Balint raised the question, in the *International Journal of Psychoanalysis*, of whether this was the best or only model for training. He was caustic about the possibility of changing the system in place at the time:

> Any justified criticism directed against training implies that some of the training analysts – especially we of the older generation – were possibly not properly trained. This is perhaps one of the reasons why it has hardly ever been openly admitted that this or that rule of our training system had to be amended, or any innovation introduced only as an experiment.[7]

But Balint understood the inherent anxiety about training and its control in the institutes. He compares this to:

> primitive initiation ceremonies. On the part of the initiators – the training committee and the training analysts – we observe secretiveness about our esoteric knowledge, dogmatic announcements of our demands and the use of authoritative techniques. On the part of the candidates, i.e. those to be initiated, we observe the willing acceptance

---

7   Michael Balint, 'On the psycho-analytic training system', *International Journal of Psychoanalysis* 29 (1948), 163.

> of the exoteric fables, submissiveness to dogmatic and authoritative treatment without much protest and too respectful behaviour. (Balint, 166)

Of course, such a claim would apply to the university medical school as well as to the psychoanalytic institute, where the final role, the acknowledgement of the student's completion of study is the awarding of the degree and the taking of the Hippocratic Oath, a residue of priestly ordination.

In 1958, Thomas Szasz – at that time a psychoanalyst rather than the *bête noire* of psychoanalysis – repeated this question in an even more pointed manner in an essay in the same journal. It began with the following quotation from Albert Einstein about education in general:

> It is, in fact, nothing short of a miracle that the modern methods of instruction have not yet entirely strangled the holy curiosity of inquiry; for this delicate little plant, aside from stimulation, stands mainly in need of freedom; without this it goes to wrack and ruin without fail. It is a very grave mistake to think that the enjoyment of seeing and searching can be promoted by means of coercion and a sense of duty. To the contrary, I believe that it would be possible to rob even a healthy beast of prey of its voraciousness, if it were possible, with the aid of a whip, to force the beast to devour continuously, even when not hungry, especially if the food, handed out under such coercion, were to be selected accordingly.[8]

For Szasz the institute model is not Balint's primitive cult but the parental dyad:

> Analytic training began as a short period of apprenticeship and rapidly evolved into a complex social structure, the modern training system. In the latter, the system and its representatives have great power over the selection of candidates and their fate. It is held that the psychological implications and effects of this sociological change in the analytic training system have not received the attention which they deserve. Indeed, to focus on the content of psycho-analytic training (e.g., training analysis, seminars, supervised analyses, etc.) while disregarding the total structure of the educational system is grossly misleading. It is reminiscent of the traditional parental attitude about raising children, according to which parents 'tell' all the 'right things' to their child and are later full of indignant 'surprise' at the human end product which results. (Szasz, 608)

---

8 Thomas S. Szasz, 'Psycho-analytic training – a socio-psychological analysis of its history', *International Journal of Psychoanalysis* 39 (1958), 598.

The basic structure of the criticism is against educational models in general and the institute as exemplary of them.

Recently, psychoanalysts such as Emanuel Berman, in his provocative book *Impossible Training* (2004), have raised this question once again. He sees himself and the development of the Israeli Psychoanalytic Society's innovative approach to training as representing the legacy of the earlier critics:

> These days, we all seem to be constantly negotiating our way between the inner world of fantasy (Freud) and the impact of family and environment (Ferenczi) as shaping personality; between drives and defenses (Freud) and self-object relations (Ferenczi) as central inceptions; between interpretation (Freud) and affective experience (Ferenczi) as our main therapeutic tools; and between viewing ourselves primarily as impartial observers (Freud) and viewing ourselves primarily as involved in a mutual intersubjective process (Ferenczi).[9]

All the above questioned not only the efficacy of the general approach to training (is a 'training analysis' actually an analysis?) but also the location of the training, seen as parochial and isolated:

> On hearing stories about the analyst, the analysand crystallizes a picture of the analyst's general (transferential) attitude to the professional community, to colleagues, and to students. The picture becomes meaningful for the analysand – no less meaningful than the analyst's direct behavior in their interaction. Following Racker's (1968) view that transference is always reactive to the analyst's countertransference, we may add a hypothesis: This general attitude of the analyst, even though it is not experienced firsthand in the sessions, also arouses transference feelings that incorporate, of course, elements from the analysand's unique inner world. (Berman, 167)

Thus there is an inherent asymmetry between the analytic claims in the clinical setting and the actual practice of the training analysts at the institute.

Such a criticism seems appropriate but Otto Kernberg has indicated that even such a critic avoids some of the discussion present in today's university:

> While all of this is very reasonable and positive, there is a striking absence, however, of any reference to scientific research, reflecting, in fact, an almost 'traditionalist' psychoanalytic attitude of suspicion toward empirical research because of its 'objectivist' quality. (Also

---

9 Emanuel Berman, *Impossible Training: A Relational View of Psychoanalytic Education* (Hillsdale, NJ: Analytic Press, 2004), 62–3.

missing is any reference to the social responsibilities of psychoanalysts in terms of the mental health challenges of contemporary society and the patient population we see.) This absence of any stress on scientific development, and the complete lack of critique of the inhibition of empirical research in traditional psychoanalytic institutes, is one of the weak points of this generally constructive and progressive approach to the problems of contemporary psychoanalytic education.[10]

Kernberg points out the disjuncture between the expectations of the psychoanalytic institutes and the university, and especially the university medical school (he is emeritus professor of psychiatry at Cornell Medical School), about science and ethics. We return here to the original claims from the 1920s about the nature of scientific research (in the university) and the weakness attributed to the institute.

The question has now been raised again within the established structures of psychoanalysis. The International Psychoanalytic Association's committee on the University and Psychoanalysis held its first conference on non-clinical programmes in 2001; the second was held under the auspices of Emory University in the autumn of 2007. Professor Adela Leibovich de Duarte of Buenos Aires, chair of the Psychoanalysis and the University Committee of the International Psychoanalytic Association, comments on the most recent conference:

> Psychoanalysis needs to reposition itself in the University. Regarding the complexity of our subject matter, working at the university on the interface between psychoanalysis and other disciplines facilitates exchange and provides the opportunity for cross-fertilization and for gaining a better understanding of the human being. In this context, it is necessary to renew and expand our involvement as psychoanalysts within academic life in order to transmit our theory and technique whose efficacy [sic] in alleviating human suffering has been demonstrated by clinical results and systematic research. (private communication)

Some things have changed radically since 1918: psychoanalysis has moved from dominating mental health treatment in the 1920s (from Vienna to Topeka, Kansas) to having a major role in the social sciences in the 1950s (from Ruth Benedict on the Japanese to Margaret Mead's *Coming of Age in Samoa*) to attaining a permanent role in the research and teaching of the humanities in the 1980s and beyond. This move meant, however, a split between 'applied' psychoanalysis and 'clinical' psychoanalysis. As non-clinicians came to dominate

---

10 Otto F. Kernberg, 'Perspectives on psychoanalysis: *Impossible Training*', *Journal of the American Psychoanalytic Association* 54 (2006), 285.

debates about 'theory' in the university, the theory debates in the institutes gave way slowly but surely to a new eclecticism in training. The former was keyed to the increased status of theory in general in the humanities and social sciences after the 1960s; the latter was to no little extent the result of the broadening of admission to the institutes after the 1980s. The shift also meant that, on the one hand, 'talk therapy' has become part of the common coin of some mental health professionals without their seeing the need for any psychoanalytic training and, on the other hand, brilliant and innovative work in applied psychoanalysis and psychoanalytic theory has developed without much attention to the realities of clinical experience.

The possibility of merging the theoretical interests of the university and the clinical demands of the institutes in the 21st century now seems feasible. The irony is that it is only possible in the 21st century because of the 'death of theory' in the university and the gradual erosion of interest in psychoanalytic training on the part of even the broader clinical audience in the institutes. Certainly, the former has to do with the regular shifts of intellectual fashion in the universities, a reflection of their Humboldtian need to keep exploring 'new' directions; the latter, at least in the United States, has more to do with the pragmatics of health care funding than clinical interests. Both also reflect the 21st century's rediscovery of so-called atheoretical, empirical 'science' (evolutionary psychology, brain imaging, genetics) and its gradual incorporation into the anti-theory perspectives of the social sciences and the humanities. Yet between them, these two facts mean that a new model which merges the clinical and the theoretical is possible today. But this model is dependent on the good will of the universities and the institutes to see common interests. Time will tell.

9. Materials for the Advancement of Conceptualization: An Introduction to Materials Library

Zoe Laughlin

Deep in the bowels of King's College London there is a space that is home to a collection of some of the most wondrous materials on earth. This space is the Materials Library, a stage for the performativity of matter. Here, materials have been gathered together not only for scientific interest, but for their ability to fire the imagination and advance conceptualization, to enable a rethinking of the stuff that makes, and is, the world around us. Materials Library aims to combine the art, science and culture of materials in order to create a place where the multidimensional world of matter can be explored by experts and non-experts alike.

Unique samples have been gathered from anywhere and everywhere: materials-science research laboratories, artists' studios, antique shops, industrial construction sites, street corners and garden sheds, as well as more formally acquired through materials suppliers and manufacturers. The collection (ongoing and growing) is a physical interface between disparate communities of practitioners with a common interest in materials including artists, architects, designers, material scientists, musicians, medics, engineers and educators. The aim of the resource is to communicate materiality by offering physical encounters with matter and to foreground a both physical and conceptual appreciation of materials as things of scientific and cultural importance.

The more celebrated materials in the library include a chunk of Aerogel from NASA's Jet Propulsion Laboratory that, at 99.8 per cent air, is the world's lightest solid; a tile of aluminium nitride that conducts the heat from one's hand efficiently enough to cut ice as if it were butter; a vial of a totally inert fluorocarbon liquid into which one can place any electronic equipment while continuing to operate it, without any ill effects. Each of these materials is more often than not encountered for the first time by visitors to the Library and greeted with curiosity, delight, intrigue and surprise. Other items, like the Bakelite telephone, the Fiestaware teacup, the ceramic knife and the uranium glass fruit bowl, are more recognizable to visitors as nameable objects with a distinct function. The conscious combination of abstract *stuff* and identifiable *thing* enables the Materials Library collection to operate as a nexus of what I have termed *material-objects*, which foreground materiality and enable visitors to discover and traverse multiple narratives in the collection. From an appreciation of sharpness or ductility to the phenomenon of fluorescence, the concept of impermanence or the colour red, visitors are able to apply their own lens of curiosity to a collection that understands the importance of – and positively embraces – multiple taxonomies.

While pre-ordained materials samples from suppliers and manufacturers are informative, and historical material artefacts culturally demonstrative, the specific territory of Materials Library (where the boundaries of material and object are explored) provides an opportunity for the purposeful creation of material-objects that explore the role of materiality in the generation of form and function. Materials Library's practice of material-object curating becomes the practice of material-object creation. The following outlines a number of the sets of material-objects made specifically for Materials Library and some of the factors that contribute to the collection physically, conceptually and methodologically.

Cubes

The first set of material-objects devised and created were cubes, each 4cm by 4cm by 4cm. About a hundred of these cubes were made from a variety of materials: lead, steel, bronze, brass, copper, clay, wax, foam, oak, Aerogel, balsa, pine, sugar, polystyrene and chocolate, to name but a few. The form of the cube was selected because it was three-dimensional enough to offer an experience of comparable masses, abstract enough to extract object function from the appreciation of the material, and simple enough to be made from a wide range of materials using a number of processes. As is the case with all items in Materials Library, the cubes were freely available for visitors to touch, lift and handle.

At their core, this set of material-objects offer a comprehension of relative densities (mass per unit volume) through experiential comparison. Over the course of their use, however, two cubes in particular came to exemplify an experiential understanding of density: the tungsten cube and the aluminium cube. Appearing to be almost identical, they are both evidently metals with smooth, shiny, metallic grey surfaces and neat hard edges, though the tungsten cube is darker in colour with a strong sheen while the aluminium cube is lighter in colour with a more diffuse sheen. Under visual examination, no remarkable difference between the materials is evident. Once lifted, however, the striking contrast in the masses of the two cubes is revealed and the two materials are thrown into opposition. The aluminium cube is lifted easily without much effort or thought given to either the action or energy required to carry it out. In contrast, the tungsten cube does not move when an attempt is made to lift it in the same manner. A much greater force is required and the greater mass of the material is thus revealed.

In each case, the material has an effect on the human body: the act of lifting is altered as a result of the properties of the material being lifted. The action performed on the cube is directly affected by the performance of the material from which it is made. Materials perform at the micro scale, which can be measured, and at the same time perform in the macro world of the physical encounter. The investigation of a material by the hand at the macro scale reveals properties accessible through haptic encounter, which are directly linked to the performance of the material at the micro scale. In the macro experiential sense, the tungsten cube is more difficult to lift; it is *experienced* as dramatically heavier than the aluminium cube. This difference in mass is the direct result of the atomic weight of the material.

Tuning Forks

The aesthetic qualities and scientific properties of sounds and our perception of them are a central part of our experience of the world around us. Sounds and their cultural resonances are built upon material relations that produce specific acoustic effects and connotations. Imagine the sound of a prisoner running a polystyrene cup along the iron bars of his/her cell, rather than the archetypal enamelled steel cup. Imagine the sound of a stick running along railings; then consider how this sound would change if the railings were glass and the stick carbon fibre. The world is filled with sonic signatures that assure us that the car-door has closed properly, inform us that the person in the flat above has replaced his/her carpet with laminate flooring, and tell us that the filament of an incandescent light bulb has blown when we shake it.

In order to demonstrate the comparative acoustic properties of different materials, the second set of material-objects made for Materials Library was a set of tuning forks. The three principal factors that influence the production of sound by a tuning fork are the shape, the density and the elastic modulus of the material from which it is made. The qualities of the sound produced are experienced as a note of specific pitch (frequency), with a particular brightness (a combinatory factor of duration and amplitude). While the cubes demonstrated density (mass in relation to volume), the tuning forks explored the effect of density in relation to other material properties in the functional scenario of tone generation and object performance. In a standard commercially available set of tuning forks, made from steel, the pitch of the note produced is changed by varying the length of the fork prongs. In the case of Materials Library tuning forks, the dimensions of the forks remained constant while the materials from which they were made varied, ranging from lead, zinc, copper and brass to walnut, spruce, nylon, acrylic and glass. Such changes in material enable the resultant differences in the performance of the forks to be judged in relation to the micro property of density and the performance of elastic modulus. Any shift in the pitch of sound produced by each fork is a direct result of materiality, rather than the form in which the material is found.

Bells and Bugles

While the object of the tuning fork is commonly recognizable as a tone generator and requires very little technique to produce the correct effect, the form itself has a degree of abstraction and is not commonly perceived as a musical instrument but rather as a specialist tool. The various acoustic effects produced by the tuning forks of varying materials do, however, tell of the materials selected for use in musical instruments. The bright tonal quality and long duration of the note produced by the brass tuning fork, for example, reveals one reason why this is the material of choice for whole families of instruments.

In order to demonstrate and enhance the musical aspect of the relation between sound and materials, a further group of material-objects was made, a selection of bells and bugles. A post-office bugle made from copper was replicated in lead, while a brass school bell was also duplicated in lead, bronze, and glass. The post-office bugle and school bell, as cultural artefacts, are very clearly objects in a materials collection. However, the act of replicating an object and varying the material from which it is made alters the way in which the artefact is perceived, highlighting materiality and foregrounding the effect of the material on the cultural and musical performance of the object. In the journey from cube to tuning fork, then tuning fork to bell and bugle, as the form of the material-object becomes more tethered to function so the object status of the set increases. The number of material variables also decreases as the exploration relies less upon the quantity of the materials and more on the quality of the effect.

Events

Quality of effect is explored in much of the work that Materials Library does outside the library space. Over the course of the last four years, Materials Library has staged a number of events and exhibitions that foreground materiality and provide the opportunity for the physical encountering of matter. Projects have included 'The Essence of Fluorescence' at the Hayward Gallery, 'The Sound of Materials' at Tate Modern, and 'Flesh' and 'Hair' at the Wellcome Collection.

In November 2006, Materials Library staged 'Materials Library Presents ... Tate Modern', a series of four materials extravaganzas that highlighted the art, science and materiality behind some of the works of art in Tate Modern's newly rehung permanent collection. Each of the events took place in the gallery space of Tate Modern, focusing in turn on the four newly hung collection areas – Materials Gesture, Poetry and Dream, States of Flux and Idea and Object – responding both to their themes and contents.

The approach used materials as a tactile language with which to explore the scientific, cultural and sensual aspects of art. Our hypothesis was that technical details enhance aesthetic experience and that, in generating physical encounters with matter, one can provide an often-forgotten way into this technical knowledge. In order to test this, Materials Conjectures were devised and created to act as physical interfaces with materials, to facilitate conversations, allowing haptic, olfactory and auditory engagement with matter.

Each Materials Conjecture was located with a specific work of art, from which it drew inspiration or to which it spoke sensorially, conceptually or materially. The content of each conjecture varied, ranging from activities and experiments specifically created for the evening to displays of material-objects taken from the Library and offered for physical encounter, as in the case of the black-and-white tables in the Sol Le Witt room in the Idea and Object gallery. In this room, Le Witt's black-and-white drawing covers all four walls. We placed two tables in the room, one covered in a white tablecloth, the other covered in a black one. On the white cloth we laid out every white item from the Library collection, as well as other white items gathered especially for the display that would then become part of the Library collection after the show. On the black table we did the same with black material-objects. People were free to handle every item, ask questions and arrange the display as they saw fit. The Conjecture brought together a wide range and variety of items, and visitors engaged in a range of improvised activities from trying to determine the blackest and whitest item on each table, rejecting some material-objects as not black or white enough, and attempting to identify the items, pick favourites and share stories and knowledge.

Another Materials Conjecture was presented in the States of Flux gallery in front of Martin Parr's photomontage *Common Sense*, in which 88 photographs are displayed in a grid. All are close-up images of selected elements from British seaside resorts, resplendent in saturated lurid technicolour. In front of Parr's work we offered 88 different types of penny sweets for people to smell, feel and taste in a synaesthetic overload.

During the course of the evenings, the cubes, the tuning forks and the bugles made star appearances alongside sculptures, sound works and abstract modernist paintings of the 1960s. In the case of the cubes, their most successful deployment was next to Lucio Fontana's sculpture *Natura*, a work that started life as a ball of clay which he then slashed and cast in bronze. A label adjacent to the work displayed the common gallery notice 'please do not touch' but, from all the gallery visitors we observed and our own impulses, it was clear that there was an overwhelming desire to touch the work. A gallery guard was stationed close by but people could not help but stretch out an arm or push forward a foot and give the sculpture a little pat or a push. Each act of touching served to test the sculpture, to investigate it materially, to know it physically. This being Materials Library's *raison d'être*, we could not ignore the opportunity to provide physical material-objects that would afford an appreciation of the relative mass of materials. The gallery label accompanying Fontana's work states it to be made from bronze and 610 mm x 730mm, but it does not say if the form is cast from solid bronze, nor how heavy the piece is. To declare that the item has a mass of 20 kilograms or two tonnes makes a great difference to the viewer's perception of the work. Equally, if a visitor is daring enough to tap the work, s/he will hear that it is in fact hollow which, once learnt, also shifts their perception of the mass of matter before them. Short of changing the content of the label, and in the spirit of the physical exploration of mass, we could not ignore the opportunity to display all the cubes alongside *Natura*, making a specific range of bronze cubes that would offer some links to the sculpture and the opportunity for imagining the implications of materials in sculptural practice.

Inside the Library space itself, or out in the context of an art gallery or museum, Materials Library devises, creates, curates and stages materials encounters that show material-objects performing as the subject *for* and *of* experience. The conception and creation of unique physical experiences that foreground materiality offer a platform for the exploration of a material's ability to mediate action, affect environments, alter perceptions, inspire creation and provoke curiosity. The hope is that after handling the lightest solid in the world, witnessing the transformation of shape memory alloys, carrying a giant lump of coal or breaking a wine-glass with sound, participants in a Materials Library experience go away thinking about, looking at and feeling the world around them a little differently.

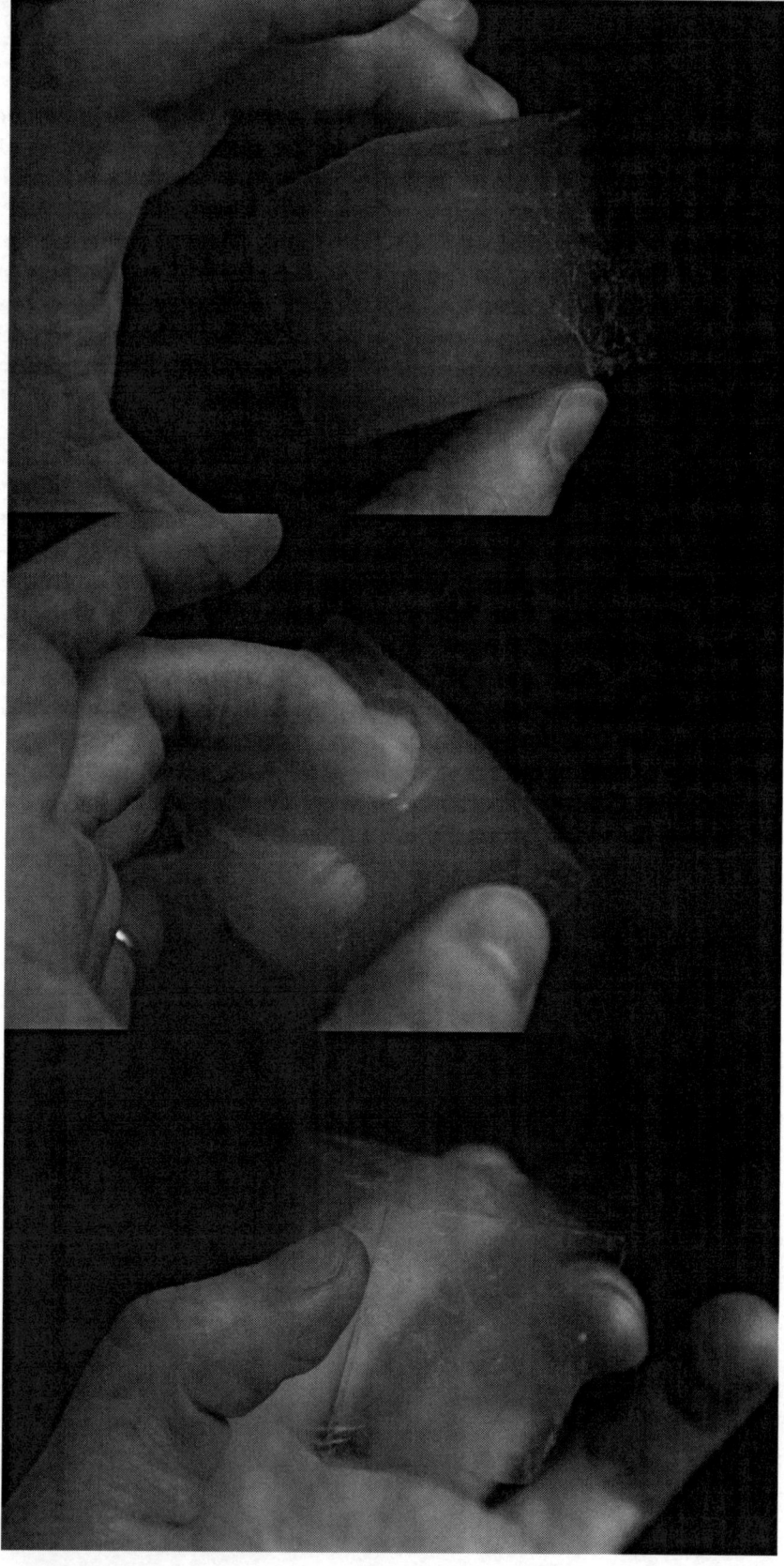

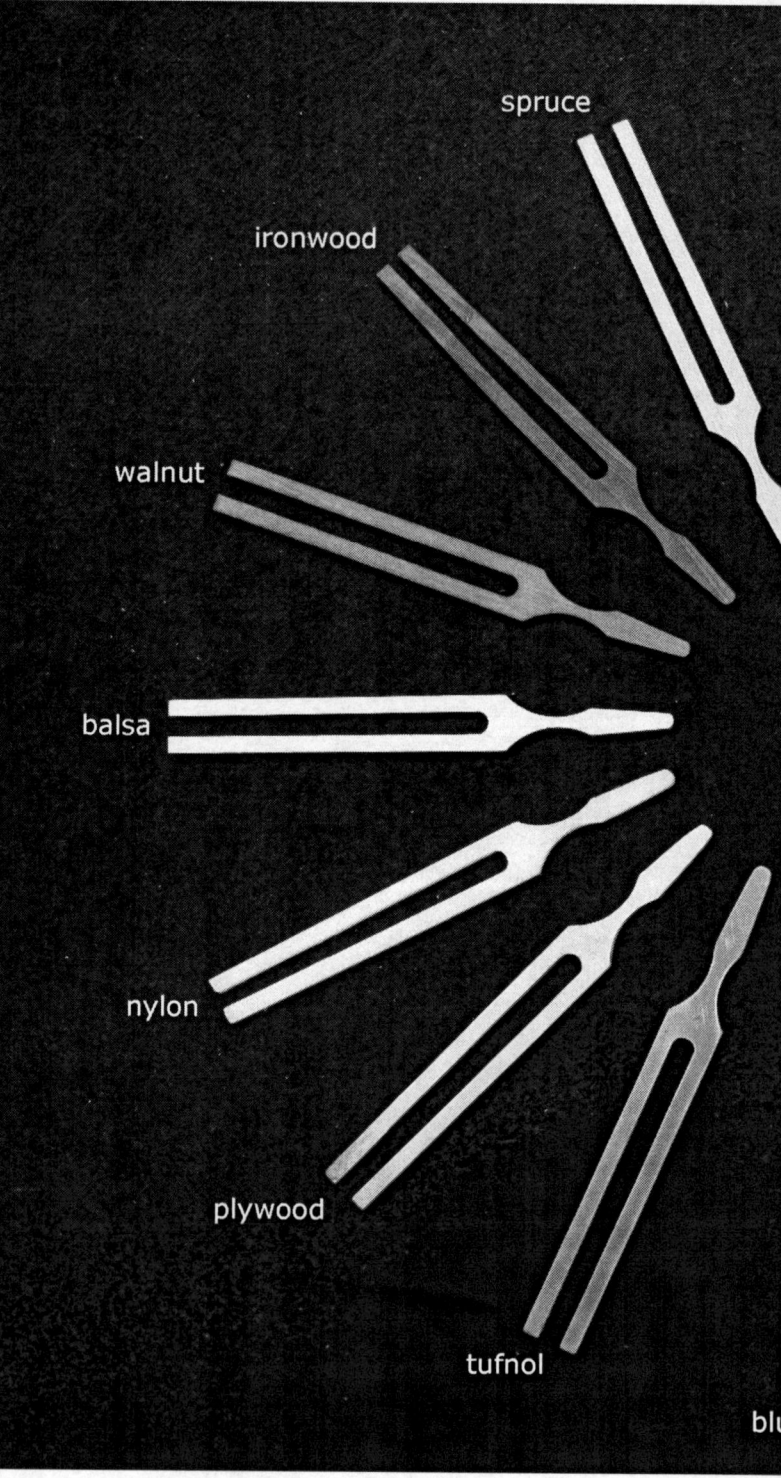

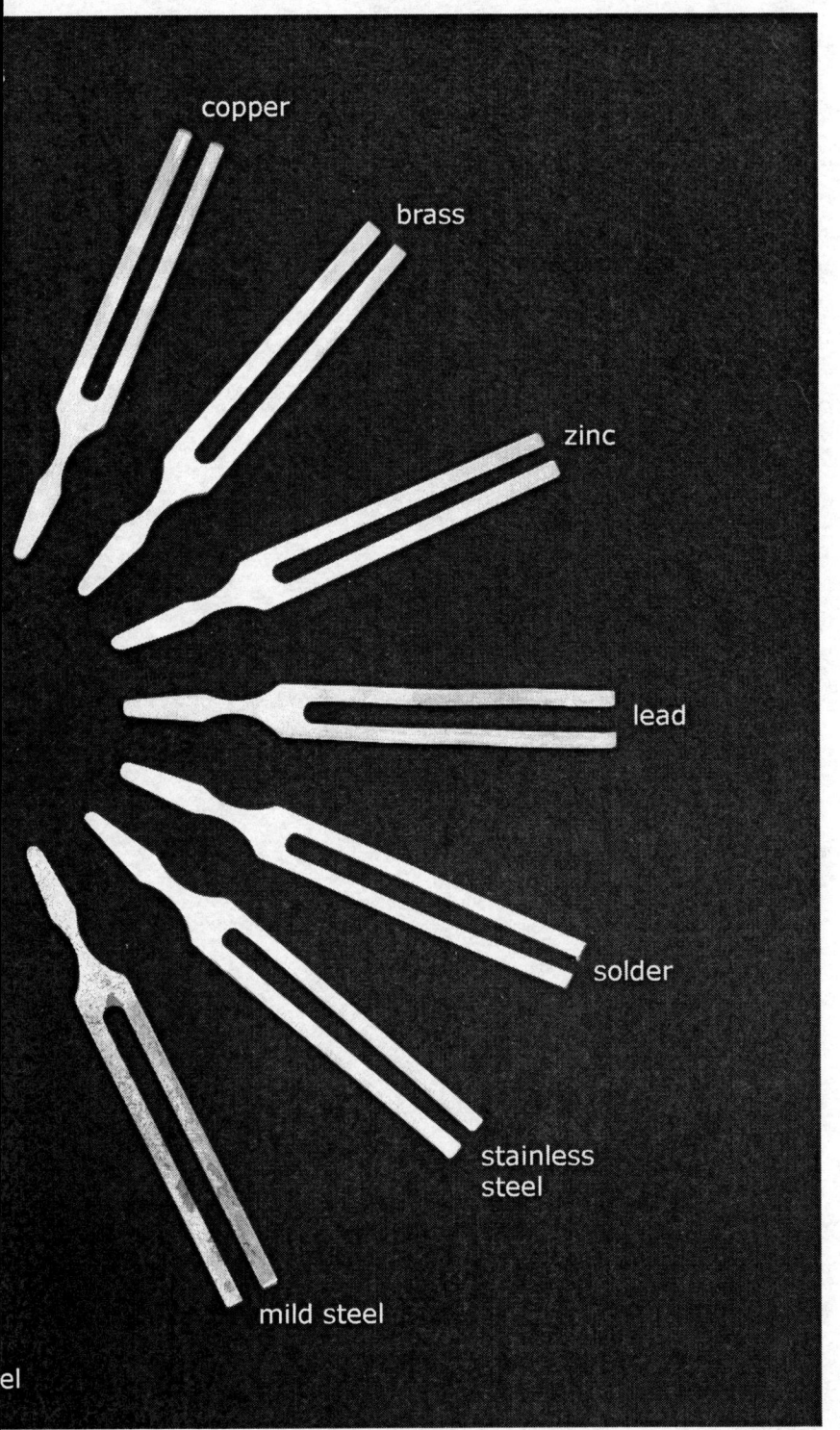

Psychoanalysis in the Spanish- and Portuguese-Speaking World

10. Speaking Experience

Alison Sinclair

Psychoanalysis as the 'talking cure' comes out of Freud's essay 'On the psychical mechanism of hysterical phenomena: preliminary communication' (1893), in which hysteria, newly perceived as not physical in origin but physical in expression, and denoting trauma, gives rise to a whole method. The phrase is that of Bertha Pappenheim ('Anna O.'), as reported by Breuer.[1] The disorder is eloquently summarized in this essay as an embodiment that resists language, that pushes language away as being unsuitable for the expression of trauma, that entices as much as it rejects. Fleshed out dramatically and tellingly in Freud's 'Psychotherapy of hysteria' (1893),[2] hysteria is a disturbing and vacant embodiment of trauma, a disorder that is full of haunting memories which can only be brought to the surface with difficulty, simultaneously gripping and elusive. Our seminars did not set out to track hysteria in the development of the thought of Freud, but uncannily the body, its meanings and its absences, pervaded both the seminar discussions and the final conference papers reproduced here.

The two essays in this section, by Hugo Vezzetti and Juan Cruz, provide a fitting and intuitively consonant finish to the themes and concerns of the Hispanic seminars held in the preceding year. Vezzetti's exposition of the nature and role of psychoanalysis in

---

1 Josef Breuer, 'Fräulein Anna O.' ['Fräulein Anna O.' [1893]], in *The Standard Edition of the Complete Psychological Works of Sigmund Freud*, 24 vols., ed. and trans. by James Strachey *et al.* (London: The Hogarth Press and the Institute of Psycho-Analysis, 1953–74), vol. 2, 30. Hereafter abbreviated SE, followed by volume number.

2 Sigmund Freud, 'The psychotherapy of hysteria' ['Die Psychotherapie der Hysterie' [1893]], SE 2, 253–305.

Argentine culture and Cruz's account of how he gave performative presence and body to the act of translation of two major works in Spanish, were not *produced* by the seminars; but they do arise, as it were, spontaneously, from the concerns that we had had from the start, and reflect in different manners aspects of the way in which we worked.

First it might be remarked that our seminars were marked by an attitude of inclusion, in that the interests of those who attended spanned a wide geographical range, encompassing both Peninsular Spain, Portugal and Latin America, particularly Argentina and Brazil. This range was, however, not a source of dissonance but rather provided a variety of platforms from which we were able to see a striking number of parallels, general themes and concerns. We also had a mixture of practitioners of psychoanalysis and people who worked in literature and culture, and more than a few who combined the two activities. This facilitated the easy move between cultural material and psychoanalytic interpretation. It also meant that our view of psychoanalysis was always grounded in specificities of time and place, and our interest was in how psychoanalysis was something that might – or might not – be used at particular times in particular places.

Our initial seminar meeting to consider our interests illustrates this mixture of variety and coherence. The predominant theme to emerge was the relationship between psychoanalysis and society, most particularly when society is in crisis, riven by war, violence and extreme political situations. Such contexts of conflict gave rise to issues in common between the different geographical areas, not least of the way in which initial trauma was such that the memory of it was characteristically repressed for the space of a generation. Looking at psychoanalysis in the countries that concerned us it was clear that we would be informed by examples of real trauma, real bodies (or absence of bodies), real gaps that would have to be bridged by language, or that might resist being brought into being through language.

We began, in fact, with language. We followed up the initial exercise, common to all the language-based seminar groups as they began life at the network's opening conference in November 2006, of considering translations of Freud's 1908 essay, 'Creative writers and day-dreaming',[3] with a further meeting on translation, where we examined in detail the vicissitudes of Freud's original through

---

3 Sigmund Freud, 'Creative writers and day-dreaming' ['Der Dichter und das Phantasieren' [1908]], SE 9, 141–53.

two distinct Hispanic lenses. These were the traditional Spanish version of the *Complete Works* by López-Ballesteros, commissioned by Ortega y Gasset in 1922, and the markedly different Argentine Amorrortu edition begun in 1974.[4] The Peninsular version has much of the best of the Strachey translation about it: it communicates the feel, the emotional tone, of Freud's original. The Amorrortu, by contrast, picks up on that other Strachey feature, the use of clearly scientific language that would later be commented on adversely by Bettelheim.[5] This feature of the Argentine edition is curious when one considers the extensive popularization of psychoanalysis in Argentina and indicates the degree to which, at the professional level, becoming popular did not equate with becoming diluted. We then devoted a seminar to reading Freud's 'Mourning and melancholia' (1917), thinking about the situations and moments that had been identified as traumatic.[6] We read this essay, intended for thinking about the individual in relation to trauma, in the light of the collective (while bearing in mind that this collective had a set of individuals, and their traumas, to deal with). This close textual work gave the seminar grounding, and we were fortunate enough to be able to triangulate our discussion linguistically through the presence of Martin Liebscher.

The key reference-points of Spain and Argentina continued throughout the seminars, periodically broadened to include Portugal and Brazil, with mentions of Chile. While moving geographically and chronologically required us to attend to specificity of situation, it also reminded us of the degree to which there were concepts and patterns that existed in an over-arching and constant way, while being inflected by their moments of occurrence. Meanwhile, in autumn 2007, the 'History and transmissions' group based in Cambridge devoted four sessions to readings on psychoanalysis in Argentina and Chile, one of the most lively being a paper on the tango in Argentine culture.

Another session – a showing of the film *Vacas* [*Cows*], introduced by Jo Evans who had just published a book on Medem, its director

---

4 Sigmund Freud, *Obras completas*, trans. by Luis López-Ballesteros y de Torres (Madrid: Biblioteca Nueva, 17 vols., 1922–34); Sigmund Freud, *Obras completas*, trans. by José Luis Etcheverry (Buenos Aires: Amorrortu editores, 24 vols., 1974–85).

5 Bruno Bettelheim, *Freud and Man's Soul* (London: Chatto and Windus, [1982] 1983).

6 Sigmund Freud, 'Mourning and melancholia' ['Trauer und Melancholie' [1917]], SE 14, 237–58.

– invited us to think in a flexible manner.[7] This complex meditation on fratricidal conflict prompted discussion of media, symbolism and gender, and particularly stretched us in thinking about the wide range of ways in which – informed by psychoanalysis – the film might be interpreted. It opens up the area of the mythical, but also of the uncanny, areas of the mind and imagination that contrast with and complement considerations elsewhere of trauma inflicted by absolutist powers, and at the same time conveys a very direct sense of the Lacanian Real.

A session on the Portuguese poet Fernando Pessoa, led by Paulo de Medeiros, brought new elements to the discussions, not least those of identity, nation, paternity and authority. Pessoa wrote under four main heteronyms, with a distinctive style, but also distinctive – or distinct – persona for each of these names, and he also had an upbringing split by changes of both residence and language. He thus presented the group with a fascinating series of issues, some of which may be borne in mind when reading what Vezzetti has to say about the heterogeneous nature of Argentina. Pessoa's example is seemingly custom-made for a psychoanalytic interpretation, whether as case-history or as providing illustrative elaboration of the disturbed mind, yet little has so far been done on his work from this point of view. This is a field ripe for exploration.

A session led by Orit Beck looked at the development of psychoanalysis in Brazil from the 1920s on. This provided us in advance with material to compare with what Hugo Vezzetti raised at the conference and writes about in this volume. This comparison works not only in terms of the early reception of psychoanalysis in both countries, but also in the later complex relationship revealed in the case of Helen Vianna Basserman and her opposition to the training in the 1970s of a man who had been a known torturer of the military regime.

Our final seminar of the series, with Mike Richards, on the problems of cultural memory in post-Civil War Spain, presented us again with issues of the unacceptable faces of public life. Graphic and telling examples illustrated the private traumas that are suffered and exacerbated by lack of public recognition, the real material of human existence and the attempts made to manipulate public consciousness and suppress private experience. This paper brought to a focus many of the strands that had been with us through the year. Though sombre in material, the energetic concepts used in it demonstrated

---

7 Jo Evans, *Julio Medem*, Critical Guides to Spanish and Latin American Texts and Films, 71, (London: Grant and Cutler, 2007).

the strengths of psychoanalysis for facilitating the interpretation of what stands outside recognized and accepted public versions of our experience.

This, then, was the backcloth to the presentations of the core programme's final conference. The two salient concerns, consisting, on the one hand, of close textual reading and, on the other, of broad consideration of public and private trauma, public and private memory, and how to deal with the disjunctions between them, had been the hallmark of our discussions. The essays that follow in this section of the book pick up on both these aspects.

Juan Cruz's enterprise, in which he set himself the task of performing a translation and interpretation of *Don Quijote* orally, to be witnessed by others, provides a singular expansion and intensification of what we had done in the early seminars. As he relates, he spent some 12 hours at this task, translating about half of this foundational text of Spanish literature. This work was simultaneously public and yet also reticent. The making visible of the process of translation provided a meeting-point of experience, an embodied mediation between a present audience and a text of immense and varied cultural significance. This performance was followed by a translation of García Lorca's lecture on the *Duende*. There are two things to note here. One is that the *Duende* lecture tells of an elusive and central force in artistic creation and performance.[8] Lorca has to describe it in terms of what it does, how it might be experienced, while never fully being able to communicate it. A bodily experience, *Duende* is a force and a process through which the artist mediates something telluric and dynamic. Vital and energizing, it is fundamental to the artistic act. But, strikingly, Cruz tells of how he both conveyed the meaning of this elusive quality Lorca referred to and produced the documentation of the translation. This recording and mediation stands in contrast with the dynamic nature of the actual translation in performance, much as our accounts within and about psychoanalysis can only be recorded in a manner that veils the vitality of the original experience. A further step is recounted in his discussion of his 2005 translation of *Don Quijote* where the element of actually performing comes to stand, in his own estimation, between himself and the

---

8   Federico García Lorca, 'Teoría y juego del duende' ['Theory and play of the *Duende*'], lecture given in Buenos Aires and Havana, reprinted in García Lorca, *Obras completas*, ed. Arturo del Hoyo, 2 vols. (Madrid: Aguilar [1954], 1980), vol. 1, 1097–109.

audience he is translating for. The element of this being a 'show' now overtakes the interest of the initial act of communication.

Hugo Vezzetti's paper, with its rich variety of approaches, produces a reading of psychoanalysis in Argentine culture that embraces virtually all the points of interest featured in the seminars. The pervasiveness of psychoanalysis in Argentina (notably, although not exclusively, a Lacanian style of psychoanalysis) is remarkable. How can this have come about? Vezzetti points out how there was 'freudismo' (practice based on the ideas of Freud) before the ideas of psychoanalysis had been more generally embraced. In the modern period, Argentina's population, strikingly, is one of immigrants. Their sense of loss and nostalgia, often related to the longings expressed in the tango, is one of the country's prime cultural themes, along with the significance of the mother, childhood and the sense of neighbourhood. The reception of Freud in Argentina is framed, as is evidenced in its initial importations, by French origins, producing quite specific habits of usage, although the version of Freud habitually used in the early decades was Strachey's *Standard Edition*. The immigrant roots of the country compounded issues of national identity that had been there since the conquest, with the result that Argentine culture was pervaded with narratives of the self and with a penchant for symbols. Because of the immigrant past, the family is there primarily as a lack, a *vacío*, something that calls to mind the recurrent symbols of absence in Medem's *Vacas*. But if Freud permits an approach to the trauma of loss, a sad retracing of a past that resists capture through memory, his adoption at a more popular level was seen as positive, in that here he was taken up as the great sexual liberator. Unsurprisingly, in both aspects, the mother – and thanks to Klein, as imported by Pichon, the terrifying mother – comes to be a prime symbol, and a strikingly apt *topos* for the myths of Peronism.

The rich, varied and highly specific reception of psychoanalysis in Argentina articulated through Vezzetti's essay thus comes to embody the full range of affective and cultural concerns that informed the Hispanic seminars as a whole. Cruz's essay, with its performance of translation reiterates for us the essential tension between the desire to speak, to engage in the talking cure, to make a bridge between languages and cultures, and the factors of otherness that will continue to make the bridging of such gaps an impossibility.

11. Psychoanalysis in Argentine Culture: A Social and Political Interpretation

Hugo Vezzetti

Psychoanalysis is ubiquitous in Argentinian culture, even in the material and symbolic geography of Buenos Aires: for years now, a neighbourhood in the northern part of the city has been known as 'Freud Town'. The many different explanations proposed for this in general refer to the idea of *destiny*: psychoanalysis was destined to take root and bear fruit in Argentine soil.[1] The causes of this destiny have been traced in Argentina's past, its origin as a society of immigrants as the Argentine Psychoanalytic Association openly admits:

> En la Argentina, el descubrimiento de Freud venía a dar una salida a una sociedad marcada por la inmigración, con el pasado perdido en Europa, en muchos casos amenazante, pero a su vez con la necesidad de reencontrarse con sus orígenes, con su historia infantil olvidada y con la posibilidad de poner al descubierto sus deseos inconscientes.

> [In Argentina, the discovery of Freud seemed to offer a way out to a society which had been shaped by immigration, which looked back to an often threatening past in far-off Europe but also longed to come face to face again with those origins, that forgotten story of childhood and to rediscover its unconscious desires.][2]

---

1 This text is a modified version of a previously published article, 'El psicoanálisis en el siglo' ['Psychoanalysis in the 20th century'], *Punto de Vista*, 88, August 2007; I am indebted to Mariama Ifode and Naomi Segal for the English translation.

2 Argentine Psychoanalytic Association, 'Historia de APA' ['A history of the APA'], at www.apa.org.ar/apa/historia/ (accessed on 24 September 2012).

In this interpretation of the subjectivity of immigration, emphasis is placed on the 'forgotten story of childhood', the search for origins; this focus creates a small myth of conspiracies and family relationships. The truncated family past and the loss of roots highlight two aspects of Argentina's 'national subjectivity' which no doubt existed before the arrival of psychoanalysis. According to this interpretation, the relationship between psychoanalysis and Argentinian society and culture, which seems so fundamental to the latter, is based on a compensatory quest to fill a void in one's origins, to repair a break with primary links and generational ties. What emerges most clearly in this line of argument is *nostalgia*: nostalgia for a past that has been permanently lost, left behind together with places, language, habits and earliest loves. The topic of nostalgia is often associated with another great icon of Argentine culture, the tango.[3] The mother, the neighbourhood and childhood are prominent themes in the poetics of the tango. Let me be clear: I am not proposing an ontological interpretation or subscribing to the simplistic notion that associates psychoanalysis with the tango because of their common preoccupation with the past. Rather, I am pointing out a motive or, if you prefer, a minor fiction that is more a theme for artists and writers than for historians: the particular inflection or situation of psychoanalysis in Argentina as a theme or motive for various stories of origin. All this is in the tale of the *Argentine Psychoanalytic Association*, which takes the form of a narrative sequence: lost past – story of childhood – unconscious desires.

Leaving these accounts to one side for a moment, I want to raise a few points about the history of Freudianism in Argentina before the introduction of psychoanalysis. Curiously, for that tale of an Argentine destiny, the first public presentation of psychoanalysis in Buenos Aires was made by a Chilean doctor, Germán Greve, in a paper entitled 'Sobre psicología y psicoterapia de ciertos estados angustiosos' ['On the psychology and psychotherapy of certain states of anxiety'], presented at the International American Congress of Medicine and Hygiene in 1910, on the occasion of the centenary of the May Revolution. Referring to this event in *History of the Psychoanalytic Movement*, Freud clearly thought that the author was German.[4] In

---

3 See Noemí Ulla, *Tango, rebelión y nostalgia* [*Tango, Rebellion and Nostalgia*] (Buenos Aires: Jorge Álvarez, 1967).

4 Freud writes: 'A physician from Chile (probably a German) spoke at the International Congress at Buenos Aires in 1910 in support of the existence of infantile sexuality and commended highly the effects of psycho-analytic therapy on obsessional symptoms', Sigmund Freud, 'On the history of the psycho-analytic movement' ['Zur Geschichte der psychoanalytischen Bewegung' [1914]], in *The*

Greve's paper and in the writings referring to Freud in the next few decades what emerges is neither nostalgia nor a familial void, but something else: a complex knot of diverse identities, relationships, languages and traditions, which emerged and were mixed together in the reception of Freudianism. Indeed, as Freudian discourse set out towards its Argentine destination, a major problem was that of appropriation and *translation*. Freud seems to expect his work to be read in German; but Freudianism arrived in Argentina initially *in French*. Germán Greve probably read Freud in German, but all his work was directed towards the argument that there were no major differences between Freud and Janet.

In fact, there is no evidence that Greve's work had any impact on the Argentine reception of Freud. However, in that first presentation, many years before the creation of the *Argentine Psychoanalytic Association* in 1942, the *French matrix* of reception was already visible as a structural and long-term feature. It is strikingly apparent in the clinical and psychopathological works of José Ingenieros as well as in the reports sent by Aníbal Ponce from Paris.[5] It is equally present in Enrique Pichon Rivière's readings of Daniel Lagache and José Bleger's of Georges Politzer.[6] In this sense, the introduction of Lacanianism at the end of the 1970s and the work of Oscar Masotta can be considered as the culminating point of a long intellectual tradition that worked to separate Freud and psychoanalysis from its relation with the German language and Germanic cultures.

What happened meanwhile to psychoanalysis in its official capacity – as an institution and in the training authorized by the international organization? The answer is, I believe, pretty well known, especially

---

Standard Edition of the Complete Psychological Works of Sigmund Freud, 24 vols., ed. and trans. by James Strachey *et al*. (London: The Hogarth Press and the Institute of Psycho-analysis, 1953–74), vol. 14, 250. Hereafter abbreviated SE, followed by volume number. Germán Greve (1910), 'Sobre psicología y psicoterapia de ciertos estados angustiosos', in *Revista de Psicoanálisis*, III (1945), 203–13.

5 Anibal Ponce, 'La divertida estética de Freud' ['The amused aesthetics of Freud'], *Revista de Filosofía*, IX, vol. 17 (1923), 89–93. 'Madame Sokolnicka y el psicoanálisis francés' ['Madame Sokolnicka and French psychoanalysis'], *El Hogar*, 10 May 1929, republished in Anibal Ponce, *Apuntes de viaje* (Buenos Aires: El Ateneo, 1942), 110–18.

6 Hugo Vezzetti, *Freud en Buenos Aires, 1910–1939*, 2nd edn., (Bernal: Universidad de Quilmes, [1989], 1996), 13–67; *Aventuras de Freud en el país de los argentinos [Freud's Adventures in Argentine-land]* (Buenos Aires: Paidós, 1996), 245–90. See Enrique Pichon Rivière, *Teoría del vínculo* [*Theory of Attachment*] (Buenos Aires: Nueva Visión, 1979). For Bleger's readings of Politzer, see José Bleger, *Psicoanálisis y dialéctica materialista* [*Psychoanalysis and Materialistic Dialectics*] (Buenos Aires, Paidós, 1958).

in London. In the conditions created by Nazi persecution and the emigration of psychoanalysts, beginning with Freud himself, the centre of gravity of the movement shifted from Vienna to London and then to New York. This move has been researched by a great historian of psychoanalysis, Riccardo Steiner.[7] In Buenos Aires, as in the rest of the world, psychoanalysis has been read in English ever since the publication of James Strachey's translations. The *Standard Edition* established a gold standard; and in the IPA's hands it became the powerful instrument of a politics of language. None of the major readings of Freud produced in Argentina used German sources despite the fact that two of the three established Spanish translations were produced in Buenos Aires – Ludovico Rosenthal's partial translation and the whole of José L. Etcheverry's.[8] These translations were brought out by non-academic publishing houses and did not provoke significant interest either from the psychoanalysts themselves or from the intellectuals in the humanities, philosophy and the social sciences who were keen readers of Freud.

Nathan Hale, an outstanding historian of psychoanalysis in the United States, has highlighted an exceptional quality of psychoanalysis – it is capable of appealing to two audiences at once: those in the field of medicine (including psychotherapies and mental health) and those in the literary and intellectual fields. Élisabeth Roudinesco also maintains this distinction in her work on psychoanalysis in France.[9] It is important to recognize that psychoanalysis is a complex subject which goes well beyond the clinical. This complexity also affects Freud's legacy. One aspect of psychoanalysis is the setting-up of training and institutional reproduction in the organization or 'movement' – Freud uses the term *Bewegung*, which is also used for

7   Riccardo Steiner, *It's a New Kind of Diaspora: Explorations in the Sociopolitical and Cultural Context of Psychoanalysis* (London: Karnac, 2000).

8   Beginning in the 1940s, Ludovico Rosenthal translated five volumes of Freud's works that were not included in the Spanish translation of Luis López Ballesteros. See Sigmund Freud, *Obras completas*, 22 vols., vols. 13 to 22 (Buenos Aires: Santiago Rueda, 1952–56). A complete new translation in 24 volumes was done by José Luis Etchererry, following the structure of the *Standard Edition*: Sigmund Freud, *Obras Completas* (Buenos Aires: Amorrortu, 1976–80). See Hugo Vezzetti, 'Freud en langue espagnole' ['Freud in Spanish'], *Revue Internationale d'Histoire de la Psychanalyse* (Paris: PUF, 1991), vol. 4, 189–207.

9   Nathan G. Hale, *Freud and the Americans. The Beginnings of Psychoanalysis in the United States, 1876–1917* (Oxford and New York: Oxford University Press, 1971); *The Rise and Crisis of Psychoanalysis in the United States: Freud and the Americans, 1917–1985* (Oxford: Oxford University Press, 1995); Élisabeth Roudinesco, *La Bataille de cent ans: Histoire de la psychanalyse en France*, vol. 1: 1885–1939, vol. 2: 1925–85 (Paris: Seuil, 1986).

a political, cultural or literary movement. But there is also a much broader notion of psychoanalysis: its ideas and methods may have a profound impact on society's thinking and its problems, on culture, aesthetics, morality and religion, and on various social groups and thought. Freud's legacy is thus very varied and cannot be reduced to just one legitimate lineage.

I would like to suggest a particular line of approach to the subject of psychoanalysis and Argentine culture, which explores not the medical or psychotherapeutic aspect but instead the forms and uses of psychoanalysis in intellectual culture and especially certain visions of society and the nation. Leaving aside that small myth about psychoanalysis, immigration and family fictions to one side for the moment, I will begin with a speculative hypothesis – in the encounter between psychoanalysis and Argentine culture, psychoanalysis is, above all, a range of positions taken in relation to the question of *interpretation*: it is about exploring certain questions about our collective condition, an obscure and complex identity, if you will. If there is a cultural *demand* for psychoanalysis, it is not for a reading at the level of content, doctrine, or theories: it is a demand for interpreters, which goes back to a time long before the arrival of Freudianism. The interpreter might take different forms – critic, moralist or prophet – but in general it has to be someone who is trying to find the answer to an uncertainty, a *subjective* dimension, a complex of problems. This search for an answer does not come from below, from the family anxieties of immigrant groups; it comes from above, from the elite – the social sector most likely to raise the question that opens a cycle of analysis. 'Who are we?', Sarmiento asked in 1883;[10] the question continues to resonate through many different interpretations in Argentina's recent history.

That question, the question of *identity*, posed both by Sarmiento and in the first interpretative essays on the Argentine nation (from Agustín Alvarez to Carlos Octavio Bunge and Ezequiel Martínez Estrada)[11] did not take its point of departure from the issue of immigration but from the Conquest, the Spanish colonization and,

---

10 Domingo F. Sarmiento, *Conflictos y armoniás de las razas en América* [*Conflicts and Harmony Between the Races in America* [1883]], (Buenos Aires: La Cultura Argentina, 1915), see especially 'Prolegómenos', 63.

11 Agustín Alvarez, *South America. Ensayo de psicología política* [*South America: An Essay in Political Psychology*] (Buenos Aires: La Cultura Argentina, [1894] 1918); *¿Adónde vamos?* [*Where are we Going?*], (Buenos Aires: La Cultura Argentina, [1904] 1952); Carlos O. Bunge, *Nuestra América. Ensayo de psicología social* [*Our America. An Essay in Social Psychology*] (Buenos Aires: A. Moen y Hermanos Editores, [1903] 1911); Ezequiel Martínez Estrada, *Radiografía de la*

above all, 'the races': European, i.e. Spanish, mixed in with the indigenous population, with Creole society and the black race of freed slaves. Early sociological literature focuses on these problems and is of course where the question of immigrants would later be introduced, with the project of creating a civilized white race, kept separate from the American native, closely tied to Europe – a society, a culture and a nation that would be in South America what the United States already was in the north, as stated in José Ingenieros's 1915 essay on 'the Argentine race'.[12]

This line of enquiry, having begun with Sarmiento, continued until Ezequiel Martínez Estrada's *Radiography of the Pampas* (1933), which aimed to unveil the *Argentina profunda* [deepest Argentina].[13] Later, Martínez Estrada would present this book retrospectively as the first social psychoanalysis of Argentina, even saying that it anticipated Erich Fromm's analysis.[14] What interests me about his examination is that it establishes an early model for the reception and appropriation of psychoanalysis in Argentine culture. He draws an analogy between the topic of deeply hidden social ills and an appropriation of Freudianism as the interpretation of what is latent. I am not concerned here with the content of his interpretations, but two aspects are particularly revealing. Firstly, his analysis goes beyond mere statements and implies the ego as a place of enunciation: there is a marked use of the first-person pronoun 'I', a feature which stands out in his work and is also present in much of his other writings. What this implies is that the exploration of the nation's latencies cannot be separated from the autobiography and self-analysis of the interpreter. Furthermore, in following in the footsteps of his predecessors – Domingo F. Sarmiento, José Hernández and William Henry Hudson[15] – he highlights the condition of the interpreter:

---

pampa [*Radiography of the Pampas*], critical edn. by Leon Pollmann (México: Fondo de Cultura Económica, [1933] 1996).

12   José Ingenieros, 'La formación de la raza argentina' ['The making of the Argentine race' [1915]], in J. Ingenieros, *Sociología Argentina* [*Argentine Sociology*] (Buenos Aires: Elmer, 1957).

13   Ezequiel Martínez Estrada, *Radiografía de la pampa* [*Radiography of the Pampas*]. Also see Leon Segal, 'La radiografía de la pampa: un saber espectral' ['The radiography of the pampas: a spectral knowledge'], in Ezequiel Martínez Estrada, *Radiografía de la pampa* [*Radiography of the Pampas*], 491–537.

14   Ezequiel Martínez Estrada, 'Sobre *Radiografía de la Pampa*', in *Leer y escribir* (México: Moritz, 1969), 134.

15   Domingo F. Sarmiento, *Facundo* (Buenos Aires: Centro Editor de América Latina [1845], 1979); José Hernández, *Martín Fierro* (Buenos Aires: Centro Editor de América Latina [1872, 1879], 1979); William Henry Hudson, *Far Away and*

exile, outsiderhood, a position of marginality and rebelliousness, all prerequisites of taking on the attitude of a critic. Secondly, the most important point is symbolic interpretation, which combines with a certain idea of the latent element to be explored: these are the 'invariants', the concentration of certain essences which only reveal themselves in the innermost density of the symbol. For this reason, it has been suggested that he seems to have Jung in mind, rather than Freud. In this version of psychoanalysis, the key things are telluric determinants, such as the land or geography embodied in certain archetypes. However, one can also see the influence of Freud in the analysis of speech and behaviour, gestures and signs, even in the analysis of everyday life.

What I want to emphasize is that the problem of the family is already cropping up in Martínez Estrada's work as a gap or negative element linked to the land and to geography: it appears before the wave of immigration as a constant, a limiting condition of the history of the Pampas population. There are no relationships, no family and no community in the Pampas, he argues. In this early interpretation, before psychoanalysis had reached Argentina, the origin of the ills of society was associated with two causes (also repeatedly found, I believe, in other analyses of interpretation), which in combination – either alternately or simultaneously – account for a collective pathology in the Pampas. These two causes are: *trauma* (a violence experienced as emanating from things unknown and unexpected) and *loss*, the melancholic core that unites native and immigrant, all equally devastated in a land of misfortune and despair, yearning for a golden age that has been lost for ever. The native yearns to renew contact with nature, which was lost after the Conquest and colonization; the immigrant yearns for a lost homeland, ties and customs. I will return to this motive later.

As we have seen, this psychoanalysis, concerned with the deep latent dimension of the nation and Argentine society, was the creation of the elite classes; alongside it, however, there was a popular, plebeian psychoanalysis, which circulated in the culture and the media and was taken up by a wider public. This amplified version of psychoanalysis was focused on *sexuality*. Of course this does not only apply to Argentina: the expansion of psychoanalysis among the non-specialist public in the western world generally takes the form of a discourse and knowledge about sexuality. In the main it was this kind of Freudianism that began to preoccupy the immigrants and

Long Ago. A History of My Early Life (London: J. M. Dent [1918] 1939); [*Allá lejos y hace tiempo*, tr. by Juan Antonio Brusol (Buenos Aires: Guillermo Kraft, 1958).

children of immigrants. Indeed this sexological inflection was already present in the work of Germán Greve, which referred to the original Freudian model, the traumatic model of the neuroses. And, together with the thesis of the pathogenic role of erotic traumas, came the idea of the talking-cure – that is, psychoanalysis presented itself, to quote Michel Foucault, as a way of making people speak.[16]

Since the 1930s, at least, there had been an extensive sexological literature that referred to Freud and which propagated certain topics from Freudianism for the masses: love and sexuality, especially childhood sexuality, hysteria and dreams. At the same time, Freud was presented to the general public as a liberator and modernizer of sexual morality, chiming in with the work of the Viennese writer Stefan Zweig, who was widely translated and read in Argentina.[17] Thus, parallel to the analysis of the age-old ills rooted in the land and the past, another appropriation of Freudianism was born in Buenos Aires: this one looked not to the past but to the *future*. This, if you like, is a more optimistic version for it seeks out and promotes knowledge and teaching on love, pleasure, relationships and happiness. This Freudianism, which was part of a sexology that went beyond psychoanalysis, was the very reverse of fatalistic: it was accompanied by a process of modernization and reform of morality and the traditional rules surrounding love relations. Starting in 1935, *Freud para todos* [*Freud for All*], a popular encyclopaedia following this line of Freudianism, edited by Peruvian poet Alberto Hidalgo, began to appear and was widely read. Even in the 1950s, in the magazine *Idilio* [*Idyll*], the psychoanalyst was a familiar figure in the problem pages offering what was then known as 'advice to the lovelorn'.[18]

Thus we have two aspects, two nuclei from the earliest reception of Freudianism in Argentina. One is focused on the past, on the 'age-old ills' of the Pampas (and by extension the absence of links, the loss or the lack of family ties); the other is related to the future, seeking in psychoanalysis a positive understanding of sexuality

16 See Michel Foucault, *Histoire de la sexualité*, t.1, *La Volonté de savoir* (Paris: Gallimard, 1976), ch. 1, 9–22.

17 Stefan Zweig, *Die Heilung durch den Geist:* [*Mental Healers*] *Anton Mesmer, Mary Baker-Eddy, Sigmund Freud* (Frankfurt am Main: Fischer Verlag [1931], 1982). The section on Freud was published separately in Buenos Aires in the 1930s.

18 See my *Aventuras de Freud en el país de los argentino*, ch. 4; and 'Las promesas del psicoanálisis en la cultura de masas' ['The promises of psychoanalysis in mass culture'], in *Historia de la vida privada en la Argentina* [*A History of Private Life in Argentina*], vol. III, ed. Fernando Devoto and Marta Madero (Buenos Aires: Taurus, 1999), 73–197.

and by extension of the family and society, and it is the basis of a reformist psychoanalysis. In sum, I want to propose, as a general framework at least, that in the development of the relationship between psychoanalysis and Argentine culture, these two nuclei and these two temporal orientations have always existed; and, of course, points of convergence and compromise also exist between them.

That minor fiction created by the psychoanalysts themselves, linking psychoanalysis with Argentine society, to which I referred at the beginning of this chapter, and which centred on a sort of failed national Oedipus who had been cut down to size by the process of immigration, is far from an adequate interpretative key in itself; rather, it needs an explanation, beginning with this intersection between the past and the future, between the sense of the absence of a family of origin and the project or, if you will, the utopia of a new family. The first point to underline is that the notion of the new family – the family of the future – is a recurrent idea in political and social writings in Argentina. As we have seen, it is present in one form or another in José Ingenieros's idea of an 'Argentine race'; before Martínez Estrada even, he picked up Sarmiento's question 'Who are we?' Furthermore, Ingenieros gives the first optimistic response. He was an immigrant and belonged to a new self-constructed elite: for him, there were no age-old ills or powerful determinisms from the past, so what is projected is a promising future. Nonetheless, the theme of the new Argentine family reappeared, particularly in the work and teaching of two authors: Gino Germani and Enrique Pichon Rivière, towards the end of the 1950s and into the 1960s. Both were immigrants and the presence of psychoanalysis is very marked in their work.

Briefly: Germani was Italian and the founder and director of sociological studies at the University of Buenos Aires. Pichon Rivière was born in Geneva to French parents; one of the founders of the *Argentine Psychoanalytic Association*, he was very much in favour of a *rapprochement* between psychoanalysis and social psychology, especially in relation to group dynamics.[19] An important point should be noted here: almost all the first generation of psychoanalysts in Argentina were immigrants or children of immigrants. In other words, they were typical of that new society that had willingly integrated foreigners, which had been a cause for concern for the

---

19 See my 'From the psychiatric hospital to the street: Enrique Pichon Rivière and the diffusion of psychoanalysis in Argentina', in *Argentina On the Couch. Psychiatry, State and Society, 1880 to the Present*, ed. Mariano Plotkin (Albuquerque, NM: University of New Mexico Press, 2003), 141–74.

elites. They also constituted palpable proof of the inadequacy of the tragic prophecies of Martínez Estrada concerning the Pampas and the metropolis. On the other hand, we should not ignore the fact that the expansion of psychoanalysis in Argentine culture and society took place during a new era of change – the 1970s. In that decade an extensive familiarity with the Freudian discipline began to take hold in Buenos Aires. If there was an Argentine school or trend within psychoanalysis in those years, it was based not in the originality of its concepts but rather in its openness towards society. It wanted to integrate itself into the reformist debate and, above all, it was curious about its role in this period of change. Psychoanalysis was dominated by a certain public vocation which was evident both in the universities and in certain experiments in the field of mental health.

I will now pick up the thread of society's hermeneutics from the viewpoint of the recurrent problem I highlighted earlier: that of the Argentine family. The first point to note is that the psychoanalysis that was practised and published in Argentina from the 1950s was suffused with family fictions. This radical *familiarisme*, to cite Deleuze and Guattari,[20] is undoubtedly a defining feature of this type of psychoanalysis. I only have space here to cite the importance of the family (a theme that is absent as such in the work of Freud)[21] in the work of four theorists: Pichon Rivière's on madness and the family; Marie Langer's on sex and maternity; the innovations of Arminda Aberastury, who translated Melanie Klein and was the first to introduce her work on the psychoanalysis of children; and the ideas and teaching of Arnaldo Rascovsky on filicide and the sacralization of the maternal role.[22] All these psychoanalysts represent the return

20 See Gilles Deleuze and Félix Guattari, *L´Anti-Œdipe. Capitalisme et Schizophrénie* [*Anti-Oedipus: Capitalism and Schizophrenia*] (Paris: Minuit, 1972), ch. 2.

21 Freud never examined in his work the subject of the family as a problem: the reader can soon spot that no chapter titles or headings include the word 'family'. This absence contrasts with the place that the family has had in the works of psychoanalysts like Jacques Lacan and Donald Winnicott. See Jacques Lacan, *Les complexes familiaux dans la formation de l'individu* (Paris: Navarin [1938], 1984); D. W. Winnicott, *The Child, the Family, and the Outside World* (Harmondsworth: Penguin, 1964) and *The Family and Individual Development* (London: Tavistock, 1965).

22 Enrique Pichon Rivière, *Del psicoanálisis a la psicología social* [*From Psychoanalysis to Social Psychology*] (Buenos Aires: Galerna, 1970), 2 vols.; Marie Langer, *Maternidad y sexo. Estudio psicoanalítico y psicosomático* [*Maternity and Sex: A Psychoanalytic and Psychosomatic Study*] (Buenos Aires: Paidós, 1951); Arnaldo Rascovsky, *El filicidio* [*Filicide*] (Buenos Aires: Orion, 1973) and Arminda Aberatury, *Teoría y técnica del psicoanálisis de niños* [*Theory and Technique of Child Psychoanalysis*] (Buenos Aires: Paidós, 1962).

to a commitment to interpreting society; and yet this hermeneutic disposition took a different form: it had lost the poignant tone of the search for origins, but it had also abandoned the optimism which imagined a future without conflicts. For example, Pichon Rivière was the author of a 'psychology of everyday life' focused on social conflicts.[23] In this book, the question of relationships and belonging reappears, but in relation to internal migrants, to the new urban population which had moved from the countryside to the city. This issue had featured centrally in Gino Germani's interpretation of the birth of Peronism. To refer to the complex of emotions and phantasies in these new working-class urban sectors, Pichon Rivière coined the expression *miedo al asfalto* [fear of asphalt], which includes its own version of Melanie Klein's early anxieties. He lists a syndrome of depression, alcohol abuse, feelings of helplessness and 'loss of identity'; in his view, melancholy did not come from the Pampas but arose from the clash with the city, that 'mythological monster full of seduction and danger'.[24] Pichon Rivière's conception of melancholy is a corrective to the optimistic mood of the 1960s; at the same time, it is easy to see that he is talking about the conditions and effects of Peronism. On the other hand, the relationship he establishes between the family and madness, a fundamental issue in his teaching, lacks the undertone of the idealization of childhood and the mother that is so marked in the works of the classics, from Sarmiento to Martínez Estrada; it is the present family rather than the absent one that dominates this alienated network. The family does not protect its own, quite the reverse: it makes them ill; it is less a source of security than a site of intolerable suffering which is discharged and displaced onto the 'mad person'.

There are two main focuses in Pichon's thought. They are representative of what psychoanalysis was inclined to think of that society, which largely equated to *Peronist* society; the two focuses are *familiarisme* and melancholy. Pichon Rivière's theory and practice of groups is based on his thesis on the family. What is most significant is that, underneath the aspects derived from the tradition of social psychology and North American's interactionism, there remains a note of tragedy: the group is a sort of substitute and corrective for

---

23 Enrique Pichon Rivière and Ana Quiroga, *Psicología de la vida cotidiana* [*The Psychology of Everyday Life*] (Buenos Aires: Galerna, 1970); see my 'From the psychiatric hospitals to the streets: Enrique Pichon Rivière and the diffusion of psychoanalysis in Argentina'.

24 Enrique Pichon Rivière and Ana Quiroga, 'El miedo al asfalto' ['Fear of asphalt'], in *Psicología de la vida cotidiana*, 111–13.

the family, and yet in both the group and the family the same thing is seen: the illness and the cure exist side by side.

In conclusion, I shall move on all too briefly from this, perhaps rather slanted, exploration centring on a set of problems: family networks, changes in society, above all the Peronist society with which Germani and Pichon Rivière were concerned. From the point of view of the ambiguities of the family and the group, one topic stands out in relation to psychoanalysis's impact on (or encounter with) Argentine culture: the mother. The doctrines of the Argentine psychoanalytic circle centred on Pichon and Langer created a *maternal* psychoanalysis based on the reception of Kleinism.[25] For instance, Pichon Rivière relates the melancholic loss experienced by internal migrants to the model of separation from the mother's body.[26] More interestingly, in the course of Marie Langer's analysis of what she terms the 'myths of Eva Perón',[27] she examines a minor urban myth that circulated in Buenos Aires during Perón's lifetime – 'the myth of the roasted child'. It was a sinister story, which everyone believed to be true, though no one could vouch for its origin: a maid was left in charge of a little boy one evening while his parents went out; when they arrived home, the young woman greeted them ceremoniously, wearing her mistress's wedding dress. She announced that she had a surprise for them in the dining room. There they found, in the middle of a table set with the greatest care, their child roasted and served on a platter. To this myth Marie Langer applies Klein's theory of 'the bad mother' projected on the servant as in the child's early fantasies. I shall not discuss Klein's theories here; they are too well known; however, there is one particular aspect which should make sense even to those who know nothing of psychoanalysis: in the Kleinian paradigm of the mother, of the maternal *imago*, there is an original discord, a flaw or hole that punctures that harmonic vision of the world of family and childhood.[28] This is transposed into an all-

---

25   Janet Sayers, *Mothering Psychoanalysis. Helen Deutsch, Karen Horney, Anna Freud and Melanie Klein* (Harmondsworth: Penguin, 1991), 3–20.

26   Enrique Pichon Rivière, *Teoría del vínculo*, 86, 105–06.

27   Marie Langer, 'El niño asado y otros mitos sobre Eva Perón' ['The roasted child and other myths about Eva Perón'], in *Fantasías eternas a la luz del psicoanálisis* [*Eternal Fantasies in the Light of Psychoanalysis*], (Buenos Aires: Hormé, [1957] 1966). See Hugo Vezzetti, 'Elizabeth I, Lady Macbeth, Eva Perón', *Punto de Vista*, 52 (August 1995).

28   In the Kleinian constellation, 'the archaic mother is the fantasy mother of the first few months of the infant's life – the paranoid-schizoid phase. Omnipotent

purpose key interpreting the latencies of Peronism and, by extension, of Argentine society in general. What is most important is the focus on the controversial representations of Eva Perón: the image of a devouring mother concealed behind the image of the saintly servant of the poor. Langer's theory was in direct contradiction to the official myth consolidated in Eva Perón's autobiography, *La razón de mi vida* [*My Mission in Life*]. In the official myth, Evita is the idealized mother; she is all the more idealized and good because, having no children of her own, her attention is not distracted from this maternal role or that of mediator between the people and the Leader. However, Langer concludes, the position of Juan Perón was actually dependent on and subsidiary to that phantasmatic means of support, the omnipotent maternal image. Paradoxically, the analysis ended up reinforcing an ultimate foundation of the myth, based on the strength of the archaic mother, and this has remained so ever since. One can set out a series in which variants of that imago return: St Evita, Evita the Guerrilla Fighter, and even Madonna's *kitsch* interpretation of Evita in the film.

I could describe many other encounters between psychoanalysis and Peronism, but there is not space to do more than point to them here. Germani deals with the position of Perón, his leadership, and his relationship with the masses, using the same kind of psychoanalytic social psychology as Erich Fromm in his analyses of Nazism.[29] There is an extensive and diverse body of texts that in some form revisit that hermeneutic interest in Peronism as a revealing subject. This is not to say that Peronism is the only subject, nor even the most important in that line of encounters between psychoanalysis and society's problems. In particular, psychoanalysts or authors inspired by their theories have had a tendency to intervene with a psychoanalytic response when faced with the conflicts and events of everyday life. I am also not suggesting that the hermeneutic position is the only one to emerge from that encounter. There was a tradition of practices in the field of mental health (for example, the psycho-hygiene of

---

and phallic, she fulfills and frustrates in equally radical measure. She is the key figure in the early stages of the Oedipus complex, and her breast, an object split into a good, nourishing breast and a bad persecutory one, is her generic attribute. It is the target of the ambivalent libidinal and sadistic oral drives of the infant in search of unlimited satisfaction, a satisfaction that, inevitably, will never be achieved', International Dictionary of Psychoanalysis, www.enotes.com/archaic-mother-reference/archaic-mother (accessed on 24 September 2012).

29 Gino Germani, *Política y sociedad en una época de transición* [*Politics and Society in a Period of Transition*] (Buenos Aires: Paidós, 1962).

José Bleger)[30] which went beyond simply interpreting collective conflicts, to try to intervene in them and reform the family, groups and society. Within that tradition a transformation of the discipline of psychoanalysis itself was found. In the revolutionary mood of the late 1960s and early 1970s, its relationship with politics changed and it began to expand its contacts with Marxism, with the aim of making psychoanalysis into a useful tool for action. In 1971 there was a double split in the *Argentine Psychoanalytic Association*: the dissident groups were marked by their integration of psychoanalysis into what in those years was considered a revolutionary process that would lead to socialism.

In sum, psychoanalysis in Argentine culture has had neither one predictable destiny nor one consistent style. The question of how we might understand the widespread presence of Freud and Lacan is not easy to decide and, above all, there is no national key to answering it. I would hazard a very general judgment: the extensive penetration of psychoanalysis has been not so much a means of advancing knowledge as a powerful ingredient in a decentralized discursive formation, a sort of multiform, open experiment in which the author is invisible and so are all attachments to a discipline or school. In this chapter, I have simply tried to trace a path within the narrative that started from that original question of identity. This is the root of a certain *discontent* that arose in that culture and society and permeated them.[31] Psychoanalysis will continue to be relevant because of the need for *interpretation*, even if it is an impure one mixed in with other kinds of knowledge. I have highlighted certain ways of answering this question, various angles that the interpreter can take, beginning with the appropriation of psychoanalysis as an essential ingredient of a hermeneutic focused on society, its culture and its politics.

---

30 José Bleger, *Psicohigiene y psicología institucional* [*Psycho-hygiene and Institutional Psychology*] (Buenos Aires: Paidós, 1966).
31 I refer of course to the translation of Freud's *Das Unbehagen in der Kultur* (1930): Sigmund Freud, *Civilization and its Discontents*, SE 21(1957).

12. Earnest Abnegation in Perpetuity

Juan Cruz

In 1996 I translated about half of *Don Quijote* orally in the basement of the Instituto Cervantes when it was housed in Manchester Square round the corner from the Wallace Collection in London. I had set up the room so that I was seated at a red formica table, lit by an anglepoise lamp. On the table was a glass on a pale blue saucer, a jug of water, a black Bic pen and some throat sweets. My bookmark was a postcard bearing an image of climbers ascending a steep and craggy cliff. I had sent out about 100 letters inviting people to come and see me do the translation between Wednesday and Friday, 1–5 pm and I had also placed a small ad in *Art Monthly*. At that time I had a job in a bookshop between the hours of 6 pm and 10 pm.

When visitors arrived at the institute the receptionist would send them down the stairs to the basement. At the bottom they would see a dim light emanating from a half-open door and hear my voice. I was working from a Spanish version of *Don Quijote*, a leather-bound edition which my aunt had given me for my first communion, and as I read I was trying to interpret the text in English and speak it at the same time. This resulted in a fragmented and ponderous delivery. I always tried to sustain the activity regardless of anyone who might be in the space and, perhaps more importantly, also regardless of no one being in the space. Often I could not tell the difference. I could hear people coming in but could not tell how many there were in any particular party. I also found it hard to discern when they had left the space and how many had done so. It was important to me at the time that the work should not be recorded because I wanted to intensify the experience for the audience who would, I hoped, get the sense that something was being performed just for them (not that they all understood how grateful they should be for this). Some people I knew would try to let me know that there was no one else there and that I could stop if I wanted to. Others whom I did not know would hover ominously over my shoulder.

In 2005 I repeated the translation but this time with some significant differences. I had in the interim engaged in other endeavours of this kind – my oral translation works – varying both the content and context of the process. In one I translated Federico García Lorca's lecture on the *Duende*, in a studio complex and art space in Rotterdam called Duende, on the 66th anniversary of Lorca's delivery of the lecture[1]. On this occasion my translation, performed in front of a seated audience, took about 45 minutes. I also recorded the translation and produced an audio CD, which I distributed to all the artists working in the studio complex.[2] In other works I recorded myself performing translations in the studio and played the recordings as components of installations involving other related elements. Because all these works were presented in the context of art I undertook a rather conventional form of photographic documentation. I now have a series of photographs of speakers, stands and amplifiers and numerous images of me sitting at tables with my forehead scrunched in concentration. When I look back through the documentation I am as aware (almost certainly more aware) of the quality of the photograph, my clothes, hair and shoes, as I am of the work, which in essence becomes a somewhat embarrassing memory.

When I did the *Duende* translation I decided only at the last minute that I wanted some photographs of the performance. It must, in fact, have been suggested by someone else, perhaps the person who eventually took the pictures. He had no slide film and so ended up taking a roll of print film. He sent me the pack of prints some time later and, to enable me to speak of the work in lectures, I turned some of the images into slides by blu-tacking the prints to my studio wall and photographing them with slide film in daylight. Later on I scanned these slides, now hairy, dusty and covered in fingerprints, in order to facilitate Powerpoint presentations. I must have consciously selected the image that now survives, the one I have come to use to represent the work, because it shows me in the background behind a member of the 12-strong audience who has his back to the camera.

1 In 1933 Federico García Lorca delivered a lecture in Buenos Aires: 'Teoría y juego del Duende' ['Game and theory of the Duende'], in which he sketched a distinctly Spanish brand of artistic inspiration bound up with the seemingly antithetical qualities of joy and suffering that dominate Spanish culture.

2 For a documentation of this work see: 'Game and theory of the Duende' [artist's pages] *Afterall*, London, Issue 3, Spring/Summer 2001.

I remember him; he was a nice guy, who was competing with the photographer for the affections of a young woman who appears, quite lovingly framed, in other pictures from the series. She is slight and a bit boyish, and not unaware of her charm. The nice guy is wearing a loose-knitted jumper, blue with an abstract and somewhat regal golden motif.

So it was with much of this in mind that I embarked on the next translation of *Don Quijote* in 2005. From the start I must have intended to undermine the portentous nature of the first translation because I called it 'Juan Cruz is translating *Don Quijote* [again]'[3] – the first time round it had the more sober title of 'Translating *Don Quijote*'. In the intervening years there also seemed to have developed a growing degree of interest in artists revisiting the possibility of making works incorporating people as material.[4] Because it appeared to me that the intensity of a confrontation with a person as an art object undermined the possibility of many other kinds of responses to a work, I decided to distance the act of the performance from the audience by making my activity visible only through a glazed window at the back of the gallery and audible only through a speaker relaying the sound of my translating voice, which was also being recorded. In order to distance the spectacle further and to make it immediately discernible as *image*, I glazed the viewing window with two panes of glass and sandwiched between them first one and then two sheets of orange gel. This was inspired by a story Joel Uden told me many years ago in Berlin about the way in which he had once advised Ed Lipski, when he was a student at Chelsea, to use two gels instead of one to intensify the colour of the light in a piece he was making involving two children's plastic chairs around a glowing institutional lamp. The idea of the room beyond a room also owed something to Mike Nelson, as well as to Vito Acconci and Michael Asher.[5]

---

3   'Juan Cruz is Translating *Don Quijote* [again]', exhibition, Peer, London, 2005.

4   An initial list of such artists might include Tino Sehgal, Santiago Sierra and Pawel Althamer, though this is by no means exhaustive.

5   For 'Studio Apparatus', his exhibition at Camden Arts Centre in 1998, Mike Nelson constructed a small, office-like antechamber through which one had to walk in order to get through to the gallery space housing the bulk of the installation. In 'Seedbed', Sonnabend Gallery 1972, Acconci lay under a false floor in the gallery space masturbating and speaking through a microphone to gallery visitors during the course of the exhibition. For his exhibition at the Claire Copley Gallery in 1974, Michael Asher simply removed the wall normally separating the exhibition space of the gallery from the office and administration area.

These structural modifications occasioned some quite significant changes in the work. From the perspective of the audience the impact was pretty much as anticipated. That is to say, it was able to view the performance while retaining a degree of critical and discursive distance. If visitors entered in pairs they were able to talk about the work in its presence and maintain some detachment from it if they chose to. Still, many of the viewers commented on the herculean nature of the task upon which I had embarked and enjoyed talking up the labour of the work to imply something about my tenacity and stupidity. Many wondered how I managed to keep going all day on this apparently mundane task without distractions. In fact, I did not. Whereas the first time round I *had* to keep going, because I had no way of knowing when people would be coming into the space, this time people had to buzz at the door to be admitted. Furthermore, there was always a dedicated invigilator who would only let people in once they had checked I was ready and in position. They also let me know when visitors had left. The unedited recordings of these days are full of hours of unrelated conversations and tea-drinking, hours that I edited out for the more austere recorded version of the work. So I behaved rather like a dancer in a peep-show, turning it on and appearing super-absorbed in my act when the punters walked in. I am sure an intelligent ear would have discerned this subterfuge through the modulations of my voice. But perhaps those intelligent enough to notice also knew better than to mention it. Not even the fact that I finished the translation within five minutes of the stated end of the exhibition schedule seemed to alert many to the fact that I may have been pacing myself in a most calculated way. The subterfuge made me feel quite uneasy, not because I was at all concerned about deceiving the audience but because the deceit placed in stark relief the rather transcendental aspirations that others seemed to want to understand from the work. I remembered hearing the porn star Ron Jeremy talk about how he could provide a money shot precisely from a countdown of ten, and I could not help feeling that my own work was beginning to engage in a sordid way with similar basic assumptions around established structures and time frames of entertainment, representation and the most banal kind of deceit.

I saw an exhibition of documentation of performances Vito Acconci had made in Italy in the late 1960s.[6] The gallery billed them as the last performances he made before turning towards other types of work – largely, Acconci seems to have stated, as a result of it becoming increasingly difficult for him to retain a sense of the

---

6 Albion Gallery, London, 2008.

audience being an audience; it became too involved for his liking, a sentiment often addressed directly in the work. Acconci had been due to exhibit a new work for this exhibition – a latex-covered bench I think – one of the quasi-semi-architectural structures in which he and his studio have recently been involved. A triple heart-bypass prevented him from having this work ready in time and he felt compelled to put together these assemblages from his archive. I am sure we all miss Acconci's early aggressive confessionals, those self-obsessed, narcissistic drives towards a kind of worthless redemption, the way in which every work was always like the last one, an *a priori* failed attempt to declare that he would never do it again, like giving up smoking or masturbating behind the stud partition. And then it just stops, and the gap is filled with an altogether more constructive engagement that sees him working with and for people, attending shamelessly and without subterfuge to their explicit needs.[7]

John Baldessari repeatedly pledged and got his students to vow: 'I will not make any more boring art'. Perhaps we misread this if we assume it to be too definitive a statement about the kind of work he is proposing *not* to make. Perhaps the statement can be understood as an acknowledgement of an ongoing reasoned disproof of the act of making; as if to say that as long as you mean at the time your declaration about giving up, and this being the very last time, then it is okay. And as long as it is always in earnest you can get away with it in perpetuity. But you have to *really* mean it. So perhaps, with the right energy levels and determination, there might remain some potential for shameful attempts towards a neo-transcendental, arduous and sentimental kind of art.

---

[7] Since the mid to late 1980s Vito Acconci has been working under the guise of the Acconci Studio, an architectural practice that has developed Acconci's early interests in the body and performance through architectural- and landscape-related projects, including designs for public street spaces, gardens, parks, public buildings and transport.

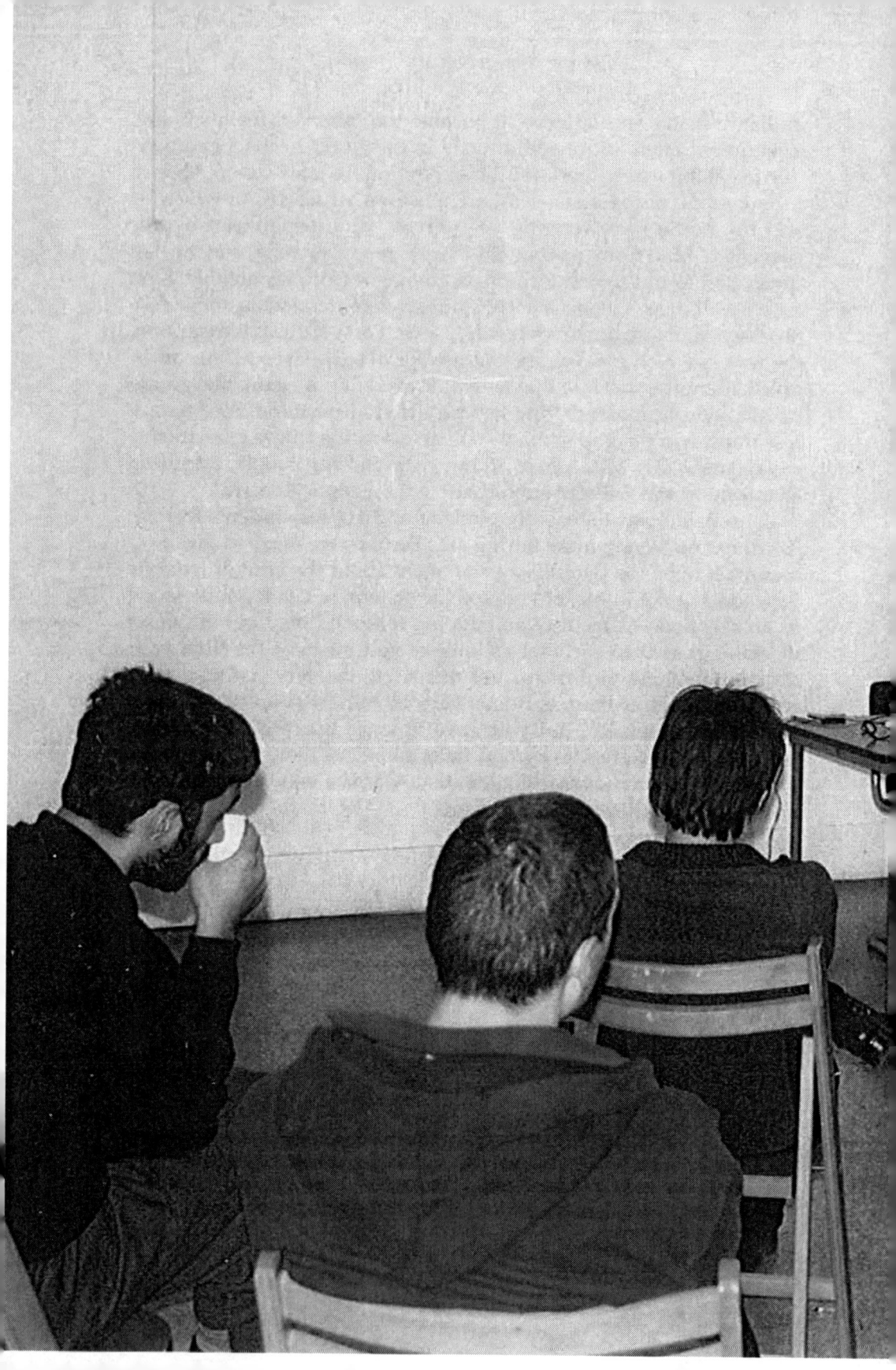

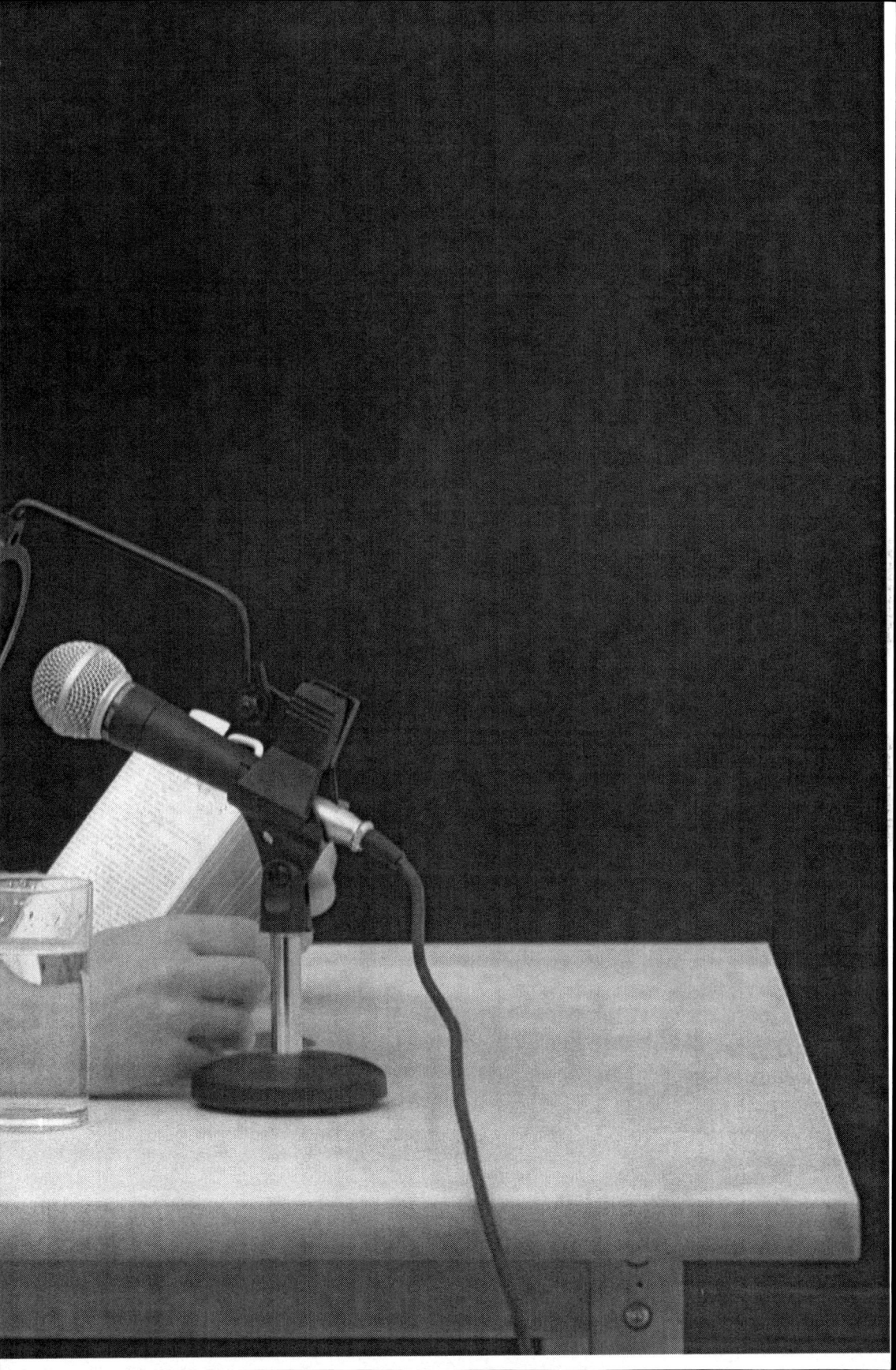

Psychoanalysis and Politics

13. Accidental Pasts and the Truth of History

Ahuvia Kahane

The question of 'psychoanalysis and politics' begins with a working assumption of two objects (whatever we make of their relation to names, especially within the ontology of psychoanalysis).[1] Of these, 'psychoanalysis' invokes the possibility, or meaningfulness, of an individual and 'politics' invokes the possibility or meaningfulness of a commonwealth. Their association, the question of psychoanalysis and politics, thus invokes and may help to problematize the relation of the one to the many, of self to other, of subject to world, of private 'law' and the law of the state, of intension to extension – there are many theoretical, methodological and disciplinary ways of formulating these terms. They are, however, some of the most basic terms of existence.

Yet, pursuing the question of psychoanalysis and politics, we may also come to question this tension between our supposed objects. Psychoanalysis involves an other. *Therapy*, to take it at its most practical, involves a *curative* intervention, but most practitioners would insist this is above all a practice of 'taking care' or 'looking after' which contains a spectrum of responsibilities in a shared space or world. The word *therapy* may be indicative here. It is derived from the Greek verb *therapein* which, unlike the verb *hiatrein* [to heal/cure] and its derivative *hiatros* [doctor], denotes not the end-product, essence or *telos*, not a finite state, but the ongoing act of 'looking after' someone or something in the manner of a *therapôn* [an attendant or caretaker]. Such care, or consciousness, or commonality, holds

---

1 The question of name and object is inherent to the issue at hand. See, for example, the brief discussion in Ernesto Laclau, *On Populist Reason* (London: Verso, 2005), 101–17.

within it societal consciousness and 'politics' (*politics* and *polis* are words with a meaning looking back to the shared space or enclosure, or citadel).[2] This is simply to suggest, as indeed many have, that the thinking of Freud – we might add Nietzsche, Marx and others – is key to the process of the dissolution (literally, '*ana-lysis*') of an interiorized point of being, of a Cartesian subject, and thus also key to a fundamental reconsideration of relations between the individual subject, the society and politics at large.[3]

Critically speaking, we find ourselves in profitable if not unfamiliar difficulty in a manner that pertains to both history and philosophy: if we choose to separate psychoanalysis and politics, together with their categories, we must answer how, if at all, the two and their inflections can relate to each other; if we choose to conflate them, we must determine whether (if we believe them to be identical) a dialectic or some other relationship is even possible, or (if the two only partially overlap) to what degree and in what manner a relationship exists between them. Either way, psychoanalysis and politics are 'good to think with'.

To the degree that the specific question of psychoanalysis and politics helps problematize basic terms of existence, its consideration would sprawl beyond the practical boundaries of this volume, let alone this brief introductory note. Yet the threat of projecting fragmented examples is inherently, perhaps even uniquely, appropriate. A partial discussion, something that disavows its capacity as complete representation, can enact a kind of *allegory* (which may be a model for being, or for the phenomenological understanding of being) or *mise-en-abyme* of the problem at hand. This is the problem of the fragment and the whole, of singularity and multiplicity. This, we may say, is also the problem of the care of the psyche and care of the body-politic. What is more, this principle also translates, happily, into the most practical action – for example, with regard to the year-long IGRS seminar that constituted the 'Psychoanalysis and politics' section of the Psychoanalysis and the Arts and Humanities project,

2 Etymology is not the buried truth of words, of course, but it can provide an interesting component of their phenomenology, especially in terms of psychoanalysis. Note that the word *curative* itself is derived from the Latin *curo*, which means 'to take care of,' 'to attend to,' in matters of one's self, of others and indeed in affairs of the state. *Curo* does *not* mean 'to heal' (see entry in *Oxford Latin Dictionary*). For the Greek see Henry George Liddell and Robert Scott (with the assistance of Henry S. Jones), *A Greek-English Lexicon*, 9th edn. (Oxford: Oxford University Press, 1996).

3 See, for example, Elizabeth Grosz, *Becomings: Explorations in Time, Memory, and Futures* (Ithaca, NY: Cornell University Press), 1999, 3.

and with regard to the essays by Juliet Mitchell and Jaspar Joseph-Lester which together comprise this section of the book. We might draw courage, for example, both in the abstract and in a practical sense, from Cornelius Castoriadis's statement: 'The world – not only ours – is everywhere in fragments, yet it does not fall to pieces. To reflect upon this situation seems to me to be one of the primary tasks of philosophy today'.[4]

Apart from exchanges during the opening and closing conferences, the 'Psychoanalysis and politics' group met to read and reflect on some basic texts. This was a collective discussion, not an exercise in the production of a commentary or an argument. The group began its readings, not surprisingly, with Freud's *Civilization and its Discontents* (1930). Discussions focused – much aided by Juliet Flower MacCannell's observations – on its melancholy, both historical (in view of the date of its composition) and perhaps inherent (when contrasted with Rousseau and others...), and its fundamental formulations of aggression, constraint, freedom and conformity. It is impossible to read this text without bearing in mind *Totem and Taboo* (1913), with its formulation of collective guilt, the killing of the father and the emergence into sociality, and *Group Psychology and the Analysis of the Ego* (1921), with its discussion of the primal father, and so on. Whatever we might say in a brief introduction to such heavily annotated texts, Freud's understanding of individual and communal neuroses constitutes one of the important inaugural moments of the question of psychoanalysis and politics. As Freud says – the matter is of course up for debate:

> If the development of civilization has such a far-reaching similarity to the development of the individual and if it employs the same methods, may we not be justified in reaching the diagnosis that, under the influence of cultural urges, some civilizations, or some epochs of civilization – possibly the whole of mankind – have become 'neurotic'?[5]

But equally, he warns, the attempt to carry our understanding of the tension between patient and environment over to the realm of culture requires extreme caution, if only because that tension may

---

4 Cornelius Castoriadis, *The World in Fragments* (Stanford, CA: Stanford University Press, 1997), vii.

5 Sigmund Freud, *Civilization and its Discontents* [*Das Unbehagen in der Kultur* (Vienna: Internationaler Psychoanalytischer Verlag, 1930)], in *The Standard Edition of the Complete Psychological Works of Sigmund Freud*, 24 vols., ed. and trans. by James Strachey *et al.* (London: The Hogarth Press and the Institute of Psycho-analysis, 1953–74), vol. 21, 144.

not exist where, as Freud says, 'all members of the group are affected by one and the same disorder'.

Without following a canonical historical or conceptual trajectory, the group went on to read Cornelius Castoriadis's short piece 'Psychoanalysis and politics' in his collection of essays *The World in Fragments* (published posthumously in English in 1997).[6] For Castoriadis, psychoanalysis, pedagogy and politics share a single structure as 'impossible' professions, disciplines that explore that question of the law of always putting the law into question. We paused, among other things, on his reading of the Freudian 'Wo Es war, soll Ich werden' ['where id/it was there ego/I shall be']. How to read Freud? How to read Castoriadis's reading of Freud? Do either Freud's formulation or its critique imply a finite progression towards the ego? Towards therapy as 'cure' rather than process? Here the group took a certain leap, deciding to read Lacan's *Ethics of Psychoanalysis* (Seminar of 1959–60) and especially his comments on *Antigone*.[7] Lacan's observations (made against the background of earlier Hegelian reading of the play and the conflict of responsibilities, state and religion, civic sphere and family) opened up another area for debate. Yet Lacan, too, in his very different way (at least in Judith Butler's account and given her critique of Lacan's structuralist patrimony), may have excluded *Antigone*, and thus also something within psychoanalysis, from the political.[8] The possibility of a breach opens up again, although our readings of Yannis Stavrakakis' *Lacan and the Political* (1999) will have provided, at least in part, a counter-argument.[9] If, as Paul Verhaeghe (cited by Stavrakakis) writes, 'all human productions [society itself, culture, religion, science] can be understood in the light of [the] structural failure of the symbolic in relationship to the real',[10] then perhaps, as Stavrakakis suggests, 'It is the moment of this failure, the moment of our encounter with the real, that is revealed as the moment of the political *par excellence*'.

6 Castoriadis, *The World in Fragments*, 125–36.

7 Jacques Lacan, *The Seminar, Book VII: The Ethics of Psychoanalysis 1959–60*, (London and New York: Routledge, 1992), 243–90 [*Le Séminaire, Livre VII: L'éthique de la psychanalyse* (Paris: Seuil, 1986)].

8 See Judith Butler, *Antigone's Claim: Kinship between Life and Death* (New York: Columbia University Press, 2000); for her critique of Lacan's structuralist patrimony see 67–68.

9 Yannis Stavrakakis, *Lacan and the Political* (London and New York: Routledge 1999).

10 Paul Verhaeghe, 'Psychotherapy, psychoanalysis, and hysteria', *The Letter*, vol. 2 (1994), 61, cited Stavrakakis, 73 (in this and the next citation, the ellipses are Stavrakakis's).

Finally, though not in the sense of a teleological movement, we read chapters from Jacqueline Rose's *States of Fantasy*.[11] Here above all, the notion of fantasy plays a definitive function in the political, not only in the context of abstract analysis, but also most practically in such historical contexts as Israel, Palestine or South Africa.

Beyond the meetings, the two chapters by Juliet Mitchell and Jaspar Joseph-Lester in this section of the project bring together, like all the other sections of this book, work anchored in academic and clinical psychoanalytic practice, on the one hand, and in artistic production, on the other. As a general principle, it seems to me that some movements across disciplinarity may themselves be viewed as an inherently psychoanalytic practice. Perhaps, as the above citation from Verhaeghe puts it, 'all human productions [society itself, culture, religion, science] can be understood in the light of [the] structural failure of the symbolic in relationship to the real', and if that is so, then a movement across disciplines, at least when it is successful, rests on a 'structural failure' of disciplinary boundaries (for instance, those between 'critique' and 'art') and their relationship to being and the work of thought.

The two essays, by Mitchell and Joseph-Lester respectively, were not created together. They are not representations or reflections of each other. Mitchell deals with the role of sibling relationships and especially sibling trauma in the formation of fundamental social identities through a pointed discussion of the case, known from the work of Freud and others, of Daniel Paul Schreber. Joseph-Lester, adopting the poetic voice of an interiorized reflection, meditates on what we might – borrowing from such terms as 'social psychology' or 'social anthropology' – describe as 'social architecture'. He speaks, without ever explicitly naming it, of the building known as the Goetheanum, the world headquarters, near Basel in Switzerland, of the Anthroposophy movement started by Rudolf Steiner. Do I, writing this introduction, have the right to name what is deliberately left un-named in Joseph-Lester's words? Perhaps as much, or as little, as I have the right to note that Mitchell, who does not speak of the Goetheanum in her essay, has nevertheless in conversation acknowledged her longstanding interest in the Goetheanum and in anthroposophy's thematizing, for example, of the transmigration of souls, which she fleetingly links to the many 'Daniels' in Schreber's family (the father Daniel Gottlob, the elder brother, Daniel Gustav, and Daniel Paul Schreber himself) and to Schreber's enigmatic reference to the 'soul murder' which his analyst, Paul (another repeated

---

11   Jacqueline Rose, *States of Fantasy* (Oxford: Clarendon Press, 1998).

name) Flechsig, had committed upon him and which Mitchell interprets, ultimately, as 'the inhabitation of one person by another' (this volume, p. 179). We are, to be sure, dealing with brief points of contact. These points, nevertheless, like the infinitesimally small tangents of a circle and a line in geometry, are points where 'touch' can occur. For Mitchell, '"sibling trauma" is the nuclear relationship on the long march towards the social.' Beyond the horizon of sibling trauma lie, as she puts it, the relationships of 'peers, affines, friends and enemies'; it is necessary to appreciate this axis of analysis for the proper appreciation of 'the politics of violence (or peace)' (this volume, p. 168). For Joseph-Lester the very substance of the building, its rough concrete, provides the 'concrete' substance of community which the building is designed to house and which bonds the individual occupant, in her or his space, to the commonwealth. Both, we might say, draw us into discussions that point in the direction of, ultimately, the political, that which belongs to the *polis*, the place of shared living.

Underlying Mitchell's short essay is a very large project indeed. Where the conventional models of analysis rely on 'vertical' relationship within the family (the father, the mother and the offspring), she is, in fact, proposing, on the basis of her careful analysis of the case of Daniel Paul Schreber and his siblings – his elder brother and sister, and his two younger sisters – a 'horizontal' model which, through its various modalities of anxiety and identification, envy and separation trauma (associated with, but different from, Winnicott's notions of separation), love and hatred, forms the self and structures our social relations. She is, in fact, intimating a 'potential new role for a so-called "social unconscious" for the ego' invested in sibling trauma (this volume, p. 184).

Where Mitchell's essay relies on some of the formalities of clinical discourse, Joseph-Lester offers us a literary fantasy. He uses – not surprisingly, but in clear distinction to 'academic prose' – what is known as 'free indirect speech', that much-studied modality of speech which brings to the fore fundamental questions of the inside and outside of the 'I' and problematizes its voice: 'He had come to see the concrete. He wanted to get to physical grips with the material that he loved. He had heard about the monumental and virile structures that had been constructed close to where he once lived. This place now stood before him.' The speaker is the 'he', the grammatical third-person, and yet clearly this is the interior voice of the first person, the 'I'. The tension between the 'he' and the 'I', we must note, is exactly the problem at the core of sibling rivalry, the dynamic setting for the 'horizontal' trauma that is the substance of Juliet Mitchell's essay. Joseph-Lester's 'He/I' voice is that of the architect in question, the elusive 'I,' we may further disclose (although this disclosure may again be inappropriate given that Joseph-Lester has chosen not to name him), is Le Corbusier. To find him, we have to search 'in the details' of Joseph-Lester's essay (God, as architect Mies van der Rohe stated or, alternatively, so the myths go, as German art historian and cultural theorist Aby Warburg said, is 'in the details'):[12] the name appears, but only obliquely, in the sign at the bottom-left corner of the image and in the reference within the caption.[13] As Joseph-Lester points out elsewhere, again in a personal communication, this 'I' voice, Le Corbusier, is supposed to have toured the Goetheanum, and apparently did not utter a word throughout the whole day of his visit.[14] Joseph-Lester's work here deals, in the form of material thinking, with the question of communal space and the enclosure of an individual within the frame of a polity (a commonwealth, a *polis*). The raw concrete, so important to the building that is the Goetheanum and fetishized by Le Corbusier, is crucial to the kind of order we are invited to imagine through the literary reflections of the architect. This concrete comes through in the prose of the architect:

> He was determined to design a place in his building where the spatial qualities of the material could be fully experienced. He believed that the roof would be the site for this; it was the space that people would share. Here would stand an elevated piazza for the use of the inhabitants of the building. It would be enclosed by a surrounding

12 The saying (and its variants, for example, 'the devil is in the details' have gone through multiple attributions and may be safely classified as 'anonymous' (see, for example, J. Bartlett, *Bartlett's Familiar Quotations: A Collection of Passages, Phrases, and Proverbs Traced to Their Sources in Ancient and Modern Literature* (17th edn., Boston: Little, Brown and Company, 2002). For attribution to van der Rohe, see *New York Times*, 19 Aug. 1969; for attribution to Aby Warburg see E. H. Gombrich, *Aby Warburg: An Intellectual Biography* (2nd edn., London: Phaidon, 1986); for attribution to Flaubert, see G. Titelman, *Random House Dictionary of Popular Proverbs and Sayings*, Random House Reference (New York: Random House, 1996).

13 See p. 198. The elision of the name is a crucial literary device, we might say. It has a long history reaching back to Odysseus's elusive use of his name in Homer's *Odyssey* and, not least, also unfolds in psychoanalysis.

14 Joseph-Lester, in conversation with AK, 3 August 2009: 'the narrative is a "fictional" account of Le Corbusier's visit to the Goetheanum (although it is known that he did visit the building) and his fetishization of the concrete or, in other words, his belief in its spiritual, social and political meaning. The text follows Le Corbusier's 'later' design and building of the *unité d'habitation* in Marseille'.

concrete wall and would be an outdoor room open to the sky. The hot summer evenings would bring people outside; here they would gather on the hard roof and watch the concrete transform into new forms (this volume, p. 190).

We are speaking, in ways that are different, and which can nevertheless be made to touch, about 'formative' elements of the social, and through the social, of the political, in the individual's mind. The result, in the case of this volume and this meeting of academic and creative discourse as in other chapters of this book, is elusive, of course. But it is only through such elusive contacts that we can mediate the individual and the community.

14. The 'Sibling Trauma' and the Case of Judge Daniel Paul Schreber

Juliet Mitchell

This chapter proposes a possible further way of understanding the psychosis and delusions of Schreber, whose *Memoirs* Freud analysed in 1911.[1] Freud's account confirmed the importance of infantile sexuality that he had spelt out in 'Three essays on sexuality' in 1905 and indicated that Schreber's symptoms derived from a conflict between his homosexual desires and the taboo on them. In the case history we read how Schreber transferred his ambivalent feelings towards his older brother on to Professor Flechsig, the first psychiatrist to treat him, and then transferred his love/hate for his father on to his concept of God in a delusion that he was a woman who, fecundated by God, would repeople the world with a new race of men. The shift from brother to father that Freud delineated was seamless: fathers and brothers (or mothers and sisters) belong, both for Schreber in his delusion and for Freud in his analysis, in the same category and the more important figure for the child to whose status Schreber had regressed is always the father of the Oedipus complex. My additional reading is based on the assumption that sometimes

---

1   See Sigmund Freud, 'Psycho-analytic notes on an autobiographical account of a case of paranoia (dementia praecox)' ('Psychoanalytische Bemerkungen über einen autobiographisch beschriebenen Fall von Paranoia (dementia paranoides)' [1911]), in *The Standard Edition of the Complete Psychological Works of Sigmund Freud*, 24 vols., ed. and trans. by James Strachey *et al*. (London: The Hogarth Press and the Institute of Psycho-analysis, 1953–74), vol. 12, 3–82. Hereafter abbreviated SE, followed by volume number. Freud's analysis of Schreber is based on Daniel Paul Schreber, *Denkwürdigkeiten eines Nervenkranken* (1903), ed. and trans. by Ida Macalpine and Richard A. Hunter as *Memoirs of a Nervous Illness* (London: W. M. Dawson & Sons, 1955).

siblings form an autonomous horizontal axis which interacts with the vertical generational one. This changes somewhat if we add siblings to the picture.

There is, additionally, a thesis beyond the scope of this essay which nevertheless prompts it in this context. I argue that what I call 'the sibling trauma' is the nuclear relationship on the long march towards the social. The human neonate is born into the social group as well as to its family of origin. When, at around the age of two, it discovers that it is no longer the one and only baby, it is forced from infancy into childhood – the older sister or brother, sometimes a unique one among unique others, sometimes just anyone among any others. This lateral relationship expands into peers, affines, friends and enemies. We cannot understand the politics of violence (or peace) if we do not develop a model of this horizontal axis. Looking at Schreber and his siblings makes only a small contribution to this task. Because we are looking at pathology, the focus is exclusively on the pains, not the very many pleasures of siblinghood.

Freud's account of Schreber's delusional system, privileged Schreber's *desires* and used analytical *interpretations* to understand these. My 'addition' explicitly and implicitly uses Freud's own later theories to stress the psychic importance of foundational *trauma* and the *(re)construction* of these in analysis. In her work on early and late Freud, Ilse Grubrich-Simitis claims that there are two great books which are infused with the insights of Freud's self-analysis: *The Interpretation of Dreams* (1900) and *Moses and Monotheism* (1939). She labels the first 'the book of desire' and the second, written under the external threat of rising Nazism and the internal threat of cancer, 'the book of the trauma'. The analysis in 1911 of Schreber's case falls under the aegis of desire.

Although desire retains its importance, to add siblings to the picture, as I wish to do, is to add trauma. This is central to this reevaluation. As understood by psychoanalysis, a trauma comes both from outside and inside; it shatters the ego which, in order to defend itself, tries to split and project but above all makes an overwhelming effort to bind the unbound energy which the traumatic impingement has released within the organism. The psychology of the trauma and its effects are not simple. In the process of recovery from the trauma, delusions and hallucinatory fantasies with their wish-fulfilment (desires) will appear which, like the daydream, '[make] use of an occasion in the present to construct, on the pattern of the past, a picture of the future'.² In one of his last papers, 'Constructions in analysis', Freud writes:

> If, in accounts of analytic technique, so little is said about 'constructions', that is because 'interpretations' and their effects are spoken of instead. But I think that 'construction' is by far the more appropriate description. 'Interpretation' applies to something that one does to some single element of the material, such as an association or a parapraxis. But it is a 'construction' when one lays before the subject of the analysis a piece of his early history that he has forgotten.³

Using a possible construction of a trauma in the past from the perspective of a trauma in the present, my 'addition' highlights the psychological illness and suicide of Schreber's older brother Daniel Gustav as an important feature of the 'historical truth' which underlies Schreber's paranoia and his delusionary psychosis.

My general argument is that the toddler aged two to three is traumatized by the expectation/arrival of a sibling. This 'sibling trauma' is another dimension of the occurrence which D. W. Winnicott described as a separation trauma – from the mother – which occurs prototypically when the new baby stands in the place of the previous one. In addition to the experience with the mother, there are plenty of feelings about the baby itself as Winnicott's own observations (but not his theory) richly demonstrate in many of his writings. I consider that the 'sibling trauma' affects all the subject's subsequent relationships. In the case of Daniel Paul Schreber's illness, I suggest that the key sibling relationship with Daniel Gustav is indicated both by the nature of the transference onto his psychiatrist, Paul Emil Flechsig, and by many features of his symptoms and his behaviour. These, together with a reading of the *Memoir*, the case history and further information about his life which was not available to Freud, enable us to offer a possible construction of Schreber's childhood sibling history. Freud used only one piece of history from outside

---

2 Sigmund Freud, 'Creative writers and daydreaming' ['Der Dichter und das Phantasieren' [1908]], SE 9, 148.

3 Sigmund Freud, 'Constructions in analysis', SE 23, 261 ['Konstruktionen in der Analyse' [1937]]. Preserving the term 'construction' rather than reconstruction indicates the putative or creative nature of the attempt. However, 'historical truth' is not only as near as one can get to the actuality of the past from the perspective of the present, it also allows us to account for the extraordinary hold that delusions have over humankind: something that underlies the distortions of delusions, really did happen. On the relationship between the illness and the treatment, Freud writes: 'The delusions of patients appear to me to be the equivalent of the constructions which we build up in the course of analytical treatment', 268.

the text of the *Memoir* and thus in this respect he was treating it as though it were an analytic patient. In using some biographical facts I am not offering a possible new psychoanalytic case history, as this would demand that one did not deploy material gained from outside the consulting-room; I am only trying to establish the importance of lateral relations along a horizontal axis. The factual data bring out elements latent within the text.

It is of course not Schreber but Gustav, the older brother, and Anna, the older sister, who will have been traumatized by the arrival of Paul (the patient), their younger sibling: 'this jealousy is constantly receiving fresh nourishment in the later years of childhood and the whole shock is repeated with each new brother and sister'.[4] However, I consider that the 'sibling trauma' which is always with the *younger* sister or brother inevitably inflects the relationship with the older – and indeed that this case history helps us to disentangle this common dynamic. Daniel Paul Schreber (the patient) had an older brother, an older sister and two younger sisters. His trauma will have been with his successor Sidonie, who I think also plays a part in the case history beyond her generic role as the bearer of the trauma. (It would have been repeated differently and to a lesser degree with Klara, his youngest sister).

Daniel Paul Schreber, a married but childless judge of a minor court, first became ill in the autumn of 1884 at the age of 42. He had recovered by the end of 1885. After about two months in the Sonnenstein Asylum he was moved to the Leipzig Psychiatric Clinic and placed in the charge of Professor Emil Paul Flechsig, where he was diagnosed as suffering from severe hypochondria. He was discharged six months later.

Some eight years further on, in 1893, he was appointed Presiding Judge of a Saxon Appeal Court but fell ill, returning again to Flechsig's clinic suffering from terrible insomnia. Persecutory ideas with sensory delusions were added to the hypochondria. Six months later he was transferred briefly to the Lindenhof Asylum and then once more to the Sonnenstein Asylum under Dr Guido Weber, where he remained until he was discharged in December 1902, after nearly nine years. The transfer from Flechsig's care in a university department to an asylum coincided with the development in June 1894 of a hallucinatory stupor. This became a full delusional system in which he was in direct communication with God and living in another world. However, the paranoid delusion gradually became isolated so that in all other respects Schreber was able to act and

---

4 Sigmund Freud, 'Femininity' ['Die Weiblichkeit' [1933]], SE 22, 123.

think normally. While always maintaining the value of his delusion, Schreber made several applications for release and, with that aim in mind, wrote his *Memoirs* during the years 1901–02. His release was granted in 1902 with the Court summarizing his persisting delusion that if he were transformed into a woman he would repopulate the world and restore it to a state of bliss. The *Memoirs* were published in 1903. Schreber's third illness started in 1907, ending with his death in April 1911. As Freud was working only with the *Memoirs*, he did not consider this last relapse; I shall mention it briefly later.

The paranoia with its persecutory fantasies was focused on Flechsig, the redeemer fantasy on God. In the first illness, both Schreber and, in particular, his grateful wife (perhaps stirring Schreber's jealousy) had shown very positive feelings towards Flechsig. However, despite the fact that Schreber was under Flechsig's supervision for only two periods of six months each within the roughly nine years of his incarceration prior to the completion of his writing, Flechsig is featured throughout the *Memoirs*. Schreber believed that Flechsig had abused him by committing 'soul murder' on him. Only at the time of his second illness did Schreber form the delusion he was a woman able to be impregnated by God. However, he recalls that he had already, while in a hypnagogic state just after his marriage in 1878, and thus prior to any illness, imagined how pleasant it would be to be a woman in coitus. For Freud this recollection is the key as it leads directly to the relationship with God. Freud focuses only on the long second illness which culminated in the *Memoirs*. If we introduce the importance of siblings, then Flechsig as 'soul murderer' takes precedence and the first illness is important.

Constructing Schreber's Sibling History

In 1956 Franz Baumeyer published his findings about Schreber's illness and his family history.[5] Although much has been researched and expanded subsequently, it is these case-notes (not, of course, available to Freud) that I shall use here. They allow us to speculate what part the 'sibling trauma' may have played and how we could offer a hypothesis about a construction of Schreber's sibling history. Under a sub-heading, 'Schreber's siblings', Baumeyer gives us information about birth-order from which I deduce the following:

> Daniel Gustav, 1839–77: three years older than 'our' Schreber
> Anna [later: Jung], 1840–1944: two years older

5   Franz Baumeyer, 'The Schreber case', *International Journal of Psychoanalysis*, 37 (1956), 61–75.

Daniel Paul, 1842–1911: the patient
Sidonie, 1846–1924: four years younger
Klara [later: Krause], 1848–1917: six years younger

Although Baumeyer, like most commentators, does not remark upon this fact, we should note that the first name of all the men in the family is Daniel. Having the same name, even among peers, is important for children: its very existence can provoke a repetition of the nightmare of the trauma that one has been replaced. Naming a child after an ancestor, though important too, implies that the child is doing the replacing and is not in danger of being replaced.

Daniel Gustav was around a year old when his sister Anna was born – he would have been too young to know why he felt disorientated and chaotic.[6] These feelings must have been focused when he became a toddler so that the next sibling, Daniel Paul Schreber, is likely to have been their recipient. Daniel Paul will have been the perfectly timed subject of Anna's sibling trauma. When Daniel Paul was a toddler, at the right age for the sibling trauma, no baby arrived. The gap of four years in a family where siblings are one to two years apart may have been caused by a miscarriage. We can surmise that Daniel Paul will have been left worrying what he did wrong not to have had a sibling at the 'right' time. His sister Sidonie is likely to have felt the delayed effects of Daniel Paul's sibling trauma.

The Trauma, the Delusion and the Analytic Construction

In *An Outline of Psycho-Analysis*, published posthumously in 1940, Freud writes:

> instinctual demands from within, no less than excitations from the external world, operate as 'traumas' [...] The helpless ego fends them off by means of attempts at flight (*repressions*) [...] No human individual is spared such traumatic experiences; none escapes the repressions to which they give rise.[7]

After Freud, psychoanalytic theoreticians of infancy have not developed this double perspective. The baby's envy and fantasized destruction of the mother in Klein's theory, though certainly powerful enough, are not conceptualized as a trauma. Nor is there in Kleinian

---

6 Anna may well have been what is called, with ethnic denigration, an 'Irish twin' to Daniel Gustav – one sibling born within 11 months of another.
7 Sigmund Freud, *An Outline of Psycho-Analysis* [*Abriss der Psychoanalyse* [1940]], SE 23, 185.

theory any external trauma, such as the mother's withdrawal, for the baby to confront. The two-year-old's 'separation trauma' (as identified by Winnicott) is, on the other hand, primarily an external trauma – the baby does not *contribute* traumatic wishes and drives from within; it *reacts* with strong emotions and 'disturbed' behaviour but only to what is done to it. Freud's late concept of the trauma of internal and external forces converging to destabilize the subject's psychic economy, is, I believe, crucial. In trauma, the external and internal forces are of great strength but also, in infancy, the protective barriers and the stage of ego development are too weak, so that the subject is overwhelmed with unbound energy which the primitive ego tries to bind.

Because a psychogenic trauma (unlike, for example, the traumatic neurosis of war) comes from within as well as from without, it has an aetiological significance: it sets up repression at the outset of psychic life in an attempt to suppress the traumatic internal demands. In *Moses and Monotheism* (1939), the period when trauma has this effect is extended backwards before the Oedipus complex to earliest infancy. This brings narcissistic and psychotic conditions within the range of its effects – as is the case with Schreber. Later trauma will repeat the effects of this earlier experience – or, rather, this earlier experience will be compulsively repeated when later traumatic occurrences arise.

Several reactions to trauma are possible: there can be some form of denial which will manifest itself in inhibitions or phobias or the trauma may persist as an un-integrated 'foreign body' in the ego, ready to 'return' compulsively at later moments. Such a compulsive repetition will occur because of the ego's failed efforts at taking the trauma on board, making it part of itself. But trauma often remains encysted, a small state within a larger one. The ego makes repeated efforts to rebind the energy in order to restore a sense of integration after the experience of disintegration or of annihilation. At first nothing can be taken in – the chaos must be expelled. Persecution often dominates so that he/she whom one has loved becomes the person who now hates one, destroying one's very being. The delusion to which Freud gives attention, is often a second stage response to trauma; it is an effort at recovery, forming a patch over the annihilated ego: this terrifyingly wonderful thing happened instead of that simple terrifying thing. The often grandiose delusion, such as Schreber's, is a hallucinatory substitutive fantasy that remakes the scene of the trauma; it stands in its place – it is, thus, as Freud claims, a step on the path of a cure: a self-cure. A 'construction' made in a psychoanalytic treatment hypothesizes the originating traumatic moment or constellation. In doing this, it repeats on a different level – that of an analytic cure – the work that the patient's self-curing delusion aspired to bring about.

The Sibling Trauma

My schema for the sibling trauma goes as follows: at around the age of two-and-a-half, weaning traditionally takes place (see, for instance, Isaac's weaning feast in Genesis). Parental sexuality is resumed and conception with the possibility of pregnancy resulting in a live (or dead) birth, takes place. Whether or not this actually happens, humankind unconsciously expects it. Taking its actual occurrence as 'normative', this will dethrone the older child who reacts with an extension of its narcissism to adore the new arrival who in its child's mind will be thought of as 'more' of itself because it was, until now, itself the 'baby' of the family. At the same time, the toddler feels a murderous hatred of the new arrival who turns out instead to be other than itself. There is a distrust of the betraying mother and a turn to the father as her substitute. It is also common for there to be illness to gain the attention of the lost mother.

The quotation I gave above from Freud's late paper 'Constructions in analysis' continues:

> it is a 'construction' when one lays before the subject of the analysis a piece of his early history that he has forgotten, in such a way as this: 'Up to your nth year you regarded yourself as the sole and unlimited possessor of your mother; then came another baby and brought you grave disillusionment. Your mother left you for some time, and even after her reappearance she was never devoted to you exclusively. Your feelings towards your mother became ambivalent, your father gained a new importance for you'... and so on. (SE 23, 261)

Winnicott's notion of a separation trauma likewise focuses on the loss of the exclusive mother. But the observations, unlike the theories, highlight the reason for the loss of the mother. This is Freud's comment:

> what the child grudges the unwanted intruder and rival is not only the suckling but all the other signs of maternal care. *It feels that it has been dethroned, despoiled, prejudiced in its rights; it casts a jealous hatred upon the new baby* and develops a grievance against the faultless mother which often finds expression in a disagreeable change in its behaviour [...] we *rarely form a correct idea of the strength of these jealous*

> *impulses, of the tenacity with which they persist and of the magnitude of their influence on later development.* (SE 22, 'Femininity', 123, my italics)

The observation of the power of sibling jealousy outstrips the theory: child analysts in particular notice its prevalence, record it but then let its explanation fit into the dominant understanding of vertical relationships. However, it is clear from the observations that the reason for the loss of the mother is not yet the claims of the father but is (or 'should be') the presence of the new baby that replaces the 'toddler' who was yesterday the baby.

I have written about the array of observations of this phenomenon elsewhere,[8] and shall only summarize enough here to provide a context for a construction of Schreber's possible experience. In this, the many and confusing identifications which the traumatized toddler makes are very important.

There is an identification between the baby whom the mother is nursing and the baby the toddler previously was; then a further identification with the previously pregnant and parturient mother as a means of not losing her. Freud's case history of Schreber, who was both a younger and an older or 'middle' child, offers a particular variation on this 'sibling trauma'. While the older child can both adore and torture the one who has apparently replaced it, the younger child will both adore and be terrified of the older one. These raw emotions of love, hate and terrible jealousy have to be socialized by what I have called 'the Law of the Mother' (Mitchell 2003), a concept whose exploration is beyond the scope of this chapter.

In my view the reason the toddler experiences the nightmare of separation from the mother (as Winnicott describes it) is because of the actual or expected advent of a sibling who displaces and replaces it. This displacement occasions the traumatic annihilation of the vulnerable ego whose omnipotence the toddler still needs, but which it must relinquish in order to realize that it is one among others. In the case of Schreber it is the older brother, I argue, who is crucial. However, the trauma of the arrival of a younger sister, Sidonie, is the ground plan on which Daniel Paul Schreber reacts to the trauma his older brother experienced when he was born. Having a younger sister and being a younger sibling to an older brother means that both as an identification with the sister and as an object of his brother's equation of his inferiority with femininity, there was a chance that his response would be in the direction of femininity.

8   See Juliet Mitchell, *Mad Men and Medusas: Reclaiming Hysteria and the Effects of Sibling Relations on the Human Condition* (London: Allen Lane & Penguin, 2000), *Siblings, Sex and Violence* (Cambridge: Polity, 2003).

Daniel Paul was the recipient of Daniel Gustav's trauma when he was born; thus, when the time came for his own 'sibling trauma' the fact that he himself has already been adored and nearly murdered by his older brother (and older sister) will affect the way he responds to Sidonie, his immediately younger sister. Sidonie's arrival will retrospectively give meaning to his own earlier experience. The case history, as I shall indicate, demonstrates the psychological imbrication of these temporally distinct events: the unconscious does not know time.

Freud acknowledges the importance of Schreber's brother but here, as elsewhere in his theory, considers that sisters and brothers belong in the same classificatory category as mothers and fathers. I suggest that sometimes they do (for instance in the nomenclature of a clan); sometimes they do not (for instance in kinship position).

Schreber's Siblings

The father of the family, Daniel Gottlob Schreber, a famous physician and educationalist, became seriously ill when Daniel Paul was 12 and died seven years later. From the hospital records, Baumeyer notes: 'His celebrated father suffered from obsessional neuroses with homicidal impulses' (70). Unaware of this, Freud concentrates on Schreber's ambivalence towards his father: he argues that Schreber greatly admired and forcefully repudiated him and this ambivalence was portrayed in his attitude towards God, on to whom he has transferred his feelings. Freud points out that Daniel Gustav, the older brother, may have taken on a paternal/patriarchal role in Schreber's teenage years. This being so then the older brother may have played God towards his younger brother.

From the viewpoint of the sibling trauma, Anna came 'prematurely' for Daniel Gustav; Daniel Paul, with whom his mother must have been pregnant while he was two, came at just the right age. So Daniel Paul Schreber will have been the object of the sibling trauma of both his older sister Anna and his older brother Daniel Gustav. He will have identified with both of them, enjoying the extension onto himself of their narcissistic love for a baby that is meant to be 'more' of themselves and terrified of their murderous hatred of him as being someone other than themselves. Between two and three years of age he will have expected a new baby and when one fails to arrive, he will wonder if his jealousy has killed it. Sidonie is born when he is four years old; she will have been a crucial object of his love and hatred. With sisters either side, there is plenty of room for feminine identification. With an older brother as an object of his aspirations, for better and worse, Daniel Paul will have had plenty to live up to.

Daniel Gustav will have wanted to kill Daniel Paul, who will have thought he killed the babies that didn't arrive (or didn't live). But to an infant killing is reversible – death is only recognized as irreversible later. Likewise the solution of 'giving birth' as a mother does, only acquires its sexed meaning later. The 'sibling trauma' comes before these later understandings of death and sex which are linked to sexed reproduction.

In adulthood his older and only brother was sufficiently mentally ill for an asylum to be considered. When Daniel Gustav committed suicide, did Daniel Paul take his place in the asylum that might have saved the life of his now dead brother? To do so, he would have to become his brother.

Schreber, the Siblings and the Illness: the Brother

Daniel Gustav Schreber died in 1877. Daniel Paul married in 1878. Although he did not become hospitalized until 1884, the clinical notes reveal that he had by then been suffering from hypochondriacal ideas for some years and that these had become worse in 1878, at the time of his marriage. Freud speculates that the marriage may have taken place as a defence against homosexuality; while Baumeyer notes that hypochondria can be understood as an expression of doubt about the marriage.[9] I would observe in addition that his marriage took place in the year following his brother's suicide; in the same period he imagines the pleasure of being a woman in intercourse. If, as is most probable, the marriage protected him from his passive homosexuality, it is likely to be the brother (not the father) who was salient in this.

Daniel Paul Schreber officially falls ill with a diagnosis of hypochondria in 1884 after his wife's miscarriages and their continuing childlessness. At the time of the sibling trauma a child falls ill frequently, and often seriously, and so may the adult in regressing to that time or at least imagining it – hypochondria. There will also be an identification with a brother who is ill. At the time of Schreber's diagnosis, hypochondria in men was thought to parallel

---

9 See Freud 1911, 45 and Baumeyer, 70. An odd feature of Baumeyer's account is that he cites the hospital notes: 'One brother paralytic, committed suicide' (62), yet his commentary only says that Daniel Gustav died from paralysis. I shall stick with what the notes say since suicide fantasies and attempts are a particularly prevalent feature of Daniel Paul's illness.

hysteria in women. It was through my examination of 'male' hysteria, in particular, that I was led to the importance of siblings in my own research.

Baumeyer makes two important comments on the role of the brother Daniel Gustav before following Freud in an entirely vertical analysis:

> Regrettably we know nothing of Schreber's relationship to his brother. It is of interest that six years later [than Daniel Gustav's suicide] Schreber repeatedly expressed the fear that he was suffering from softening of the brain. It is conceivable that this and other hypochondriacal fears originated in guilt feelings about his brother. (Baumeyer, 70)

He also notes: 'it should be remembered that, following the death from paralysis of his elder brother, the dread of madness ran like a red thread through Schreber's manifold hypochondriacal fears' (72). Indeed it does. When ill for the second time in 1893, Schreber thinks he is suffering from 'softening of the brain', fears he is going to die, has persecutory notions that they have made a lunatic of him, that he is dead and decayed so that he is no longer in a fit state to be buried; and makes many suicide attempts – all bringing to mind what little we know of the brother's history.

The case-sheet of the Leipzig-Dosen Asylum, where Schreber returned in 1907 and died in 1922, comments: 'One brother paralytic, committed suicide' (62). His youngest sister Klara had written to the clinic on 21 March 1900 that Daniel Paul Schreber, once ill himself, had failed to recognize 'the progressive psychosis of our dear eldest brother' (68). This must refer to the 'unofficial' illness of Daniel Paul as by the time he is hospitalized, Gustav has committed suicide. Probably Daniel Paul could not recognize Daniel Gustav's illness because he was enacting it in a hysterical identification.[10] I suggest Daniel Paul is first terrified that he is like, and then terrified that he actually is, his brother. He imagines that he is this brother not only in the near-present of his brother's psychosis and suicide but also in the time of their childhood. I think there may be one explicit reference to his brother in Freud's citations of Schreber, an indirect naming: Schreber is preoccupied with the fact that both he and the soul-murdering Flechsig had warring ancestors, so he asks about the dates of King Gustav's reign in the 17th century.

10   She was alive at the time of his death, dying in 1907 just prior to Schreber's final period in an asylum from 1907 until his death in 1911. We do not know her reaction to Daniel Gustav's death – but whatever it was, it is likely to have triggered Schreber's memories of his childhood sibling experiences.

The childhood of Daniel Gustav and Daniel Paul will most likely have been in this connection both the childhood of torturing games played by brothers and of the sibling trauma when Sidonie arrived. Schreber's identification with the baby is both with Sidonie and with his own babyhood, when he had himself arrived to the shock of Daniel Gustav. Schreber suffers the fate assigned him in his infancy by a jealous older sibling. This is played out most fully in the fraternal transference to Flechsig.

Flechsig has, according to Schreber, committed 'soul murder', the main charge of his persecutory fantasies and a notion that has attracted a great deal of critical attention subsequently. Schreber addresses his *Memoirs* at start and finish to Flechsig. Yet Schreber was only in Flechsig's clinic for two short periods of about six months, before writing his *Memoirs*. At no point is the portrait of Flechsig that of a father; he is, rather, either a point of identification with Schreber himself – the two Pauls – or his brother.

In his fantasies, Schreber both becomes his ill and dead brother and reenacts his childhood self in his transference of the brother onto his psychiatrist, Emil Paul Flechsig. This reenactment was quite probably of the torture to which his brother may actually have subjected him in childhood and to which his own sexual excitement and sexual love for his brother will have contributed. 'Complains that Flechsig disturbs him by calling for him and shouting "Holy Thunder!"' (Baumeyer, 63). At times Flechsig is not his persecutor brother but his suicidal brother; at times, too, Schreber thinks he himself is the one who sexually abuses Flechsig. In childhood both the brothers would have been recipients of identification and objects of the other's illicit desires. What we have here are the sexual desires, assaults and bullying, the sort of persecutions seen in schoolboys' mutual torments and anal, masturbatory games. For instance, the adult Schreber complains that when he needs the lavatory, someone is sure to have got in first to keep him out so that he even faints through violently suppressing the need to defecate. He sometimes takes the imagined effeminate and passive role but he shifts between being assaulted and being ecstatic – as may well have been the case in mutual boyhood, particularly anal, masturbation. What is 'soul murder' but the inhabitation of one person by another as could have been experienced in the mutual identifications of orgasmic boyhood masturbation?

In the complex disguise of hallucinations and delusions, what Schreber experiences is commonplace between brothers or peers in fraternal-type relationships in childhood. They may persist into adulthood. Christopher Isherwood describes the advent of sexuality in his close friendship with W. H. Auden: the sophisticated adult friends were embarrassed by 'the schoolboy sex partners', who were nevertheless immensely important.[11] Letters between Sándor Ferenczi, Freud and Jung, while Freud was at work on this case history, have the homosocial frisson of their being 'all boys together'. I mention these outside instances in order to convey that there is nothing Oedipal about Schreber's sexuality from the side of either a man or a woman.

This relationship, however, was not just based on the real abuse Daniel Paul may have suffered and in which he most likely participated, it was profoundly influenced by his own 'sibling trauma' when his sister Sidonie was born. Here Schreber is a mix-up of the toddler he actually was at the time of her birth, the baby he had been until her birth and the baby he wants to be – the baby girl, Sidonie, who is getting all the attention.

Schreber, the Siblings and the Illness: the Sister

Schreber will have experienced the sibling trauma of feeling annihilated when his sister was born. At that moment he will have wanted simultaneously to be her – the loved baby – and to get rid of her, his hated replacement. The identifications are featured in the feminine positions he assumes; his ambivalence will have contributed to the negative associations with which he regards girls as well as to the pleasures he has in 'becoming' one of them.

Like the traumatized toddler, the adult Schreber wants to be the baby again. Hypochondria is the mark of an adult regressing to the frequent illnesses of the sibling trauma. In the clinic, Schreber suffered from 'retardation of speech', his eating was disordered; he often wet the bed and 'dirtied' himself. There is the anality which characterizes the displaced two-year-old who is identifying with the beloved new baby – smearing himself with faeces. In the regression there is also the anger of feeling and behaving 'like shit'. The adult Schreber, like the regressed toddler, felt too weak to walk and wanted to be carried.

In childhood his brother may well have called him 'sissy', just as he imagines Flechsig deriding him as '*Miss* Schreber', but when he retaliates with '*Little* Flechsig' it is more likely that this is how he derided Sidonie. He both scorns anything 'girlish' such as the 'talking birds' (Freud deciphers these as bird-brains = girls) who

---

11 See Charles Osborne, *W. H. Auden: The Life of a Poet* (London: Eyre Methuen, 1980).

inhabit heaven and he also acts in girlish ways, perhaps imitating his older sister Anna, whom he may have admired but who would also have been perceived with hostility because of his hatred of his younger sister Sidonie.

Freud emphasizes how Schreber wanted to be a woman, yet what Schreber insists is not that he is a woman but that he is a young girl frightened of indecent assaults. In the second illness he looks in a mirror and sees his breasts growing: 'April 1899. His occupation with feminine pursuits (sticking with paste, sewing, decorating with gaily coloured ribbons) continues' (Baumeyer, 64). In dismissing him as 'the baby' did Daniel Gustav, very typically for a three-year-old boy (and of our cultures generally), also equate babyhood with effeminacy? Did Schreber identify with Sidonie and Anna as he adorned and adored himself, thus turning the pain of Daniel Gustav's taunts into the products of the love and hate he felt towards his sister(s)?

When Schreber's wife miscarries and perhaps gives birth only to dead babies, these fatalities will replicate the wish to kill his younger sister to which he has regressed. His mother may also have miscarried or had dead babies, which would contribute to the dread that his murderous jealousy may have succeeded. It is maybe in an echo of this that Freud's Schreber considered – unusually for the time – that he was partly responsible for his wife's (mother's?) 'failure' to produce live children.

The Siblings' Mother

A toddler's dominant identifications overlap and coexist and these will be played out throughout childhood. The regression of the adult patient, although it is typically to the period around two to three years old, will also take on the tonus from later relationships – certainly those that are important in the adulthood of the present day, but also ones from other periods of his or her life, such as puberty. Thus Schreber is a young girl preening herself in front of a mirror as his adolescent sisters may well have done. He is a sexually ambiguous person being abused anally by his older brother, as he himself may have experienced in latency. He also derides girls and accuses himself of being an abuser again; whether this really happened or was only a fantasy, in either case it will probably be from later childhood. He has regressed to these positions from the status of an adult and socially powerful male.

Regression to the 'sibling trauma' also entails an identification with the mother. The toddler has 'lost' the mother to the new baby;

one way of not losing is to become the other: Freud describes the small child who, following the death of a cat, went around mewing, lapping from saucers and so on. Schreber becomes his pregnable mother. But for him the identification is ambivalent: he rages against the missing mother as well as worshipping her. For Freud, the ambivalence is towards the father. But such violent repudiation and oscillating adoration is typical of the 'dethroned' child. Baumeyer comments on Schreber's continual 'bellowing' (which Freud does not address): 'By the bellowing, God would be compelled to draw nearer to him again. Schreber behaved like an infant calling for his *mother*' (Baumeyer, 71, my italics).

It is important that Baumeyer introduces the mother but is he right in suggesting the child 'bellows' for her? Might not the bellowing Schreber also *be* the parturient mother? In the *Memoirs* (though not the case history) 'bellowing' is the most persistent feature of Schreber's behaviour – an appalling note of agony that emerges from some unidentifiable depth of his being. The same word is used for the cow-like agony of the mother in labour. Is Schreber howling both because the little boy cannot bear his mother's new pregnancy and wants her all to himself, and also because he thinks he can give birth as she does? Thomas Mann describes Jacob's wife Rachel in the throes of giving birth: 'urgent pain grabbed the mother-to-be [...] when things grew worse, she did scream – monstrous, savage cries [...] she was not in her right mind, no longer herself, and they could easily tell by her hideous bellowing that it was not Rachel who was screaming, because the voice was utterly strange, the voice of demons'.[12]

We do not know whether Schreber's mother gave birth to his younger sisters at home (almost certainly) or whether Schreber was in the house (quite likely) or was sent away, no idea whether she had miscarriages or stillbirths – but Schreber's constant bellowing resembles this account of Rachel's. When Schreber feels he is also responsible for his wife's miscarriages it may be because he has reached the male climacteric (as Freud suggests), but it may also be because he believes that as a murderously jealous toddler he caused his mother's miscarriages and therefore is repeating this trauma with his wife. Two-year-old Schreber will have wanted to be the mummy, like the little girl whom Winnicott calls 'the Piggle' (after her own

---

12 Thomas Mann, *Joseph and his Brothers* [*Joseph und seine Brüder* [1933–42]], trans. by John E. Woods (New York: Alfred A. Knopf, 2005), 279.

self-naming), and desired to have given birth to babies like Freud's 'Little Hans'.[13]

Unlike the silly girl, whom Schreber becomes when he feels he is sexually and violently abused by Flechsig/Daniel Gustav, this maternal identification may at first appraisal seem a more positive association of femininity as it produces the delusion of creating new lives. However, the sibling trauma also alerts us to the fact that this illusory identification with the procreative mother is threatened by the strength of the toddler's ambivalence. We see here the child's violent rejection of the disloyal mother; if she has to be shared with the new baby, the mother topples. Looked at from the perspective of the sibling trauma, the identification with the mother is both reassuring (omnipotently giving birth) and terrifying – risking not only torturous pain (bellowing in agony) but also death – both these positions are exemplified in the 'self-cure' of Schreber's delusion. The possibility of real death for the parturient mother is *informed* by the experience of death/annihilation and the murderous hatred which belongs to the sibling trauma.

In Freud's analysis, Schreber's surge of tabooed homosexual libido moves seamlessly from an abusive relationship with the brother (transferred to Flechsig) to impregnation by the father who is perceived as having been transferred onto both God and the sun. Freud points out that the sun is the male counterpart to mother earth. However, if we take more seriously the fact that, in German (the language of Schreber and Freud) *Sonne* [sun] is feminine in gender, then other possibilities open up. Schreber insists that both God and the sun are whores, that is, faithless women, just like the toddler's mother.

According to Schreber's fantasy, God only has commerce with corpses. Schreber asks, of his own condition, 'whether he has not been dead for a long time?' (Baumeyer, 62). His mother may not only have betrayed him by giving birth to Sidonie and by her possible miscarriages; she also may have preferred her eldest son and have continued to do so after his death. For Schreber and the pre-Oedipal child, 'God' is as much the mother as the father; or, if the father, then the father who replaces the toddler's 'lost' mother rather than the father of the Oedipus complex.

---

13 See Sigmund Freud, 'Analysis of a phobia in a five-year-old boy' ['Analyse der Phobie eines fünfjährigen Knaben' [1909]], SE 10.

The Trauma in the 'Sibling Trauma'

Freud's examination of the Schreber case seems latent with certain specific emphases he made in his final writings. The difficulties inherent in the case suggest the need for an additional focus. We can select a number of instances that indicate some new directions and which, I would argue, could benefit from inserting siblings into the analysis. My suggestion of a generic sibling trauma implies a potential new role for a so-called 'social unconscious', for the ego, for trauma and for siblings themselves.

A year after the Schreber case, Freud wrote *Totem and Taboo* (published in 1913), which posits a human pre-history: the group of brothers murder the father who has hitherto monopolized all the women. Then they have to form the first social contract amongst themselves to stop internecine strife and to share out the women equably. Though an original take on the theme of the formation of a social mind, this mythology endorses the observation that children band together as a social group when they learn that the father will not love them if they hate their siblings, whom the father also loves. In 1914, in 'On narcissism', Freud added the ego as the object of self-love to provide another dimension to the picture of unconscious psychic life. Freud's notion of 'His Majesty the baby' is the narcissistic baby just before the birth of the new baby. This ego is shattered when there is (or 'should' be) another baby occupying its place. World War One brought to the fore the question of traumatic neurosis and hence a renewed interest in trauma.

The case of Daniel Paul Schreber, one of psychosis, is important not only for what it says but for what it opens up that still needed and needs saying. I have not considered other theorists because I believe, as group analysts also maintain, siblings are essential for understanding the formation of social groups and such groups are the sine qua non of political considerations. In this 1911 text, Freud promised the understanding of a social unconscious; such an understanding, I argue, needs siblings who indeed hold that position in Freud's own work, yet it is a position which is clinically observed and mythologized but never theorized. In *Group Psychology and the Analysis of the Ego* (1921), Freud notes the identity of an individual and a social mind. These new themes were signposts which could only lead somewhere at the end of Freud's life, in *Moses and Monotheism*, the *Outline of Psychoanalysis*, 'Constructions in analysis', 'The splitting of the ego in the process of defence' (1940) and the other last papers and written fragments.

For Schreber, I suggest, a particular occasion in the present that triggers his illness is the present-day trauma of his older brother's psychosis and suicide. Using the incestuous-sibling desire and the probably normative or excessive abuse of his childhood sibling-relationships, he identifies with his ill/dead brother and his little-girl sister and manages to construct the delusion of a future on the model of the past in which he, a new and parthenogenetic mother, as he imagined when he was a toddler, will save the world by giving birth to a new race of humankind. The present trauma retrospectively uses the complex constellations around the old, original one and, by deferred action, the old one acquires retrospective meaning.

In the Schreber case, Freud wrote about the truth of Schreber's delusion, referring to the fact that the patient, like the analyst, was confirming the importance of infantile sexuality. In 1937 he writes in almost the same words of the *historical* truth of the trauma that underlies psychopathology in general and the delusion in particular. A construction made in psychoanalytic treatment reaches back to the trauma beneath the delusion. In *Moses and Monotheism*, he wrote that the important traumas of childhood take place between the ages of two and four and are inaccessible to memory except as occasional flashes of screen memories, a memory of an imagined instance that stands like an icon of a wider crucial experience. The traumas, he claimed, relate to impressions of sexual and aggressive acts, and 'no doubt also to *early injuries to the ego (narcissistic mortifications)*' (Freud 1939, 74, my italics). Between the 1911 case history and the last writings, the importance of the death drive and aggression and a new model of the ego had been put in place. These are crucial for the 'sibling trauma' in which the toddler experiences an annihilation of its ego to which it may respond with aggression, sexual violence and/or depression as a turning inwards of the aggression.

Homosexuality, Incest and the Mechanism of Paranoia

Freud begins his discussion of the mechanics of paranoia by arguing that the Oedipus complex is at stake in all psychogenic 'illnesses'. Specific to paranoia is the formation of delusions of persecution to defend against a sudden increase in homosexual libido. Thus, referring to the confirmatory research of Jung and Ferenczi, he writes: 'Yet we were astonished to find that in all of these cases a defence against a homosexual wish was recognizable at the very centre of the conflict which underlay the disease' (Freud 1911, 59). He decides from this and other work, to make the following generalization:

> delusions never fail to uncover these relations and to trace back the social feelings to their roots in directly sensual erotic wishes. So long as he was healthy, Dr Schreber, whose delusions culminated in a wishful fantasy of an unmistakably homosexual nature, had, by all accounts, shown no signs of homosexuality in the ordinary sense of the word. (Freud, 60)

This observation refers also to Freud's thesis that the social mind arises from a sublimation of male homosexual desires. Much has subsequently been written to complicate, add to and dispute Freud's explanation. Here I am only concerned with what adding siblings and an early sibling trauma would do to this explanation.

If we place Schreber's original trauma and its resolution in his adult delusions as dating from roughly the age of two to three (the moment of the 'sibling trauma') then the division which Freud is making into a homosexual and heterosexual orientation is not pertinent. In the present time of the adult illness, assuming a female position may be equivalent to a homosexual stance; however, the adult patient has regressed to the cusp of infancy/childhood and for the toddler the distinction between 'same' and 'other' sexual desires is not pertinent – nor is it for the mother who, from her position as the 'law', forbids the child's sexuality, whether same sex or other sex. Interestingly, when Freud referred his own relationship to Wilhelm Fliess and Carl Jung back to the death of his brother Julius when he was scarcely a toddler, he wrote not of his own 'homosexuality' with his male friends and colleagues but of his 'femininity'. Although the heterosexual model dominates in our adult minds, small children are sorting out their gender positions before the 'sexual difference', which is the psychic facilitator of sexed reproduction, is symbolically acquired with the castration complex.[14] My thesis argues that it is this, the gender femininity of girlhood, not the reproductive womanliness of 'sexual difference', that Schreber enacts.

What is taboo or forbidden in the earlier phase therefore is not homosexuality but incest, *'incastus'*, unchastity for a member of one's kin, a relative defined as very close, of either sex. Incest taboos are not only notoriously variable, but definitions of incest are also mobile. From the viewpoint of analysing it psychoanalytically, it is important

---

14 See my 'Procreative mothers (sexual difference) and child-free sisters (gender)', in *The Future of Gender*, ed. J. Browne (Cambridge: Cambridge University Press, 2007). In 1911, Freud, though en route there through analysing Little Hans, had not yet formulated the castration complex.

to distinguish adult from childhood meanings. Childhood sexuality persists or is regressed to in differing degrees by everyone and it forms a part (normatively subsidiary) of adult sexuality. However, it is useful to delineate analytically what in real life is a mix-up. In the western world, sexuality between same-sex or other-sex children is equally prohibited. Looking from the perspective of psychoanalysis, I propose to call 'incest' any tabooed sexual intra-family relations whether same- or other-sex. We may think of incest as heterosexual because we link it to reproduction, but it is more inclusive than this. Schreber, like the toddler, is involved in a parthenogenetic birth: the impregnation by God is an immaculate conception, the putative parturition, a virgin birth. This is what Winnicott calls 'a pre-genital pregnancy'.[15]

When Freud discusses soul-murder, his associations, though not his argument, suggest sibling incest following the sibling trauma. Thus he is on Byron's track: 'I have searched [*Manfred*] in vain for the expression 'soul-murder'. But the essence and secret of the whole work lies in an incestuous relation between a brother and a sister. And here our thread breaks off short' (Freud 1911, 44–45). Freud's footnote to Byron (who committed sibling incest as well as writing about it) concludes with the observation (repeated later) that Schreber says in addition that it has occasionally been claimed that both Flechsig and Schreber himself are guilty of 'soul-murder'– it takes two to incest. If Schreber has sexual desires for his brother or father, these must, by any definition, be incestuous. The 'Law of the Mother' prohibits incest, either same-sex or other-sex, but does not prohibit homosexuality. Prohibitions must have a generic provenance. Attitudes to homosexuality are extremely diverse and I suggest that any taboo is not 'universally' there *ab initio* – we read it back post-oedipally as an effect of that constellation. Cultural prohibitions and taboos cause the repression of illicit wishes in such a way that they become *unconscious* – unconscious processes are the object of psychoanalytic enquiry.

After Freud the processes of splitting and projection that characterize paranoia have been situated as arising in pre-oedipal constellations. However the framework has remained both the ascription of tabooed homosexuality (which I am arguing is post-oedipal) and the vertical axis: Schreber and his father or mother.

I suggest that though the adult may be terrified of his repressed homosexuality, this masks a universal taboo however diversely

---

15   D. W. Winnicott, *Playing and Reality* (London: Tavistock Publications, 1971), 75.

expressed: one cannot kill one's brother or sister except in particular circumstances. Pre-genital sexuality and children's invariable fantasies of parthenogenetic reproduction as those aspects of sibling relations which become (most often) forbidden and tabooed as incest; thus it is incest and not homosexuality that breaks through in Schreber's paranoid symptoms and redeemer phantasies. That one can be enjoined to kill, particularly a sister and sometimes a brother, and to marry and reproduce with a sibling, suggests an important difference from the prohibitions of Oedipus but not a difference of kind.

Sexual and aggressive/death drives are central as a response to the trauma. Schreber's delusion, which forms a patch over his trauma, is redolent with his claim to be dead: this is the experience of his own ego's annihilation as he failed adequately to move in this part of his mind from omnipotent infancy to social childhood. In the misery and triumph of his paranoid delusion we see the persistence of his narcissistic wish to have and be his brother and be and have his sister and the violent rejection of, and identification with, the adored and treacherous mother who was the God of his early siblinghood.

15. Spirit

Jaspar Joseph-Lester

He had come to see the concrete. He wanted to get to physical grips with the material that he loved. He had heard about the monumental and virile structures that had been constructed close to where he once lived. This place now stood before him. The vast concrete exterior of the building immediately inspired him. He began to ask himself what it might mean to build an entire city. The concrete captivated him. Here, in its richly textured surface, he imagined a new future. He touched the walls. He believed that concrete could determine the way that people lived: its blank, grey surface produced powerful experiences; it fostered a sense of community; it generated new relations. He could see all of this as he wandered around the interior of the building. The physical scale of the internal spaces, the stairs, the walls and the floors were all joined together as if the space had been carved out of a single lump. Looking out, he observed the other buildings. This wider community of architectural forms repeated the same organic structures. The lines of the houses followed the contours of the surrounding hills; their forms occupied the landscape like sculptural objects.

Returning to France, he began to work on a new design. It was to be built in the south, in a city on the sea. The scale and vision of this concrete structure would take time to realize and the demands would be different from those of the buildings he had studied. The concrete was the thing that was most important to him. He knew that it would change lives: he had seen this happen. The concrete would allow him to structure and shape the activities of the people who were to live in his building. It would dissolve difference. It would produce unity. In every moment he worked on his drawings he remembered how the concrete embodied something more. This immaterial supplement was as physical as the monumental structures it supported; its ghostly spirit addressed him directly. It produced meaningful affects in him.

Unlike the curved and moulded forms he had experienced in Switzerland, his building would take the modular units of the golden section. Two interlocking squares would be cut out in the part of the bare concrete façade containing the lift tower. This same section of façade would feature a row of six rectangular windows, repeated on each of the 17 storeys. The domestic spaces would be efficient and well-designed. Each would have access to a balcony where the huge concrete walls could be encountered directly. The physicality of the overall structure would be present in each of the apartments and would generate a strong sense of the whole.

He designed the lift to carry the inhabitants through the inner concrete structure of the building. The automated movement provided the necessary circulation and opened onto both residential and public spaces. This mechanized movement led towards the sky. He wanted to build a structure for a new age. It would house a community that would never need to leave its walls. Young people, families and single people, the entire community would live and work under one roof. They would share this space, joined by a deeper understanding of the material qualities of their homes. They would be bound together in the reinforced walls of the building.

He was able to think in this way because he had come to understand the process more fully. His new design would reveal the hidden secrets that he had experienced first-hand. The surface of the concrete mapped out the process of its casting; it spoke of human ingenuity and occupied the space in a way that reflected the humanity of the people who lived in it.

For him, concrete was something to be celebrated. He was determined to design a place in his building where the spatial qualities of the material could be fully experienced. He believed that the roof would be the site for this; it was the space that people would share. Here would stand an elevated piazza for the use of the inhabitants of the building. It would be enclosed by a surrounding concrete wall and would be an outdoor room open to the sky. The hot summer evenings would bring people outside; here, they would gather on the hard roof and watch the concrete transform into new forms.

He decided to travel back to the place that had first got him thinking. He would travel alone. He needed to explore the building more fully. On arrival he was again struck by the presence of the concrete. This time it addressed him differently.

Spirit

He headed straight for the auditorium. The large internal space was situated at the centre of the main building. The tall concrete walls were painted in bright colours and the vibrant stained-glass windows refracted a spectrum of tinted light on to the hard interior surfaces. It was here that he saw the concrete move. The dancing, flickering shapes captivated him. For the first time he could see what he understood to be the spirit of the material. He had always sensed it but now he could see it moving before his eyes.

When he left the main building he saw how the smaller surrounding houses were also moving. In his eyes, they began to dance. The relation between these spaces was determined by an incommunicable order. The concrete allowed this. The space of the theatre and the spaces where the people lived were joined together as a single life force. A living, breathing organism. The community was governed by an agreement. The aesthetic of the spaces occupied reflected the politics of the community. The people spoke through the spaces that they had come to inhabit. They were transfixed by the structures of their making.

The inauguration ceremony took place on 14 October 1952. He took the grand opening as an opportunity to pay homage to the building tradesman Sarde (who was an expert in concrete construction) and Bertocchi (who was the master concrete worker in charge of the constructions and sculptural mounds on the roof). He also spoke of the political, moral and social ideas that were embodied in the building. The speech was followed by a ceremony involving a young dancer dressed in white fur. She performed a folk ritual on the concrete stage below the monumental screen. This was a celebration to mark the completion of the building, a construction that would act as a basis for the needs of the community. Here, on the roof, the inhabitants would pass beyond the reality of the world below.

He was now able to experience the space he had only imagined before. The tall concrete screen stood before him as a monument to his love of the material. The flickering images that danced over its surface gave form to the qualities that normally were only sensed. The inhabitants gathered to stare at its surface. The skyline of the city and the sea behind it acted as a backdrop to the serenity and force of the concrete. The surrounding wall, which circled the edge of the roof, blocked out the surrounding city. Here, in this space, the monumental screen appeared as a public sculpture in the grand piazza. The tactile and earthy qualities of the material eclipsed any architectural function; in place of the systemized domestic units, there emerged something more. The concrete performed in a way that pleased him, it was just as he had first experienced it. It did not speak of his beliefs and he was not sure if it even spoke for the community that lived in it. He no longer cared, he only wanted to be close to it, to watch it dance before him. The concrete was all that interested him.

Psychoanalysis in the German-Speaking World

16. Constructions in the Humanities: the German-field Seminars

Martin Liebscher

William Cobbing's artistic exploration of Freud's interpretation of Wilhelm Jensen's novella *Gradiva* fits perfectly with the interests of the German-field seminar group. This is because the text marked not only the beginning and the end of the series but also accompanied all of our presentations and debates in some way. The final discussion revealed the development of a certain *Denkbewegung* [movement of thought] which we had undergone the preceding year. One might say that this last discussion was an analytic act in itself, insofar as we brought the underlying unconscious stream of interest into the light of day.

'Bringing into daylight' is a metaphor widely used to describe the analytic process of transmuting unconscious contents into conscious thoughts – a process of expressing something in figurative language which simultaneously involves an element that by definition cannot be known, the unconscious; hence, the excessive use of metaphorical speech in psychoanalysis from Freud onwards. One of the allegories that Freud drew on stems repeatedly from the realm of archaeology: he compared the therapeutic process with the archaeological excavation of an historical site. This was the starting-point of our series when Dora Osborne, Lucia Ruprecht and Andrew Webber approached Freud's 'Der Wahn und die Träume in W. Jensens *Gradiva*' ['Delusions and dreams in Jensen's *Gradiva*'] from different angles, triggering a discussion on space, memory and the city.[1]

---

1 Sigmund Freud, 'Der Wahn und die Träume in W. Jensens *Gradiva*' [1907] ['Delusions and dreams in Jensen's *Gradiva*'], in *Gesammelte Werke*, 19 vols. (Frankfurt am Main: S. Fischer, 1987), vol. 7, 29–122, hereafter abbreviated GW,

Following Freud's allegorical description of Rome in *Das Unbehagen in der Kultur* [*Civilization and its Discontents*], Andrew Webber examined the triangular scheme of psyche, [city]-space and body,[2] something that can also be detected in Freud's understanding of Gradiva's footprint. He used Freud's allegory as the basis of a psycho-topographical approach to the city – in his current work, this is the city space of 20th-century Berlin.[3] Of course he finds himself confronted with the task of clarifying the link between topography and memory and, as one can see in Jensen's text, memory is psychoanalytically attached to the place, 'and the obsessive memory-fetish of Gradiva's step always has to be thought in its relation to place: a figure bound to and partly lifted up from, ground'.[4]

Dora Osborne's contribution examined the validity of archaeology as a metaphor for psychoanalytic work, as can be found in Freud's reading of *Gradiva*. Following the analogy between the archaeological excavation and the psychoanalytic work, she demonstrated that 'this necessarily raises questions of appropriation and violation and [...] of distortion'.[5] This becomes evident in the analyst's work of (re)construction – similarly to the archaeologist, s/he is confronted with the belatedness of posterity. As in the case of Gradiva's footprint, both can only produce a copy of something that was never given to them in its original form.

The third initial presentation was given by Lucia Ruprecht. Her starting-point was the choreographic aspect of the novella and Freud's obvious unwillingness to deal with the question of fetishism in his essay. From here she engaged with the dialectical opposition between *Wissenschaft* [science] and *Kunst* [art] or, to be more precise, psychoanalysis and aesthetics. In the case of Jensen's protagonist Norbert Hanold, archaeological knowledge is opposed to and interacts with the realm of dreams, hallucinations, fantasies, delusions and fetishism: his *Wissenschaft* becomes subordinated to

followed by volume number, in *The Standard Edition of the Complete Psychological Works of Sigmund Freud*, 24 vols., ed. and trans. by James Strachey et al. (London: Hogarth Press and the Institute of Psychoanalysis, 1953–74), vol. 9, 7–93. Hereafter abbreviated SE, followed by volume number.

2 Sigmund Freud, *Das Unbehagen in der Kultur* [1930] [*Civilization and its Discontents*], in GW vol. 14 and SE vol. 21.

3 Andrew Webber, *Berlin in the Twentieth Century: A Cultural Topography* (Cambridge: Cambridge University Press, 2008).

4 Andrew Webber, 'Psycho-cultural topography', paper delivered to the IGRS German-field seminar group, 26 February 2007.

5 Dora Osborne, 'Unearthing archaeological constructions', paper delivered to the IGRS German-field seminar group, 26 February 2007.

his fantasies. According to Lucia Ruprecht, this echoes Freud's own approach in his interpretation of Jensen's text. Freud's analysis is an expression of his fascination with the original text and can be seen as a 'selective, distorting and embellishing mimicry' of the novella. In keeping with Freud's understanding of literature, his interpretation is a pleasurable repetition and gives him the chance to work through his own complex in relation to literary writers, as admitted to in a letter to Wilhelm Fliess in 1899.[6] As Ruprecht put it: 'The cure from literature (by turning it into case material) is a first-rate literary spectacle itself, just as Hanold's cure from fetishism is staged as a fetishistic feast.'[7]

The discussion of the dialectic between psychoanalysis and aesthetics continued at a rare screening of G. W. Pabst's film *Geheimnisse einer Seele. Ein psychoanalytischer Film* [*Secrets of a Soul. A Psychoanalytic Film*] (1926). As Freud refused to be involved in this project because of his doubts about the future potential of the film medium, Hanns Sachs and Karl Abraham stepped in as consultants to the director. It was probably the only time that psychoanalytical principles were explicitly presented in a pedagogical way through the aesthetic categories of film – though one might question whether this attempt was true to the psychoanalytic cause at all. In contrast, we are familiar with interpreting films through using psychoanalytic categories. Unlike Norbert Hanold in Jensen's novella, and Freud in his subsequent interpretation, Pabst does not subordinate the *Wissenschaft* to his fantasies, but restricts art to the purpose of disseminating the theory of psychoanalysis – which makes for a rather odd propaganda movie. Pabst's later works, such as *Die Büchse der Pandora* [*Pandora's Box*] (1929) or *L'Atlantide* (1932) would reverse this relationship and become milestones of psychoanalytic film-making.[8]

Following Andrew Webber's contribution on the relation between psyche, space/body and memory, the group discussed the question of mnemonics from Simonides onwards, thereby linking memory and space. In *Zur Genealogie der Moral* [*Genealogy of Morals*], Friedrich

---

6 Letter from Sigmund Freud to Wilhelm Fliess of 11 September 1899, in *The Complete Letters of Sigmund Freud to Wilhelm Fliess, 1887–1904* (Cambridge, MA and London: Belknap Press, 1985), 370–2.

7 Lucia Ruprecht, 'The pleasure of re-telling', paper delivered to the 'German-field' seminar group, IGRS, 26 February 2007.

8 For the psychoanalytic aspects of Pabst's *Pandora's Box*, see Andrew Webber, 'Pan-Dora's box. Fetishism, hysteria and the gift of death', *Die Büchse der Pandora*', *International Journal of Psychoanalysis*, 87 (2006), 273–86.

Nietzsche brought together memory and the body – memory being inscribed into the body in the manner of the relationship of debtor and creditor.[9] Interestingly enough, the Viennese Psychoanalytic Society dedicated its meeting of 1 April 1908 to the third part of Nietzsche's *Genealogy*, followed by only one other session on a Nietzsche text, that on *Ecce Homo*, 28 October 1908.[10] Duncan Large and Martin Liebscher introduced the group to the debate in the Freud circle as recorded by Otto Rank in the protocols of those meetings. Freud's explicit unwillingness to acknowledge Nietzsche's philosophy as a forerunner of psychoanalysis seems to reveal a complex towards philosophy similar to the one we have seen him show towards literature.

Accordingly, the position of psychoanalysis in the philosophical tradition was the topic of the next presentation. Johan Siebers examined the rift between philosophy and rhetoric from a psychoanalytic perspective and traced a history of rhetorical or dialogical thinking, beginning with the Socratic dialogues and locating Freud's theory in this tradition. Special attention was given to temporality and to metaphor as a basic structural feature of the unconscious. The rhetorical *genera* which Aristotle linked to past, present and future were interpreted in the light of psychological structures, and the role of enunciation in therapeutic dialogue was examined in reference to Lacan and more recent work in psychoanalytic theory.

Having focused on two major aspects where Freud's unconscious complexes influenced the shape of psychoanalysis, namely his relation to literature and philosophy, the group invited Michael Mack to introduce another famous 'exclusion' of Freud's *Wissenschaft*: religion and especially his relationship to the Jewish faith. We discussed Freud's correspondence with Oskar Pfister and key passages of *Der Mann Moses und die monotheistische Religion* [*Moses and Monotheism*].[11]

---

9   Friedrich Nietzsche, 'Zur Genealogie der Moral' ['On the genealogy of morals'], *Kritische Studienausgabe*, 15 vols. (Berlin, Munich: de Gruyter, DTV, 1988), vol. 5, 295, trans. by Walter Kaufmann and Reginald J. Holingdale, in *On the Genealogy of Morals and Ecce Homo* (New York: Vintage, 1967), 61.

10   *Protokolle der Wiener Psychoanalytischen Vereinigung* [*Minutes of the Vienna Psychoanalytic Society*], ed. and trans. by M. Nunberg, H. Nunberg and E. Federn, 4 vols. (Frankfurt am Main: S. Fischer, 1967–75; New York: International University Press, 1962–75), vol. 1, 354–61 at 338 (meeting of 1 April 1908), vol. 2, 25–34 at 28 (meeting of 28 October 1908).

11   *Sigmund Freud, Oskar Pfister: Briefe 1909–1939* [*Psychoanalysis and Faith: the Letters of Sigmund Freud and Oskar Pfister*], ed. and trans. by Ernst Mosbacher, Ernst L. Freud and Heinrich Meng (Frankfurt am Main: S. Fischer, 1963; London: Hogarth Press and the Institute of Psycho-Analysis, 1963); Sigmund Freud, *Der*

At our final meeting, it became obvious that the historical outlines of our seminar topics were inseparably intertwined with our initial reading of Freud's interpretation of *Gradiva*. Our undertaking was indeed a reconstruction – similar to the task performed by the archaeologist and the analyst – and it was no coincidence that our series ended with Freud's 'Konstruktionen in der Analyse' ['Constructions in Analysis'], in which Freud described the work of the analyst as follows:

> Er hat das Vergessene aus den Anzeichen, die es hinterlassen, zu erraten oder, richtiger ausgedrückt, zu *konsturieren*. [...] Seine Arbeit der Konstruktion oder, wenn man es so lieber will, der Rekonstruktion, zeigt eine weitgehende Übereinstimmung mit der des Archäologen, der eine zerstörte und verschüttete Wohnstätte oder ein Bauwerk der Vergangenheit ausgräbt.'[12]

> [His task is to make out what has been forgotten from the traces which it has left behind or, more correctly, to *construct* it. [...] His work of construction, or, if it is preferred, of reconstruction, resembles to a great extent an archaeologist's excavation of some dwelling-place that has been destroyed and buried or of some ancient edifice.]

It is not only the analyst's task that resembles that of an archaeologist: reconstruction is also at the heart of the humanities. It could be argued that when humanities scholars are dealing with psychoanalysis they are reconstructing their fantasy of psychoanalysis.

Gradiva's footprints and the subsequent process of reconstruction are also central to the two articles that follow. Both provide an account of the interplay between space, memory and art: William Cobbing gives an insight into his Gradiva project, which was exhibited at the London Freud Museum; and Herbert Lachmayer introduces us to his exhibition concept of staging knowledge, which is deeply ingrained in Freudian thought. Following the traces of Gradiva, both the artist and the curator are concerned with the 'archaeological' or 'psychoanalytical' construction which is at the centre of any exhibition space, each seeking in his own way to challenge gridlocked historical preconceptions of psychoanalysis.

Mann Moses und die monotheistische Religion [1939] [*Moses and Monotheism*] GW vol. 16, 101–246, SE 23, 6–139.

12 Sigmund Freud, 'Konstruktionen in der Analyse' [1937] ['Constructions in analysis'], in *Studienausgabe*, 11 vols. (Frankfurt am Main: S. Fischer, 1975) Ergänzungsband, 396f, in SE vol. 23, 258.

17. Staging Freud: Reflections on *Gradiva*, the Muse of Psychoanalysis[1]

Herbert Lachmayer

In the early days of psychoanalysis, Sigmund Freud and the group of colleagues who attended his regular Wednesday Salon were inspired by Wilhelm Jensen's symbolist novel *Gradiva* (1903). It tells the story of a young archaeologist called Hanold who falls in love with a young woman and is at the same time obsessed with an ancient Roman relief of a striding nymph: the point of the tale is that Hanold mixes up his scholarly fascination (with the archaeological image) with his erotic obsession (with the real young woman). It is extremely interesting to see how, through a combination of empathic ability and analytical voyeurism, Freud developed his relationship with the artist's strategy of poetic production as a way of beginning to make the processes of the unconscious comprehensible to psychological rationality.

For the circle of men at 19 Berggasse this novel became a focal object of what I shall call 'cognition desire'. Through a shared empathic phantasy, the group of male investigators, seeking to understand eroticism as an irritant in the function of causal reason, used this fiction to uncover the basic workings of the unconscious – not least because, symbolizing the process of affect-regulation between repressed drives, the imagined world and classical kitsch, it offered them the opportunity to indulge their erotic fantasies under the pretext of exploring the imagination in the service of science. They found a way of communicating this erotic power of the imagination and at the same time analysing it reflectively, without collectively breaking the taboo of entering too deeply into a sexual

---

1 I am indebted to Naomi Segal and Morwenna Symons for the English translation of the successive drafts of this essay.

phantasy. Thus the unconscious was investigated, not only through the reported case-histories of patients, but also, more importantly, by describing instances of psychical deviancy in the same way that poets, composers and visual artists communicate them to us. After all, the 19th-century division of the intellectual realm into the sciences and the humanities, into reason and irrationalism, abstraction and sensuality, rational causality and the unconscious,[2] had left a 'monumental deposit' whose sediment is perceptible up to the present day.

In the late 18th century, the 'ordering reason' of enlightened absolutism was the supreme *reality principle* but, from the beginning of the 19th century, the above-mentioned distinctions between theoretical abstraction and imaginative intuition became the basic structures for the development of individuality. We should not forget that, for the most part, the later bourgeois morality and regulation of sexuality did not exist at the revolutionary end of the 18th century: rather, it was dominated by a kind of 'rebellious enlightenment' with a *sensus communis* of what I propose to call 'pornosophic phantasies',[3] by which I mean that a great variety of polymorphous-perverse sexual habits were integrated both into the conversation of the aristocratic salons and into everyday communication. In the 19th century the domain of the unconscious and the irrational was handed over to the 'romantic genius', who took the role of a 'professional in the business of suffering' and was both privileged and condemned to create aesthetic counter-worlds as essential models of inwardness and individualism for the bourgeoisie.

The early 19th century was a society defined by superego and guilt and, while the unconscious was gradually solidifying into a Pandora's box that seemed to be positively waiting for Freud to discover it, it was largely left to the artist and to a prudish legal system to exercise control over the erotic power of the imagination. Cultural creativity, as sublimated libido, was also often subject to a dialectics of shame and morals: as the core of bourgeois identity, the ego was a perpetually overcharged psychological authority, on the one hand dominated by the overweening demands of the superego,

2   The noun '*Unbewusste*' ['unconscious'] was first used by the Romantic artist and medical doctor Carl Gustav Carus in his book *Psyche – Zur Entwicklungsgeschichte der Seele* [*Psyche: A Developmental History of the Soul*] (Pforzheim: Flammer und Hoffmann, 1846).

3   The term 'pornosophic' was first used by Pia Jauch, *Damenphilosophie und Männermoral: Von Abbé de Gérard bis Marquis de Sade* [*Ladies' Philosophy and Men's Morality: From the Abbé de Gérard to the Marquis de Sade*] (Vienna: Passagen, 1990), 95.

on the other destabilized by the id and its uncontrollable dynamics. In contrast to the bourgeois, the bohemian was already tugging at the moral corset of a society of hypocrites – the artist was idealized as a hero of unrestrained emotionality and later on as an idol of sexual liberality. Thus the artist as hero and his work as the product of genius, rather than industry, became the essential medium of bourgeois cultural life – they believed in art as a religion, a sort of profane spirituality, the way to deal with all the great questions of life, love and death. Conversation became the central medium of bourgeois cultural interaction – the bohemian's conversation at the coffee-house as much as the over-refined small-talk of Marcel Proust's Faubourg St-Germain salons – and this conversation was concerned above all with inventing artistic strategies to satisfy the drives, or at least to find an illusory replacement for them. Freud's interest in studying the productive sensibility of the artist's poetic strategies through a 'projective identification' with both the author (Wilhelm Jensen) and the protagonist (young Hanold) – exploits the work of art in order to comprehend what one might call its play with the unconscious.[4]

As he invented psychoanalysis, Freud came to understand mythology or creative writing as an 'aesthetic material' in which the psychological structures of the human mind, affects and emotions are highly condensed: as a manifestation of the unconscious, art turned, for him, from an object of aesthetic enjoyment into an object of serious scientific interest. This was a powerful move, not least because the professional process of scientific study conventionally forbade such a reliance on 'artistic subjectivity' as a method of 'objective' cognition. It meant that the 'productive decadence' of *fin-de-siècle* Vienna became conditioned by a new 'scientific artistic spirit', as Sigmund Freud broke down the one-dimensional notion of the domination of 'masculine' rationality by ascribing an equal level of importance to the 'feminine' reality of dreaming. In so doing, he became, in Klaus Heinrich's words, the 'enlightener of the Enlightenment'.[5]

With the worldwide influence of Freud's creative work as a form of therapy, his significance as a critical theorist of culture, a

4 For the term 'projective identification', see Melanie Klein, 'Bemerkungen über einige schizoide Mechanismen' ['Notes on some schizoid mechanisms' [1946]], in *Das Seelenleben des Kleinkindes und andere Beiträge zur Psychoanalyse*, ed. Hans A. Thorner (Stuttgart: Klett-Cotta, 1983), 141.

5 Klaus Heinrich, 'Festhalten an Freud. Eine Heine-Freud-Miniatur zur noch immer aktuellen Rolle des Aufklärers Freud' ['Cleaving to Freud. A Heine-Freud-Miniature on the ever-new role of Freud as Enlightener'], *Zeitschrift für Psychoanalytische Theorie und Praxis*, 3 (2007), 376.

philosopher and cultural anthropologist has been underestimated. These days, society seems less and less inclined to grasp history as a critical and self-critical process of experience and learning, a process we depend upon to 'arrive at the present' in a theoretical, practical and above all sensually concrete sense. In particular, we urgently need to bring today's young people into closer contact with the notion of a reflective historical consciousness, for they tend to live in a kind of all-encompassing 'permanent present' into which the dimension of the future is incorporated – very different from the generation of 1968, for example, for whom the future was situated in some 'distant utopia'. Young people today are more likely to think: 'Utopia, sure – it'll happen the day after tomorrow, or maybe even today.' It is also true that 'the distant future' no longer exists in the way it did for the generations in the second half of the 20th century, whose lives were defined by a single career-path. Today's future options need multi-tasking abilities, an intuitive reason and a poetically inspired rationality: even the past of 'cultural memory' (to borrow a term coined by Aleida and Jan Assmann in 1980)[6] is part of the all-encompassing present. Thus cultural knowledge as the presiding *sensus communis* of bourgeois society no longer structures time as past, present and future. Culture itself is no longer a sphere for finding solutions to the major problems of human life. Freud realized that culture is incapable of putting a brake on humankind's incredible powers of self-destruction, both individual and collective.[7] This is still relevant today. After Freud's 'Copernican revolution' in modern thought,[8] it is especially important for our time that we do not forget the socio-cultural premises of psychoanalysis. Contemporary art, too, may be able to throw the light of a little more understanding on the shadowy terrain of the repressed unconscious structures that are cemented nowadays by the global media of affirmation – and which make the notion of the 'Enlightenment of the Enlightenment' just as essential today.

---

6   Aleida and Jan Assmann, *Schrift und Gedächtnis: Beiträge zur Archäologie der literarischen Kommunikation* (Munich: Fink, 1983).

7   Sigmund Freud, '*Das Unbehagen in der Kultur*', ['*Civilization and its discontents*' [1929–30]], in *Studienausgabe Bd. IX: Fragen der Gesellschaft, Ursprünge der Religion* (Frankfurt am Main: Fischer, 1974), 191–270.

8   Sigmund Freud, *Introductory Lectures on Psychoanalysis: Lecture XVIII 'Fixation to Traumas – the Unconscious'* [1917], in *The Standard Edition of the Complete Psychological Works of Sigmund Freud*, 24 vols., ed. and trans. by James Strachey et al. (London: The Hogarth Press and the Institute of Psycho-analysis, 1953–74), vol. 16 (1963), 284–5.

If we think of the processes of both aesthetic creativity and its reception, what genuine form of understanding can artistic experience offer us? In order to answer this, we need to cast our minds back to the pre-disciplinary knowledge-based society of the 18th century, when the sharp distinction between the human and cultural sciences, between philosophical reflection and musical creativity, did not yet exist in that particularized form in which it appears from the end of the 19th century onwards. These structural tendencies of particularization have an affinity to similar developments at the beginning of the 19th century. In the history of the development of subjectivity in the modern era, the emergence of modern individuality in the latter part of the 18th century is of key importance. Philosophers, scientists and, above all, court-artists played a major role in the invention of modern individualism – the latter because of their contribution as *producers of symbols* in absolutist courts where the aristocrats demanded endlessly renewed festivities. Librettists like Metastasio or Da Ponte were just as important as confectioners, butchers, musicians, architects or painters. After all, without opera a proper wedding was unthinkable and without music food would not have tasted anything like as good. In this courtly enactment, the function of artists was to refine the sophisticated taste of their audience, inculcating an *intelligence of taste* that constituted a central element of individuation in high aristocratic circles. The challenge for the great composers and librettists was to find ever-new and surprising elements in order to differentiate their work from the standard conventions of the time – anything else was dismissed as boring. The artistic productions of the court were a key ingredient in keeping that court society up to date in its symbolic-aesthetic representation of the world, so that it could also make decisions and take action in the political reality of absolutist omnipotence. Court artists played an essential part in enabling this absolutist aristocracy to demonstrate its power on a personal level – alongside the structural network of objective conditions that, as Michel Foucault points out, constitute the main enactment of power.[9] It was only on the basis of their privileged position as participants in the aristocratic *know-how of ruling* that they could compose an *opera seria* or *opera buffa* in which the aristocracy might poke fun at their emperor or themselves.

At the end of the 18th century, then, science, artistic genius, military and political strategy and tactics did not operate in separate educational faculties but were grouped more flexibly within a

---

9 Michel Foucault, *Surveiller et Punir* [*Discipline and Punish*] (Paris: Gallimard, 1975).

common field of imagination in which they might even change places. Aesthetic judgement and rationality were connected to each other in the dimension of *taste intelligence*, passionate reason and inspired ingenuity – theory was not 'grey' and life 'green' as Goethe wrote in *Faust I*.[10] The definitive psychic authority of the ego did not yet exist as it would in 19th-century bourgeois society, a society constituted by the superego and guilt, as suggested above. The self-confidence of a non-aristocratic freelance court-artist like Mozart was based on audacity: he believed he was, by virtue of his genius, more than the equal of the prince and that, by developing and realizing not only his own individuality but also that of the sovereign and the nobility, he could develop as an artist and enjoy a more extensive, more historically lasting subjectivity than the prince himself could ever attain – for all the privilege of the latter's birth, blue dynastic blood and absolute power. It is as a unique non-aristocratic personality – a genius – that the artist might reflect the conditions of freedom (the ability to be creative) with which he was obsessed. Both Mozart and Haydn are defined by this dynamic, each in his own way, as their very different attitudes and career strategies show. Mozart was a child prodigy, a solo virtuoso from his earliest days, achieving one success after another all over Europe, even though he never secured the court position which his father insisted was the only route to financial security. Haydn's world fame was achieved in his lifetime through an entirely different strategy: he spent a significant proportion of his life in the service of the princes of the house of Esterházy in Eisenstadt, composing at a healthy distance from the hectic, hysterically competitive turmoil of the imperial city of Vienna. Despite his 'splendid isolation' in Eisenstadt, he became famous all over Europe by publishing his compositions in Vienna, Amsterdam, Berlin, Paris and London – for instance, he was celebrated as a musical star in Paris without ever setting foot there. Each of these composers had his own strategy for fulfilling an obsession with individual freedom by subverting the absolutistic privilege of the nobility: Mozart chose to confront authority personally, for example when he broke with the Salzburg archbishop Colloredo, while Haydn ignored his contracts with the princes of Esterházy (which stipulated that he should create music only for their noble ears) by publishing his compositions in the emerging European music market. In their time music was a way of modulating affect and developing modern

10 In Johann Wolfgang von Goethe, *Faust I*, Studierzimmer 2 [Study 2], Mephisto says: 'Grau, teurer Freund, ist alle Theorie, Und grün des Lebens goldner Baum' ['Dear friend, all theory is grey, and green the golden tree of life'].

formats of emotionality – the unique creations of music belonged to the sphere of the unconscious which was, so to speak, *dissolved* in the interactions of everyday life.

In order to grasp the exceptional significance of Freud in the history of science and culture, we must understand his invention of the unconscious from the perspective of enlightened rationalism of the late 18th century. As one of the foremost 'enlighteners' of the 20th century, Freud radically reformulated the role of the 'enlightener of the Enlightenment'. He also radicalized the Romantic concept of 'depth' – for Freud, 'depth' was not the opposite of 'surface' but an element of all expressions of thought or action. The repressed, that which is *not yet overcome*, returns in a different form – such as in the figure of the *Doppelgänger* [double], or the 'repressed part of the ego'.[11] For Freud, enlightenment was a continuous and interminable process, in which both the individual and the human race must constantly seek a new equilibrium. Freud the 'enlightener' dethroned the categorically restricted philosophy of consciousness of the Enlightenment, for which the drive was the declared enemy[12] – in this way, though it was not explicit, he found other means of pursuing the tradition of a rebellious-pornosophical enlightenment (that of the Marquis de Sade, La Mettrie, the Marquis d'Argens, and so on) which had been repressed in the 19th century. Irrationality became the central, radical element in Freud's enlightenment: the theory of the unconscious undermined the claims of rational logic to be able to deal with affects and emotional structures as though they were verifiable facts. The idea of a contract between analyst and analysand, working together to create a 'common enlightenment', is derived from Rousseau's social-contract theories.[13] Yet the communication between analyst and analysand dispenses with any traditional rational rules, insofar as everything has to be communicated – even or especially anything the analysand produces by pure association, without knowing its meaning; this approach is the very opposite of rationalistic restriction. Because it elevates dream and irrationality

---

11   Sigmund Freud, 'Das Unheimliche' ['The uncanny' [1919]], in *Studienausgabe Bd. IV* (Frankfurt am Main: Fischer, 1974), 24–75.

12   Cf. Klaus Heinrich, 'Festhalten an Freud' ['Cleaving to Freud'], *Zeitschrift für psychoanalytische Theorie und Praxis*, 3 (2007), 365–87.

13   Jean-Jacques Rousseau, *Émile ou de l'éducation* [*Émile, or On Education* [1762]] (Paris: Garnier-Flammarion, 1966) and *Du contrat social ou Principes du droit politique* [*The Social Contract, or Principles of Political Right*] (Amsterdam: Chez Marc Michel Rey, 1762).

to the level of reality, it places the 'reality of the rational' under the direct threat of outing itself (or being outed) as *surreality*.

The basis in cognition of the European philosophy of consciousness goes back to Descartes' declaration that every piece of knowledge must be defined as 'claire et distincte' ['clear and distinct'][14] – but the fact is that the most long-lasting and inspiring concepts, even in philosophy, have been clear without being distinct, beginning with the term 'reason' itself. All such concepts take hold through the dialectic of rational analysis and the production of myth, a continuous process of enlightenment since Hesiod's time. Returning to the 18th century, Kant's interpretation of Descartes' 'cogito ergo sum' ['I think, therefore I am'] leads to a distinction between two egos which are both present in the act of *cogito*. On the one hand, *cogito* represents the existential personality of the human individual who is able to think – on the other hand, it represents an instance of self-reflexivity, since the act of thinking is the highest manifestation of that individual's sovereignty of freedom (self-cognition) which suggests that the self-reflexive part of the *cogito's* ego is controlling the other, existential one. This structure can also be found *en correspondance* in Goethe's concept of a 'double life'.[15] Kant's philosophizing could be seen as an arduous path to self-understanding through the application of Enlightenment,[16] and it could also be compared with Freud's self-analysis, which includes a sort of self-communication with the internal 'Wächter'[17] ['watchman'] that represents the ambiguity between dreaming and wakefulness, the very productive state of hypnagogia that leads to insight for the psychoanalyst as well as inspiration for the artist. Kant unflinchingly thematizes the fact that there is a price to pay for clarity of consciousness – reflected in his observation that we continuously use our consciousness at the borderline between

---

14 René Descartes, *Discours de la méthode: Von der Methode des richtigen Vernunftgebrauchs und der wissenschaftlichen Forschung* [*Discours de la méthode pour bien conduire sa raison et chercher la vérité dans les sciences* [1673]], ed. and trans. by Lüder Gäbe (Hamburg: Meiner, 1997).

15 Johann Wolfgang von Goethe, 'Julius Cäsars Triumphzug – gemalt von Mantegna' ['The triumphs of Caesar – painted by Mantegna' [1822]], in *Werke. Hamburger Ausgabe*, ed. Erich Trunz, 14 vols. (Munich: C. H. Beck, 1999), XII, 182–202 ; and Gert Mattenklott, '"Mantegnas Doppelleben" als Muster für Goethes Späte Ästhetik', in *Bausteine zu einem neuen Goethe*, ed. Paolo Chiarini (Frankfurt am Main: Athenäum, 1987), 135–47.

16 Immanuel Kant, 'Beantwortung der Frage: Was ist Aufklärung?' ['Answering the question: what is Enlightenment?'], *Berlinische Monatsschrift 2 (1784), 481–94*.

17 Sigmund Freud, *Die Traumdeutung* [*The Interpretation of Dreams*] (Vienna & Leipzig: Franz Deuticke, 1900), 161.

phenomenen and *nuomenon*, so that our 'pure reason' allows us to make unambiguous *a priori* distinctions[18] – while the aesthetic judgment of taste intelligence enhances our rational cognition with the dimension of ambiguity. To some extent, this is the price of the 'split ego' in Freud's concept as well: there is another doubling-effect in the tension between the ego-fragment which is the result of the repressed unconsciousness and the critical ego as the representation of consciousness.[19] Freud's unconscious is metaphorically located beyond all rational distinctions: absolute boundaries are dissolved, even between life and death. The 'unconscious' is, in a totally ambivalent sense, the basis of our life – setting it in a permanent state of turmoil. The conception of such a 'science of experience', which is what psychoanalysis ultimately is, is groundbreaking. It definitively supersedes the one-dimensional, rationalistic Enlightenment of the 18th century, in which the unconscious (in the form of mythological demons and so on) was viewed as a compulsive force descending on rational thought like a horde of barbarians and 'tarnishing' its *claritas*. The latter could only be corrected by a good education able to tame and order the modulation of affects. With psychoanalysis, Freud introduces a process of understanding that combines science, art and creative productivity and is balanced between dreaming and waking consciousness. The ambiguities of our existence actually have a highly inspiring and productive effect on Freud.[20]

The 19th century was heir to the Enlightenment and as such, with the development of bourgeois society, industrialization and capitalism, it was ruled by the all-encompassing authority of rationality – economics, the natural sciences, technology, military logistics, the humanities, medicine and social studies (statistics) were presided over by the definitive reality-principle of *reason*. What united scientists and humanities thinkers was the aim of finding a method that could 'give objective form' to the manifold 'phenomenon' of reality; this method was intended to bring order to the overwhelming 'universe of experience' and replace warring mythologies with psychology, which would relativize them through analytic comparisons. Gradually these 'phenomena' became domesticated, turning into the 'Haustieren unserer Subjektivität'

---

18 Immanuel Kant, *Kritik der reinen Vernunft* [*Critique of Pure Reason*] (Riga: Johann Friedrich Hartknoch, 1781).

19 Sigmund Freud, 'Das Unheimliche' ['The uncanny' [1919]], in *Studienausgabe Bd. IV* (Frankfurt am Main: Fischer, 1974), 241–75.

20 Klaus Heinrich, 'Festhalten an Freud' ['Cleaving to Freud'], *Zeitschrift für psychoanalytische Theorie und Praxis*, 3 (2007), 365–87.

['household pets of our subjectivity'].[21] As mentioned before, the demons of the irrational, such as spirits and ghosts were handed over to professionals, the artists living the bohemian life. With the rise of the modernist avant-garde, this polarization between intellectuals and radical artists became even more extreme. Unlike the court-artists of the waning 18th century, who had been occupied in devising a symbolic universe for the everyday life of the aristocracy, they had an immanent function within that world as the figures of art and its creations. The existence of the Romantic genius was justified by the professional work of internalizing the suffering of society, creating psychical 'alternative worlds' in the form of an aesthetic cosmos, and acting out 'extremist subjectivity' for a bourgeoisie starved of feeling and desperate for a religion of art – this was particularly true of late 19th-century Vienna.

For Freud, as we have seen, mythology, bridging the conscious and the unconscious, enabled the discovery of new kinds of meaning. This was thematized in the exhibition '*Gradiva*: Muse of Psychoanalysis', held in Vienna in 2012, a continuation of my exhibition series, 'Staging Knowledge – performative dissemination of culture and imaginative rhetorics', which was created as a response to the urgent need to build bridges between science and art. The events held so far in this series have been cultural-historical exhibitions on the relevance of the 18th century for our times;[22] they are also an attempt to develop a new kind of research practice for the humanities, following the principle that any strategy for communicating knowledge is potentially a research strategy, and vice versa. Thus we staged a 'knowledge-space' which was also – following Aby Warburg's idea of the 'Bilderatlas' ['picture atlas'][23] – a 'thinking-space' into which conversations with academics,

---

21   Klaus Heinrich used this term in a conversation with the author, Berlin 2006.

22   Previous 'Staging Knowledge' exhibitions: 'Beschwörung nationaler Identität – Das Bernhardzimmer: Neugotik im Herzen des Klassizismus' ['Conjuration of National Identity – The Bernhardzimmer: Neo-Gothic at the Heart of Classicism'] (Weimar 2009–10); 'Haydn Explosiv' (Eisenstadt 2009); 'Wozu braucht Carl August einen Goethe?' ['What Does Carl August Need a Goethe For?'] (Weimar 2008); 'Mozart. Experiment Aufklärung' ['Mozart. Experiment Enlightenment'] (Albertina, Vienna 2006); 'Wolfgang Amadé – ein ganz normales Wunderkind' ['Wolfgang Amadé – Quite a Normal Child Prodigy'] (Zoom Kindermuseum, Vienna 2006); 'Lorenzo da Ponte – il poeta di Mozart' ['Lorenzo da Ponte – Mozart's Poet'] (Jewish Museum, Vienna 2006); 'Salieri sulle Tracce di Mozart' ['Salieri on Mozart's Path'] (Palazzo Reale, Milan 2004).

23   See Aby Warburg, *Der Bilderatlas MNEMOSYNE* [1924–29], ed. Manfred Warnke and Claudia Brink (Berlin: Akademie Verlag, 2000).

helpful in this as well, not so much by being a source of inspiration as by strengthening both the connections and the distinctions between a brilliant analytic intelligence and a phantasmagoric intuition – this at least is our hypothesis as curator. At the same time, 'Staging Knowledge' is a way of broadening the practice of research in the humanities, extending the routine limits of traditional discourses by the enrichment of an experimental dimension. I can vouch from experience for the fact that, as scientists and artists work together in close collaboration to create a common project based on a common concept, from the opening of the exhibition to the completion of all the connected performative-rhetorical 'projections', the horizons of possibility for scientific thinking really are broadened.

18. Gradiva Project

William Cobbing

I visited the Museo Chiaramonti in the Vatican to see the Gradiva bas-relief firsthand during my artist's residency at The British School at Rome.[1] Part of the motivation for this visit was curiosity, simply to be able to confirm the existence of the sculpture exactly where Sigmund Freud had gazed at it on 24 September 1907, a century before. In a letter to Martha, his wife, Freud writes: 'I saw today in the Vatican a dear familiar face! The recognition was one-sided, however, for it was the Gradiva, high up on a wall.'[2] To stand in the Museo Chiaramonti in front of the Gradiva bas-relief is to assume the same vantage point, to see Gradiva as Freud did, as if in his shoes. Freud had a plaster-cast of Gradiva in his study in Vienna, which he brought to London with many of his other possessions when he and his family fled Nazi persecution in 1939. The fascination this sculpture held for Freud derived from Wilhelm Jensen's gothic novella *Gradiva* (1903), in which a young archaeologist, Hanold, dreams of the figure in the bas-relief coming to life from stone only to be buried alive underneath the ash of Vesuvius when it erupted in 79 CE. Hanold becomes enthralled with the figure's distinctive gait ('Gradiva' meaning 'beautiful step'), deluding himself that the fantasy of his dream could be played out in the reality of his waking hours. Freud was interested in the novella's archaeological dream narrative, metaphorically relating it to his own

---

1 Arts Council England Helen Chadwick Fellowship at British School at Rome and Ruskin School, University of Oxford, September 2005–March 2006.
2 Sigmund Freud, *Letters of Sigmund Freud 1873–1939*, ed. Ernst L. Freud (London: The Hogarth Press, 1961), 276.

psychoanalytic enquiry, namely 'burial by repression and excavation by analysis'.[3]

Over two months after first visiting the Museo Chiaramonti, my interest in making a work based on Gradiva took shape via an unrelated encounter at the Ruskin School with the scholar Federico Caprotti. During our conversation I became intrigued by his research into the fascist street alterations Mussolini imposed on Rome from 1922. Besides the prominent fascist monuments and statues which still highlight the past, more subtle indicators are the *Era Fascista* (E.F.) insignia, which adorn certain manhole covers, street lamps and other municipal markers in the city. Beyond the reference to Mussolini, the discussion led me to think about manhole covers, something I had rarely considered before, even though I walk over these inconspicuous iron plates every day. This interest was awoken primarily because of my perspective of looking at the cover as a kind of cast-iron sculpture, with a tread pattern and the embossed insignia of a local authority, water or gas company, and keyholes to lift it out of the ground. This triggered a leap of association between a manhole cover and the bas-relief of Gradiva, since in different ways they are both shallow relief-forms emerging from a two-dimensional plane. This observation represented the moment of a fortuitous confluence of two seemingly disparate entities, leading to the idea of embossing a bas-relief of Gradiva onto a manhole cover.

The initial idea was to superimpose and then blend a shallower copy of the Gradiva bas-relief onto a cast of an SPQR manhole cover;[4] these are ubiquitous on the streets of Rome. I made a plaster-cast of one, forming the bas-relief on to it with modelling clay, before taking it to an industrial foundry to be cast in iron.

It seemed conceptually appropriate that the manhole cover sculpture should function much like any other in the street, rather than be displayed in a gallery context. To enable this, I purchased a pair of iron lifting keys to raise up an SPQR cover situated on via Gramsci in Rome, and temporarily replaced it with the Gradiva Project sculpture. It remained in position for only a few minutes, emphasizing the fleeting action of installing it rather than its quality

3 James Strachey 'Editor's note' in Sigmund Freud, 'Delusions and dreams in Jensen's *Gradiva*' ['Der Wahn und die Träume in W. Jensen's *Gradiva*' [1907]], in *The Standard Edition of the Complete Psychological Works of Sigmund Freud*, 24 vols., ed. and trans. by James Strachey *et al.* (London: The Hogarth Press and the Institute of Psycho-analysis, 1953–74), vol. 9, 4–5.

4 SPQR is the acronym for 'Senate Populusque Romanus' ['The Senate and People of Rome']. SPQR insignia appear on certain manhole covers, water hydrants and other municipal markers in Rome.

as an autonomous object. I repeated this in Pompeii with the help of three Pompeian site workmen, further echoing the locations in Jensen's *Gradiva*, when Hanold dreams of Gradiva being brought to life on the archaeological site. At first, however, the existing cover stubbornly remained in place, leading the workmen to attempt ever more robust ways of trying to prise it out. The resulting documentary video plays out like a slapstick routine, with the workmen bumping into each other in the confined space, eventually using hammers and a crowbar to force the cover out. When installed, the mud and grit from the archaeological site quickly accumulated on the Gradiva Project cover, making it look as if it had been in place much longer than it really had. Reflecting on the installation of the cover returned me to the inevitable and frequent act of stepping on a manhole cover on the pavement, considering the connection with Jensen's depiction of Gradiva as 'the one who walks' or 'beautiful step'. Transposing the Gradiva bas-relief from the wall to the pavement as a manhole cover can be likened symbolically to the shadow cast on the ground by a person standing up. This involves a reorientation from a vertical to a horizontal plane, and perhaps even a shift in its cultural value from high to low status. The classical bas-relief of Gradiva on the wall of the Museo Chiaramonti is recreated in the more common form of a manhole cover in the street.

After I had started the Gradiva Project in Rome and Pompeii, the main settings for Jensen's novella, the most fitting destination for the nomadic work was the Freud Museum, London, where the project could come full circle. The reason for choosing to exhibit here was of course its rich association with Gradiva, from Freud's own plaster-cast of the bas-relief displayed on his study wall to the museum's having hosted the 1994 conference at which Jacques Derrida spoke of Gradiva's imprint and traces, later published as *Archive Fever*.[5] As a venue for exhibiting art, the Freud Museum is the antithesis of a 'white cube' gallery space. Not only is it a fully furnished house, but it is also Freud's house, with all the symbolism that this entails. The particularity of the venue required the negotiation of numerous conceptual and practical factors in the installation of the works.

I had garnered a large amount of raw material for the Gradiva Project in Rome and Pompeii, including hundreds of photographs and several hours of video footage of the manhole cover being put in place. Significantly, the project had reached this provisional stage

---

5 Jacques Derrida, *Archive Fever: A Freudian Impression* [*Mal d'Archive : une impression freudienne*], trans. by Eric Prenowitz (Chicago: University of Chicago Press, 1995).

through an unfolding of events, rather than as a planned course of action. I wanted to preserve this freedom in the way I worked, despite the defined outcome of a museum exhibition. Whereas the project had previously been nomadic, journeying around Italy, its location was now fixed in the grounds of the Freud Museum. Although the covers had previously been installed in Pompeii and Rome for a matter of minutes, a new manhole cover could potentially be placed in the museum grounds for a much longer time. I replaced an existing cover on the pathway of the museum's front garden, with a newly cast one from the Gradiva Project, where it stayed for the duration of the exhibition and where it will remain as a permanent work. Being exposed to the elements, it expresses passing time more slowly, through its gradual oxidisation, forming a distinctive coat of orange rust that eats away at the surface layer of the iron. Robert Smithson notes that rust:

> is caused by oxidisation [...], as during exposure to air or moisture; it consists almost entirely of ferric oxide, Fe_2O_3 and ferric hydroxide, $Fe(OH)_3$. In the technological mind rust evokes a fear of disuse, inactivity, entropy and ruin. Why steel is valued over rust is a technological value, not an artistic one.[6]

As in the above comments, the Gradiva Project manhole cover referred to entropy, ruin and memory, not in a negative technological sense of fearing obsolescence, but in an artistic way of drawing attention to the effect of the passage of time on objects.

Over the course of the 18 months prior to the exhibition I was primarily concerned with developing new works, in tandem with considering how and where they would be placed in the Freud Museum. The question of installation and context was a significant challenge, as I had previously had solo exhibitions in galleries that were far more neutral contexts for showing works. Because the museum is so steeped in Freudian history and symbolism, it is imperative for an artist to develop a strategy to negotiate this highly subjective venue. As it is a fully furnished house, there is little space exclusively set aside for works of art, with it often being necessary to set sculptures and television monitors between the existing paintings, photographs, bookshelves and Austrian peasant furniture in the rooms. To a certain degree, I felt like an interloper, forced to tread delicately around this highly personalized, even haunted, living space to showcase my works. This poses a dilemma for both

---

6   Robert Smithson, *Robert Smithson: The Collected Writings*, ed. Jack Flam (Los Angeles: University of California Press, 1996), 106.

curator and artist, expressed in the following observation from the exhibition's curator, Jon Bird:

> Curating contemporary art in the Freud Museum is now a well-established practice – an ongoing conversation between the Freudian archive and the work of art that, given Freud's caution over the use-value of applying psychoanalysis to art, might more be seen as art's reply to psychoanalysis: a riddle which, like the peculiarity of *Gradiva's* walk, invites and resists interpretation.[7]

Whereas art exhibitions at the Freud Museum may be a 'reply to psychoanalysis', Freud did not 'reply' to the artists who responded to this theories, as is evident in his ambivalence to André Breton and the surrealists.[8] Now Freud is gone, the only form of communication left open is one of 'replying', often by positioning art practice in such a way as to create a 'riddle' between engagement in and independence of psychoanalysis. The silence which greets the 'reply' of artists to Freudianism is highlighted by Beth Williamson's observation that 'contemporary works sit among the furniture and artefacts in Freud's old London home and we wonder what he might have made of them'.[9] This intriguing thought often crossed my mind while working on the project at the museum. The intangible presence of Freud still permeating the museum means that works of art exhibited there tend to be affected by this aura. Joanne Morra writes:

> It must be peculiar to have an exhibition at the Freud Museum. An exhibition in such a complex space must make it difficult, if not impossible, to read the work outside of this context. A concern for any artist showing their work here must be how to engage with what the museum is and stands for, while not having the work subsumed by it.[10]

---

7   Jon Bird, *Gradiva Project*, ed. William Cobbing (London: Camden Arts Centre, 2007), 3.

8   Breton set up Galerie Gradiva in Paris in 1937, and several of the surrealist artists responded to the narrative of Gradiva, notably Max Ernst, Salvador Dalí, and André Masson. As part of the Gradiva Project exhibition, I made two manhole covers featuring bas-reliefs based on Masson's *Gradiva* painting and *Acéphale* drawing, installed on the forecourt of Camden Arts Centre, near the Freud Museum.

9   Beth L. Williamson, 'William Cobbing: Gradiva Project', *The Art Book*, vol. 15, Issue 3 (August 2008), 23.

10   Joanne Morra, *Gradiva Project*, ed. William Cobbing (London: Camden Arts Centre, 2007), 26.

Morra makes the point that to place a work of art in the Freud Museum is to accept that a reading of it will be conditioned by the context, as if it is viewed through the prism of Freudianism. Bearing this in mind, how can an artist engage with this context and preserve the autonomy of his/her work? My experience with installing the Gradiva Project in the museum is that this varies from work to work, and even from room to room. Walking around one feels Freud's presence reverberating in subtly different ways and to varying degrees, most acutely in his study. Here, I chose to exhibit 'Excavation': on a television monitor on a small tabletop in front of Freud's bookshelf, a figure chips away with a hammer and chisel at a craggy mass of concrete enveloping its head. The activity appears distressing but is also darkly humorous, and continues without resulting in the expected breakthrough, only looping repetitively. I have exhibited this work on a number of occasions, mainly in more generic 'white cube' spaces including Milton Keynes Gallery, Netwerk Centre for Contemporary Art, Aalst, and Z33 in Hasselt, Belgium. 'Excavation' seemed like a completely different video, compared to when it was screened at these venues, since its location in Freud's study had a reductive effect on how it was interpreted. In a more neutral setting the video can be considered in a more nuanced way, with the chipping away of concrete regarded as having several possible connotations, such as a wry reference to the cliché of the traditional sculptor chipping away at a block of stone in his atelier, or the futility of Sisyphus pushing a boulder up a mountain only to let it roll down again. If a visitor to the museum walks into Freud's study to discover the video, there is a possibility that it will be regarded primarily in terms of the archaeological metaphor, with the chipping away read as burial and excavation of emotion or memory.

I installed several other sculptures and videos between the furniture in less conspicuous areas of the museum than Freud's study, and this led to them being viewed as if out of the corner of one's eye. The 'Untitled' concrete body cast, plumbed in to the unused doorway of the upstairs exhibition and television room, was partially obscured from view when visitors entered the room. The pile of 'London Brick' sculptures rested on a wooden pallet between wall, floor and a chest of drawers and below a painting from Freud's collection. Even the Gradiva Project manhole cover was situated outside the side-door, so a visitor walking up the path to the main door would have to glance at it in a sideways direction. Morra considers the act of drawing attention to what is in one's peripheral vision as linked to the premise of psychoanalysis itself, giving the example of Freud's Gradiva cast:

The *Gradiva* bas-relief was hung askance in Freud's consulting room in Vienna and then in London. It was placed in such manner as to engage the peripheral vision of those occupying the rooms, in the same way as psychoanalytic treatment encourages the foregrounding of peripheral thoughts and fragments. (Morra, 30)

In the move from Vienna to London, Freud's cast of Gradiva was no longer situated in the study, as it occupies the narrow wall in the library that is passed before entering the study. Nevertheless, one could still make Morra's remark — about it being peripheral — about its current new location, as it is more likely to be glanced at sideways on the way into the study. With the Gradiva Project manhole cover remaining in place, it may also continue to attract the peripheral vision of those visiting the museum, serving as a reminder of the significance of hidden thoughts and memories.

Psychoanalysis and Transmission

19. Transmission Impossible?

Andrew Webber

For the 'Histories and transmissions' group in the Psychoanalysis and the Arts and Humanities Network, transmission was always understood as at once spatial, temporal and conceptual: mapping the physical and disciplinary travels of psychoanalysis across the globe over the last century as well as across substantial parts of the academy. Three exemplary domains are featured here: psychoanalysis and anthropology, psychoanalysis and cinema, and psychoanalysis and Latin America. This short chapter consequently tracks the transmission of psychoanalytic ideas into a disciplinary territory (anthropology) that has neighboured it from the beginning. It progresses into a cultural medium (film) of which the same can be said and then into a far-away continent (Latin America) but is also in particular respects neighbouring – albeit in ways complicated by colonial and postcolonial relations – for Europe as the home continent of the movement. Each area has a special, proximate relationship to psychoanalysis, similar to the sibling one Juliet Mitchell analyses in this volume: difficult and changeable, subject to vicissitude, if not impossibility. This chapter outlines the vicissitudes in question, suggesting that they offer particularly telling evidence of the status and possibilities of psychoanalytic thinking in both historical and contemporary terms, as it is transferred or transmitted to and through other disciplinary, formal and cultural-geographical domains.

Since its origins psychoanalysis has been concerned with transmissions of knowledge, whether from the personal unconscious into consciousness, classically in the interlocution of the consultation room, or from that most immediate territory of psychoanalytic enquiry into other epistemological domains. And disciplinary transmission operates in parallel with the travelling of psychoanalytic ideas and practices from their home terrain in Vienna around 1900 to other places and times. This section of the volume is concerned with the often- interlinked routes of transmission and the difficulties – if not impossibilities – associated with them. These were the preoccupations of the scholars and analysts in the aforementioned 'Histories and transmissions' group when it met in 2007–08 at the Cambridge University Centre for Research in the Arts, Social Sciences and Humanities (CRASSH); and they are the subject of the next two chapters, by the Argentinean historian of psychoanalysis Mariano Plotkin and the London-based artist Uriel Orlow.

Let us begin by taking an image in a medium that, behind and alongside its motion-picture counterpart, has particularly appealed to psychoanalytic thinking: Sharon Kivland's photograph of the staircase at Berggasse 19, Freud's address in Vienna, which features on the cover of this book and first appeared as part of her work *L'Esprit d'escalier* [*Spirit/Wit of the Staircase*].[1] It records a kind of transitional space, leading to the iconic site of the formation of psychoanalysis, but one that is not recognizable as such and could just be a generic, late 19th-century staircase in the central European style. It could for instance – if the buildings in question had survived – be the sort of staircase that Walter Benjamin describes in his *Berlin Childhood around 1900*, a kind of extended threshold between exterior and interior haunted by bugbears for the infant subject and the recollecting adult.[2] The staircase seems to suspend the historical dimension in a particular way, as a potential site for the reenactment of original scenes. It is a space for coming and going on an everyday basis and also for more permanent departures or evacuations. For both Benjamin and Freud it is the starting-place for emigrations, in the latter's case leaving the living-space as what would come to be a museum and memorial, though with much of its interior having migrated elsewhere. The staircase is always, potentially, a site for ghosting, for phantom experiences. It is a particular space of psycho-topographical anxiety and desire: a space of anticipation, in the fantasies that precede encounter, and of after-life, in those that follow it. In a particular sense, this is what it is both for the analysand mounting or descending the stairs to the consultation room, and

---

1   Sharon Kivland, *L'Esprit d'escalier* (York: information as material, 2007). '*Esprit*' here suggests at once wit, spirit/mind, and perhaps, by association, phantom.

2   The different versions of Benjamin's text were written between 1932 and 1938. For a more extensive reading of *Berlin Childhood*'s threshold hauntings, see my *Berlin in the Twentieth Century: A Cultural Topography* (Cambridge: Cambridge University Press, 2008), 61–103.

for the analyst. That is, if the staircase is a transitional space, it is also inhabited by kinds of second-order transference: the sorts of extension of the dynamics of the clinic that are inevitably transmitted into the life-worlds of the individuals concerned.

The staircase is thus also a transitional space in the sense that it represents communication with others. In Kivland's photograph it is, after all, not just Freud's staircase but a communal place of passage over time. And it seems that it can serve as an appropriate allegorical image for considering the transmissions of psychoanalysis in a broader sense, always recalling that allegory – in Benjamin's understanding of that master-trope – incorporates an element of historical damage and loss in its logic. If psychoanalysis seeks to attend to historical and case-historical damage and loss, its transmission into the wider world is certainly not free from these, and the break in the continuity of the staircase's historical space marked by forced emigration can be seen to represent this.

The image represents a view down the staircase over three floors: a *mise-en-abyme* and, as such, a suitable emblem for the sorts of structure in and beyond the apparent structures of psychoanalytic thinking that concerned the Psychoanalysis and the Arts and Humanities Network as a whole. The edifice of psychoanalysis in itself could be represented by such an image of the poetics of space, following Freud's architectural, archaeological and topographical imagination in his first fashioning of the movement. And it could certainly be represented thus in its various disciplinary translations and transmissions – the systems of historical, cultural and conceptual transaction that have characterized the travels of psychoanalysis. Beyond the analyst's consulting room, then, are other rooms, other suites and passages and doors opening upon the world.

The image also represents the idea of vicissitude, not least as it might apply to the transmission of a body of thought such as psychoanalysis. A staircase is a guiding structure, a conduit, allowing transmission through architectural form and a certain control of the process of transmission – a space at once open and closed. Kivland's image also has a questioning function for that process of transmission: it plays with depth and plane – the dimensions of the steps collapse vertiginously as you behold them. It also plays with dark and light – the bright light-source here is an isolated reflection on, rather than diffusion from, the lamps. And the guiding structure of the handrail – part biomorphic, part mechanical – seems designed to overwhelm that function with its elaborate form. The conduit or passage thus impinges on any movements through it, reminding us that transmission is always under pressure from its environment. There is something here of what Anthony Vidler has called the architecture of the uncanny: a space for stumbling upon the familiarly unfamiliar.[3]

The image made an appealing frame for the 'Histories and transmissions' group's programme. Of course, the impossible project of scoping the historical transmissions of psychoanalysis needed to be contained. Hence the decision to explore three floors of the massive edifice, with psychoanalysis and anthropology, psychoanalysis and cinema, and psychoanalysis and Latin America set as consecutive levels in the light of our programme.

The first sequence or flight of readings, then, concerned anthropology – in a broad sense – and included works by Freud, Malinowski, Mannoni, Fanon and Said.[4] The history of bilateral transmissions between the two domains is a complex and often ambivalent one insofar as Freud's interest in anthropology from the origins of psychoanalysis onwards is concerned and the exploration of psychoanalytic ideas in the work of anthropologists after Freud. Its ambivalence turns most particularly on a fundamental question that marks all psychoanalytic moves into other disciplinary domains but is particularly acute for one that is concerned with other cultures: what limitations does the cultural-historical specificity of psychoanalysis impose upon its transmission to other times and places? In the context of anthropology, which can itself be seen as rooted in imperial projects, the cooperation with psychoanalysis, however cautious and complicated, might also transport imperialism with it. The traffic between the disciplines took the group in the direction of colonial and postcolonial politics, as intrinsic to both disciplinary territories and particularly acute in their combination. The final move was through a communicating door into the work of Judith Butler, following Freud's anthropological writings, on discourse and contagion in

---

3 Anthony Vidler, *The Architectural Uncanny: Essays in the Modern Unhomely* (Cambridge, MA: MIT Press, 1992).

4 Sigmund Freud, *Totem and Taboo* [*Totem und Tabu* [1913]], in *The Standard Edition of the Complete Psychological Works of Sigmund Freud*, 24 vols., ed. and trans. by James Strachey et al. (London: The Hogarth Press and the Institute of Psycho-analysis, 1953–74), vol. 8 (1948), 1–161; Bronislaw Malinowski, *Sex and Repression in Savage Society* (New York: Harcourt Brace, 1927); Octave Mannoni, *Prospero and Caliban: The Psychology of Colonization*, trans. by Pamela Powesland (London: Methuen, 1956); Frantz Fanon, *The Wretched of the Earth* [*Les Damnés de la terre* [1961]], trans. by Constance Farrington (New York: Grove, 1965); Edward Said, *Freud and the Non-European* (London: Verso, 2003).

the constitution of individual and collective identities.[5] This opened up the possibility of considering how a system like psychoanalysis constitutes itself performatively through its dialogues with, and its resistances to, other discourses such as anthropology and how it might, with its communal structures and ritual behaviours, itself be an object of ethnographic study.

The second flight of readings was concerned with transmissions between film and psychoanalysis – how psychoanalysis has been historically transmitted by the medium of film since their shared cultural birth at the end of the 19th century and how film and film theory have in their turn been transmitted by psychoanalytic theory. Our readings here included work by Jacques Lacan, Slavoj Žižek and Stephen Heath, along with an essay by Todd McGowan on Lacanian film theory and its vicissitudes.[6] The characteristic vicissitude of finding the best way round our edifice intervened at this point, as we were diverted by our reading of Heath on the role of fantasy in the parallel histories of cinema and psychoanalysis. Here, we read classic accounts of the construction and functions of fantasy by Freud, Isaacs, Lacan, and Laplanche and Pontalis,[7] concerning ourselves with how it might figure in the movements of psychoanalysis into other territories. The programme of film-theoretical readings, which we interrupted for our side-step into fantasy, was then resumed in that light. This led to a CRASSH-sponsored conference on

---

5 Judith Butler, 'Contagious word: paranoia and "homosexuality" in the military', in *Excitable Speech: A Politics of the Performative* (New York: Routledge, 1997), 103–26.

6 Jacques Lacan, 'Of the gaze as *objet petit a*' ['*Du regard comme objet petit a*'], in *The Four Fundamental Concepts of Psycho-analysis* [*Les quatre Concepts fondamentaux de la psychanalyse* [1973]], ed. Jacques-Alain Miller, trans. by Alan Sheridan (London: Vintage, 1998), 65–119; Slavoj Žižek, 'The Hitchcockian blot', in *Looking Awry: An Introduction to Jacques Lacan through Popular Culture* (Cambridge, MA: MIT Press, 1991), 88–106; Stephen Heath, 'Cinema and psychoanalysis: parallel histories', in *Endless Night: Cinema and Psychoanalysis – Parallel Histories*, ed. Janet Bergstrom (Berkeley, CA: University of California Press, 1999), 25–57; Todd McGowan, 'Looking for the gaze: Lacanian film theory and its vicissitudes', *Cinema Journal*, 42.3 (Spring 2003), 27–47.

7 Sigmund Freud, '"A child is being beaten": a contribution to the study of the origin of sexual perversions' ['"Ein Kind wird geschlagen": Beitrag zur Kenntnis der Entstehung sexueller Perversionen' [1919]], in *The Standard Edition*, xvii, 175–204; Susan Isaacs, 'The nature and function of phantasy', *International Journal of Psychoanalysis* 29 (1948), 73–97; Jacques Lacan, 'Le fantasme au-delà du principe de plaisir', in *Les Formations de l'inconscient* (Paris: Seuil, 1998), 233–48; Jean Laplanche and Jean-Bertrand Pontalis, 'Fantasy and the origins of sexuality', *International Journal of Psychoanalysis*, 49 (1968), 1–18.

cinema and psychoanalysis under the title 'Transmission: Cinema/ Psychoanalysis', held in Cambridge in September 2008, with speakers including Mieke Bal and Kaja Silverman.

The final flight explored the reach of psychoanalysis in perhaps its most significant 'foreign territory', a continent that is as it were at once light and dark, home and colony, for the psychoanalytic project – Latin America. Here, we concerned ourselves both with the case-historical and other work of analysts, and with historical accounts of the discipline's development in different Latin American countries. Our reading included the historiographical work of Mariano Plotkin,[8] along with theoretical essays, especially by Latin American analysts of an object-relations persuasion, ranging over various themes, from the psychoanalytic frame, via transference, perversion and persecution, to the culture of tango. The discussion was enriched by the participation of scholars in Latin American studies, who were able to ask questions about the development of psychoanalysis in a specific set of cultural and political framings. With a recurrent focus on questions of migration, exoticism and colonial and postcolonial civil strife – the work of analysis under states of exception – it mapped back onto our anthropological readings in interesting ways.

So, to return to Kivland's image, we chose a certain, necessarily limited route through a vast edifice of historical transmissions, translations and dialogues – a tower of Babel perhaps. On each floor, we selected certain rooms to explore more carefully and, in each case, found or stumbled upon reminders of spaces from other floors. And what we discovered on those floors also threw the passage between them – the staircase – into a new light, a less standard, more than functional perspective. These new ways of looking at processes of transmission were productively extended by the contributions of Mariano Plotkin and Uriel Orlow to the Network's concluding conference, the first concerned with the culture of psychoanalytic theories and practices in their Latin American emigration, and the second with the artist's filmic and photographic work on the performance of ethnography and on the transmission work of archives after genocide.

The chapters by Plotkin and Orlow that follow this introduction represent extensions of their concerns with the vicissitudes of historical transmission. Both address, from different angles, the interactions between history and memory in the understanding of cultural migration and place-making. Plotkin considers how

---

8 Mariano Plotkin, *Freud in the Pampas: The Emergence and Development of a Psychoanalytic Culture in Argentina* (Stanford: Stanford University Press, 2001).

psychoanalysis operates as a transnational system and how its global movements are always co-determined by local differences of cultural and political environment. If psychoanalysis was coloured at its origins by the local culture of Vienna around 1900, its subsequent moves to London, New York, Paris, Rio and Buenos Aires each involved a complex dynamics of transmission. In Plotkin's account, psychoanalysis as a system all too easily conflates the historical complexities of those transmissions with its corporate memory, which we can understand as inevitably a kind of screen memory, needing analytic work to be properly differentiated and apprehended. The task of the historian is to complicate that memory narrative and for Plotkin this involves a certain kind of ethnographic turn: viewing psychoanalysis through a necessary frame of critical alterity. In the case of the emigration of the psychoanalytic system to Latin America and to Argentina in particular, where it inhabits so much of cultural and political life, there is a particularly acute need to view it first as other, at a critical distance, before proceeding to enter into dialogue, or consultation, with it. Part of this critical process involves revising the assumption that Latin American psychoanalysis must always be seen as a (colonial) derivative of a European original. The need for critical distance is all the more compelling when we consider the operations and inevitable accommodations of a transnational cultural system like psychoanalysis in times of crisis and coercion. Thus the different histories of psychoanalysis in National Socialist Germany and in an Argentina haunted by political disappearances are limit cases, particularly poignant and troubling chapters of a vicissitudinous history of transmission.

Orlow's chapter is also profoundly concerned with the relations between history and memory in a psychoanalytic light. He, too, wants to question the transmissions between historical record and the works of collective memory and – taking his cue from Benjamin, Nora and Laplanche – he argues for a heightened critical attention to the depositions of historical experience in spatial sites. The interior spaces of the Café Odeon in Zürich, as a historical station of cultural migration and collaboration, echo back to the staircase in Kivland's image. These are images of sites of memory, melancholy and haunted spaces, which might threaten to transfix understanding in mythological structures, but which can also function as a necessary cognitive counterpart and corrective to the continuity-edited narratives of history. That is, they can act as dialectical images in the sense developed by Benjamin, establishing a lightning link between then and now, there and here, which illuminates and transmits the processes of history.⁹ The Café Odeon is a vicissitudinous site of historical transmission, of encounter and passage; and in the artist's psychoanalytically-inspired encounters with it and reworking of it, as transmitted by and between image and text, it is cast as Benjaminian *Schauplatz* [scene of spectacle]. It is a place of showing and seeing cast between historical transit and the capture of memory. Within and between Orlow's aesthetic memory work and Plotkin's critical historiography there are spaces where the appropriate transmission of psychoanalysis in view of its vicissitudes and in the unsettling presence of its ghosts seems possible.

9 See Walter Benjamin, *The Arcades Project*, ed. Roy Tiedemann, trans. by Howard Eiland and Kenneth McLaughlin (Cambridge, MA: Harvard University Press, 1999), 473.

20. On Psychoanalysis and its History: Some Reflections from the South

Mariano Ben Plotkin

This chapter includes some methodological reflections on the study of the history of psychoanalysis or, more generally, on the possibility and problems inherent to historicizing it, particularly in and from cultural spaces where it has occupied a central place. Although most of the concrete references that illustrate my discussion refer to Argentina (the case I know best), I hope that it will provide some ideas for a historical approach to psychoanalysis in general.

While the diffusion of psychoanalysis is one of the cultural phenomena that has defined the 20th century, in some specific cultural and national spaces a true 'psychoanalytic culture' has emerged. If, for instance, we consider the relatively little known case of Argentina – and more specifically of the city of Buenos Aires – the manifestations of that culture are not limited to the fact that one in every 190 *porteños* (as those living in that city are known) is a psychologist practising some form of psychoanalytic therapy. Its existence also becomes evident in public discourse, where psychoanalytically inspired neologisms are constantly used in conversation, and in the fact that psychoanalysts are perceived, and perceive themselves, particularly in times of crisis, as 'public intellectuals' whose knowledge is in high demand for expert explanations and authorized opinions on a variety of social and political issues. This was particularly evident in the economic, political and social crisis that Argentina endured in 2001–02, when psychoanalysts became a regular presence in the media and press, replacing other intellectuals and experts whose knowledge had lost some of its former legitimacy.[1]

1 Mariano Plotkin and Sergio Visacovsky, 'Saber y autoridad en las intervenciones de los psicoanalistas en torno a la crisis en la Argentina'

From TV stars to politicians, or even generals, everyone uses ideas and concepts inspired by psychoanalysis. Let us remember that in the mid 1990s, when General Martín Balza, the then Argentine Army Chief of Staff, made an unannounced appearance in a popular television show to offer his public apologies for the crimes committed by the armed forces two decades earlier, he did not apologize in the name of God or the Fatherland; instead, he used a number of terms and concepts that he, or whoever had written the speech for him, knew would be intelligible to his target public. The general spoke of the need to 'work through' the process of mourning for the dead and the disappeared, and he used such terms as 'collective unconscious' (with a Jungian, rather than a Freudian resonance, but that is another issue), and others that referred to a psychoanalytic way of understanding social trauma. It is worth noting that the repressors of the 1970s, even though they considered Freud to be an 'intellectual subversive', had also made use of psychoanalytically inspired ideas and concepts for propaganda purposes.

The omnipresence of psychoanalysis in countries like Argentina makes it difficult to define and delimit it as an object of study. Throughout its history, psychoanalysis has been appropriated and used in a large variety of forms for different and, in many cases, seemingly incompatible purposes.[2] Moreover, its nature as a discipline is both unique and multi-faceted. On the one hand, from its very beginnings, psychoanalysis has been conceptualized as a psychological theory aimed at the research of a specific object, the unconscious – whose existence can, however, only be captured by means of the method that postulates its existence, that is, psychoanalysis. On the other hand, it has also been conceptualized as a therapeutic technique and as a theory of the mind. However, beyond that, psychoanalysis has become, at least in some cultural spaces, a *Weltanschauung*: a vision of the world, a system of beliefs.

The epistemological status of psychoanalysis is far from clear.[3] It does not fit comfortably among the social sciences, the biological

---

['Knowledge and authority in interventions of psychoanalysts around the crisis in Argentina'], *Estudios Interdisciplinarios de América Latina y El Caribe* 18: 1 (2007).

2 For a thorough discussion of the different appropriations of psychoanalysis see Joy Damousi and Mariano Plotkin (ed.), *The Transnational Unconscious. Essays in the History of Psychoanalysis and Transnationalism* (London: Palgrave Macmillan, 2009).

3 Much has been written on the epistemological status of psychoanalysis. Particularly enlightening are: Adolf Grünbaum, *The Foundations of Psychoanalysis: A Philosophical Critique* (Berkeley, CA: University of California Press, 1984); Grünbaum, *Validation in the Clinical Theory of Psychoanalysis: A Study in the*

sciences, or the humanities, although it has influenced their development. Moreover, in contrast to other contemporary systems of ideas and beliefs, psychoanalysis has also become a profession. Nevertheless, it is a peculiar one which eludes most models proposed by different currents of the sociology of professions. Generally speaking, psychoanalysis is not a state-regulated profession. However, its practitioners, unlike those of other non-regulated professions such as economics or sociology, have achieved something close to a monopoly of their practice and their reproduction through the creation of autonomous training institutions and the strict rules for training they have established. The legitimacy of analysts' professional practice is based on their belonging to an international institutional network and on the successful generation of a belief system that validates all these mechanisms of legitimacy, at least among their potential clients. Nowadays in Argentina, for instance, no academic or professional title is required to practise it and yet only those who have undergone training in one of the many psychoanalytic institutions that proliferate in the country are socially recognized as psychoanalysts.

Having said all this, how can such a complex object be approached? How can we define it in a way that maintains its complexity and at the same time turns it into something delimitable? Considered as a psychological theory, the history of psychoanalysis belongs to the history of ideas or of science (regardless of whether it could be considered a real science under current paradigms). From this point of view, its history is connected to a genealogy of theories of the mind that originated in the 18th century, as Henri Ellenberger showed decades ago.[4] Here, however, without ignoring this dimension of psychoanalysis, I want to focus on another one that transcends it. In pursuit of my interest in the discipline as a broadly defined cultural artefact and practice which provides legitimacy to other discourses and practices, I would like to revisit the concept of 'psychoanalytic culture'. According to Sherry Turkle,[5] this could be defined by the way in which metaphors, concepts and forms of thought inspired

Philosophy of Psychoanalysis (Madison, CT: International University Press, 1993); Jürgen Habermas, *Knowledge and Human Interests* (Cambridge: Polity, 1987). Original title: *Erkenntnis und Interesse* (Frankfurt am Main: Suhrkamp Verlag, 1968). For a critical assessment see John Forrester, *Dispatches*, ch. 6.

4 See Henri Ellenberger, *The Discovery of the Unconscious. The History and Evolution of Dynamic Psychiatry* (New York: Basic Books, 1970).

5 Sherry Turkle, *Psychoanalytic Politics: Jacques Lacan and Freud's French Revolution* (London: Free Association Books, [1978] 1992).

by psychoanalysis penetrate everyday life, discourses and practices. Thus 'psychoanalytic culture' refers not only to a canonized psychological theory or therapeutic practice but to all social and cultural practices and discourses that seek to base their legitimacy on a supposed psychoanalytic inspiration, regardless of whether or not this inspiration is 'accurate'.

The ability that a certain system of knowledge or of beliefs has to generate a 'culture' is derived from those intrinsic qualities of that system, qualities that are, to some extent, linked to its transnational nature (I will return to this). These qualities include: its capacity to address issues of everyday life; its capacity to generate an easily appropriable discourse that provide concepts that are 'almost tangible' (Turkle, xvi); and the existence of an institutional apparatus and a body of evangelists ready to spread the word in many different cultural spaces and from many different disciplinary viewpoints. It is noteworthy that at the beginning of the 20th century there were other systems of thought in the international market of ideas that addressed many of the problems and issues that would later be appropriated by psychoanalysis, some of which were at one point or another more prestigious than that discipline. However, they have not enjoyed the long-term success of the system created by Freud. One of the key differences between psychoanalysis and its potential competitors was, probably, its accessibility and the way in which the Freudian texts define and involve their readers. In the second edition of *The Interpretation of Dreams* (1909), Freud points out that his target public is composed not of his colleagues nor his detractors, nor even his followers; his ideal reader, as John Forrester notes, consists of a broad circle of educated and curious readers, that is to say, potential dreamers, patients or Freudians who would become such after, and as a result of, reading the book. As Forrester puts it: 'The strategy of the dream book requires one to partake in the experience of analysis in both positions: as interpreter (which shades overt into the almost irresistible urge to one-up Freud) and as dreamer' (166, 179).

Another important aspect of psychoanalysis is its transnational nature. I suggest that a system of ideas or beliefs can be considered transnational if and when it fulfils at least the following three criteria: first, when it circulates across national and cultural boundaries; second, when its theoretical concepts transcend cultural limits; and third, when its centre of production and diffusion, as well as the languages in which it is mainly diffused, change over time and therefore its development is not associated with any specific cultural and national space. Judged by these criteria, psychoanalysis clearly qualifies as a transnational system of thought. Its ideas and categories have circulated throughout the world. At the same time, it claims that its analytic categories – the unconscious, childhood sexuality, the Oedipus complex, and so on – transcend cultural boundaries. According to most practitioners, psychoanalytic categories and concepts are not attached to or defined by any particular cultural setting. Finally, following its origins in the German-speaking world, the centres of production and diffusion (and consumption) of psychoanalysis shifted first to the English-speaking world and, more recently, to France and especially to Latin America.[6]

Sciences, some political movements (such as Marxism) and some religious movements are obvious examples of transnational systems. Nonetheless, psychoanalysis does not belong to any of these categories. It does not fit well among the sciences, since its mechanisms of validation are different and the possibility of disproving its theories limited.[7] Regarding the 'religious nature' of psychoanalysis, it is possible to find elements of the sociology of religions formulated by Max Weber, and later reformulated by Pierre Bourdieu, that could fruitfully be applied to psychoanalysis.[8] However – and anthropologists always point out the importance of taking seriously the 'native perspective' – no psychoanalyst or patient would characterize his/her practice as a religion. Finally, while the relations between psychoanalysis and politics are very complex, no one would characterize the former as an essentially political practice. Psychoanalysis, therefore, constitutes a category unto itself of transnational systems of thought and beliefs.

However, transnationalization cannot be understood without also taking into consideration the local dimension. The ways in which a particular psychoanalytic culture develops or, more generally speaking, the manner in which a set of patterns associated with a system of beliefs and thought is implanted in a specific cultural space

---

6 See Joy Damousi and Mariano Plotkin, 'Introduction' to *The Transnational Unconscious* (2009).

7 For a sometimes-biased recent discussion of the scientific flaws of psychoanalysis which summarizes classical points of view by Popper and others, see Catherine Meyer (ed.), *Le livre noir de la psychanalyse. Vivre, penser et aller mieux sans Freud* (Paris: Les arènes, 2005). For an alternative vision, see Habermas, *Knowledge*, ch. 10.

8 See Max Weber, *Ensayos sobre sociología de la religión* (Madrid: Taurus, 1986); Pierre Bourdieu, 'Une intérpretation de la théorie de la religion selon Max Weber' ['An interpretation of the theory of religion according to Max Weber'] *Archives européennes de sociologie*, XII, 1, 1971, 3–21. Original title: *Gesammelte Aufsätze zur Religionssoziologie* (Tübingen: J. C. B. Mohr, 1920–1).

is not a homogeneous process. It is criss-crossed by local traditions, ideological orientations, gender and class issues and, in general, it has to do with what Norbert Elias characterizes as 'national habitus'.[9] This can be clearly seen, for instance, in the early diffusion of psychoanalysis in Brazil, where the reception of Freudian thought was linked from the very beginning to the 'racial question' which has constituted an important aspect of the Brazilian national *habitus* since colonial times. One might query, therefore, whether various psychoanalytic cultures – the one developed in France since the 1960s, that originating in the US in the 1930s, the Brazilian and the Argentine ones, different as they are from each other – are in fact parts of the same global phenomenon. The tensions between the transnational and the local dimensions of the diffusion of psychoanalysis become apparent when particular cases are examined.

Even in each cultural and national space, the reception of psychoanalysis takes place at different levels and at different speeds. One should, for instance, distinguish its circuits of reception in medical circles from those by which Freud's ideas have been disseminated among writers and literary critics, or the way it has been diffused in popular publications. Nonetheless, these different forms of diffusion are usually interconnected. Thus, the history of psychoanalysis exemplifies very well the problems and limitations inherent in the traditional distinction between 'popular' and 'high' culture. Psychoanalysis is a system of ideas that emerged in a scientific environment but whose diffusion has taken place in cultural circuits that are much broader. Furthermore, it has become a form of knowledge legitimized through its supposed scientific origin but which, at the same time, embraces and legitimizes other forms of knowledge. Psychoanalysis has turned out to be expert knowledge on the unconscious and sexuality but also a popular discourse on dreams, literature and the origins of culture. Traditions and cultural patterns that are unique to each cultural space open up certain paths of reception and close others. An analysis of the development of a psychoanalytic culture should, therefore, take into consideration the various levels of reception, circulation and conceptualization, addressing tensions and dialogues between them.

---

9   Elias defines 'national habitus' as the way in which 'the fortunes of a nation over the centuries become sedimented into the habitus of its individual members'; Norbert Elias, *The Germans. Power Struggles and the Development of Habitus in the Nineteenth and Twentieth Centuries* (New York: Columbia University Press, 1996) [*Studien über die Deutschen Machtkämpfe und Habitusentwicklung im 19. und 20. Jahrhundert* [1989]], 19.

It is my belief that the study of a transnational system of ideas and beliefs such as psychoanalysis also forces us to reconsider and problematize accepted hierarchies. First, we should question the hierarchies that are internal to the field. In order to understand why and how such a system of thought and beliefs turns itself into a 'culture' (such as the 'psychoanalytic culture' defined above), it is crucial to examine carefully not only the 'authorized views' formulated by canonical intellectuals – doctors, and psychoanalysts themselves – but also what other means of diffusion such as popular publications, magazines, radio and, later, television have to say and how they have conceptualized psychoanalysis. This multidimensional analysis is important since psychoanalysis does not mean the same to everyone, and issues like class and gender (and ethnicity where it is a central dimension of social interaction) need to be taken into consideration.

Moreover, it is necessary to articulate the transnational dimension (understood both as a quality inherent to the object and as a methodological approach that emphasizes circuits and networks of the circulation of ideas, people and goods beyond national borders)[10] with specific forms of local reception. This articulation may be a source of surprise since it breaks down the usual distinction between 'centre' and 'periphery'. Where is the centre of practice and diffusion of the Lacanian version of psychoanalysis located today: in France, where it originated, or in Latin America, where it is today widely practised and discussed? Jacques-Alain Miller was enormously surprised that, on one of his numerous visits to Argentina (where he enjoys a large audience), a customs officer recognized him as 'Lacan's son-in-law'... However, beyond mere anecdotes, there are other kinds of reason to question the opposition between 'centre' and 'periphery'. Let me take again the case of Argentina, a country which, in spite of the central place psychoanalysis occupies in its urban culture, has been generally recognized as being at the periphery of the transnational psychoanalytic community. Argentina has been perceived as a space of reception or, in the best cases, of circulation of psychoanalytic thought within Latin America. According to the canonical version, psychoanalytic ideas always travel from North to South and from East to West. However, Argentina became an international centre of diffusion of Freud's and Lacan's theories beyond Latin America.

---

10 For a thorough discussion on transnational history see C. A. Bayky, Sven Beckert, Matthew Connelly, Isabel Hofmeyr, Wendy Kozol and Patricia Seed, 'AHR conversation: on transnational history', *American Historical Review*, vol. 111, no. 5 (December 2006), 1441–64. See also Akira Iriye and Pierre-Yves Saunier (eds.), *Dictionary of Transnational History* (London: Palgrave Macmillan, 2009).

Readers may be surprised to learn that Melanie Klein's theories were known in France through translations from Spanish of the works of Argentine Kleinian analysts before her works were available in French translation.[11] Similarly, the introduction of Lacan's psychoanalysis in Spain – despite the fact that Lacan had himself visited that country on several occasions – took place mainly because Argentine exiles were living there. Anthropologist Sergio Visacovsky has recently studied how Spanish and Argentine Lacanian analysts established a similar genealogy for their discipline.[12]

The historicization of psychoanalysis thus presents significant difficulties which are inherent in all systems of thought and beliefs of this complexity. However, there have been particular problems associated with the task of looking at psychoanalysis from a historical point of view. To begin with, it could be said that many members of the various psychoanalytic communities, starting with Freud and his close disciples, have proved unable to historicize their discipline. Several psychoanalysts have conceptualized the uses of the past – to a larger extent than practitioners of other disciplines – as tools providing the basis for a system of self-legitimation. Its 'official history' has been an empty one: psychoanalysts sought to construct the legitimacy of their discipline through a genealogy in which psychoanalysis had no antecedents, being the fruit of the isolated effort of a lonely genius. As Freud pointed out, for instance, thus explicitly ignoring all the previous work to which he was heir, the interpretation of dreams before psychoanalysis had 'made very little advance'.[13] Because most psychoanalysts take their discipline for granted as something without links to the past, it is difficult for them to think about it historically. For many, its history is just a question of validating the institutions, schools or sects to which they belong. Thus the past has been used to establish and defend one or other orthodoxy: history is conflated with memory. However, while no one can demand of memory that it must problematize its object, it is the task of history to do so. This is probably why some of the

11 Alejandro Dagfal, 'Paris-London-Buenos Aires: the adventures of Kleinian psychoanalysis between Europe and South America', in *The Transnational Unconscious*, ed. Damousi and Plotkin, 179–98.

12 Sergio Visacovsky, 'Origin stories, invention of genealogies and the early diffusion of Lacanian psychoanalysis in Argentina and Spain (1960–1980)', *The Transnational Unconscious*, 227–56.

13 Sigmund Freud, *Die Traumdeutung* [*The Interpretation of Dreams* [1900]], in *The Standard Edition of the Complete Psychological Works of Sigmund Freud*, 24 vols., ed. and trans. by James Strachey *et al.* (London: The Hogarth Press and the Institute of Psycho-analysis, 1953–74), vol. 4, 1.

most rich and fruitful pieces of work on psychoanalytic history have been produced outside the profession's community. Only those who can adopt what could be characterized as an 'external viewpoint' (regardless of whether or not they actually are psychoanalysts) are in a position to enrich our historical knowledge of the discipline. This external view consists not just in the ability to critically observe the social conditions of the production of psychoanalytic knowledge, but also (and more importantly) to be able to problematize the very existence of their object instead of taking it for granted.

Some of the problems inherent in this historicization – evident not only in the works produced by psychoanalysts-turned-historians, but also in those produced by some professional historians – manifest themselves in the uncritical use of categories internal to psychoanalysis to explain it. Most such histories, for instance, take for granted the existence of the unconscious as an analytic category. And yet the unconscious is a very peculiar construct because it can only be inferred with the tools provided by the discipline that postulates its existence. We could say that the existence of the unconscious is a hypothesis and not a proven fact. Writing a history of a form of knowledge is most fruitfully done when the historian problematizes the discipline and the objects it defines, rather than using them as a point of departure or as explanatory categories.

Let us now move on to another concept also originating in psychoanalysis and which has had a large impact in its historiography: the idea of 'resistance'. According to psychoanalytic theory (I am aware that I am brutally simplifying things, but this is not the place and I am not the best qualified person to discuss the theory's foundations), psychoanalysis generates resistance – it must do so, in order to be effective. If the patient immediately accepted the truth revealed by it, the therapy would not progress as it should. Freud and his followers soon extended this central idea, according to which patients show resistance to Freud's discoveries, to the whole of society. From this point of view, societies will likewise resist the revelations of psychoanalysis. This conceptualization fits into the movement's myth of origin very well (indeed, could be said to be constitutive of it), according to which it developed as the result of the work of an isolated genius who fought against social obscurantism to impose a new and revolutionary truth which, because it was revolutionary and true, his contemporaries refused to see and understand. Freud himself was sceptical and suspicious of the rapid and wide diffusion that his ideas enjoyed in the USA. The concept of resistance also became a (tautological) weapon against those who questioned the new knowledge from within or without. Given that psychoanalysis predicted that it was bound to come up against resistance, any questioning of the theory or of a particular orthodoxy within it amounts to a confirmation of it, since these deviations or questionings can be (and usually are) interpreted precisely as resistance or, even worse, as resistance born directly out of neurosis. Freud used a similar strategy as a methodological tool in *The Interpretation of Dreams*. Those dreams that did not easily fit into his hypothesis that dreams are the fulfilment of wishes paradoxically confirmed it because they manifested the dreamer's desire to show that Freud's ideas were mistaken.

A significant proportion of the historiography on psychoanalysis has taken the idea of resistance as its point of departure. Thus, a category originated within the body of ideas that is to be analysed is utilized uncritically for that purpose as an analytic tool. A good example is Élisabeth Roudinesco's otherwise monumental history of psychoanalysis in France, whose very title, *La Bataille de cent ans* [*The Hundred Years' War*] is revealing.[14] Even John Forrester, one of the most lucid students of psychoanalysis and its history, considers that the incessant and almost atemporal 'battle' between Freud and his critics should be understood as being similar to the 'combat' between the analyst and his/her patient.[15]

However, if we consider the publication of *The Interpretation of Dreams* as the founding moment, what we find is that the history of psychoanalysis, far from being determined by resistance, was an exceptionally successful one. It originated as a theoretical body of knowledge, in the declining capital of a declining empire, resulting from the work of a Jewish doctor of provincial origins and a group of collaborators who occupied a rather marginal position in the professional (medical) and academic fields. Although its purpose – to treat certain mental diseases and at the same time to provide a new methodology for research on the mind – was ambitious, its origins were modest. What should really strike us, therefore, is not so much the 'resistances' that psychoanalysis generated as the fact that in less than 20 years it became a transnational discipline, anchored in an international institutional apparatus with a presence in at least three continents. By that time psychoanalysis had vastly overflowed its original scope and its original project. Freud himself

---

14 Élisabeth Roudinesco, *La Bataille de cent ans. Histoire de la psychanalyse en France*, 2 vols. (Paris: Fayard, 1986 and 1994).

15 John Forrester, *Dispatches from the Freud Wars. Psychoanalysis and its Passions* (Cambridge, MA: Harvard University Press, 1997), 3.

(always so inclined to emphasize his solitude and the rejection generated by the system he had created) was forced to-acknowledge in *An Autobiographical Study* (1925) the already broad influence of psychoanalysis on a large variety of disciplines and fields of knowledge. Its diffusion had transcended national and cultural frontiers and the discipline was practised and discussed in countries as far away from the new Republic of Austria as Peru, India and, of course, Brazil and Argentina. Although it is true, as Carl Schorske has suggested, that psychoanalysis is a child of its time and place, it is also true that it became a transnational system of thought and beliefs amazingly quickly.[16] If this is the case, what requires explanation is not so much the resistances (which of course will appear every time a new system of thought challenges accepted paradigms and professional hierarchies), as the secret of its unprecedentedly rapid global success.

As can be seen in the examples discussed above, the difficulty of distinguishing between (as the anthropologists would say) 'native' and 'analytical' categories constitutes a severe limitation for the historicization of psychoanalysis. In order to be understood as a broad cultural phenomenon, psychoanalysis must be studied both from the perspective of cultural history and from a historical-anthropological point of view, though without losing sight of its multi-dimensional nature. It is crucial to take into consideration the different cultural levels and spaces in which psychoanalysis manifests itself as a practice and as a system of beliefs. In order to do so, it is essential to question its fundamental categories. However, this is not an easy task, since many of those categories are constitutive elements of the Western culture of the 20th century. As John Forrester has suggested, following Richard Rorty: 'in the domain of moral reflection, of the creation (rather than recognition) of the self and in the arena of sex, there is as little chance of going back to pre-Freudian beliefs as there is of going back to pre-Copernican beliefs' (2). For good or bad, Forrester concludes, there is something irreversible in the Freudian revolution.

If there are always problems inherent in the task of historicizing psychoanalysis, doing so from a cultural space where it occupies a central place – as is the case with the urban centres of a country like Argentina, but also of France and, to some extent, of Brazil – presents additional difficulties. The question thus is: how should the history of psychoanalysis be studied in a country where it has become a

16 Carl Schorske, *Fin-de-Siècle Vienna: Politics and Culture* (New York: Vintage Books, 1981).

component of that portion of reality that sociologist Peter Berger has defined as 'the world taken for granted'?[17]

In the particular case of Argentina, psychoanalysis itself is beyond questioning – and here I will take the liberty of introducing a personal anecdote. When I started working on the history of psychoanalysis in Argentina, some 15 years ago, I was initially surprised by the abundance of studies on the subject, both in general and focused on specific countries, even those where psychoanalysis did not have a massive diffusion. On thinking about it further, I realized that the existence of this mass of literature was not difficult to explain, since psychoanalysis has been one of the most influential systems of thought and beliefs of the 20th century. Our ideas on subjectivity and sexuality and our conception of the mind are inspired, to a considerable extent, either by psychoanalysis or in opposition to it. I would like to emphasize that my use of the 'we' is inclusive, since I am referring not only to what is usually known as the western world of which Latin America is one of the extreme 'outposts'. However, what I found more surprising was the almost total absence of a substantial body of scholarship on the history of psychoanalysis in Argentina, a country which was already recognized at that time as one of the world capitals of the practice and consumption of Freudianism (and Lacanianism). Needless to say, since then the situation has changed dramatically and today considerable numbers of first-class scholars are working on different aspects of the history of the 'psy' world, in both Buenos Aires and several cities in Argentina's interior. Nevertheless, my initial surprise at the lack of historical studies on psychoanalysis in my own country made me think about the subject from a different perspective, associating this lack with the famous case in which Sherlock Holmes discovers who carried out the murder because the victim's dog failed to bark when he entered the house. The detective was using negative evidence which allowed him to draw a positive conclusion: the murderer must have been an acquaintance of the victim and therefore known to the dog and this is why it did not bark. I started wondering what the striking absence of interest in something that was actually so omnipresent could mean.

The relative absence of curiosity about the development of psychoanalysis in Argentina suggested that its centrality in Argentine culture was more important than I had thought. Nobody asks questions about what is not perceived as problematic. We do not question that portion of reality that is part of 'the world taken for

17 Peter Berger, 'Towards a sociological understanding of psychoanalysis', *Social Research*, 32 (1965), 30.

granted', that is to say, the part of the social world that is naturalized in the social imaginary. The main conclusion we can draw from this is quite obvious: in order to be able to approach a problem fruitfully one must first recognize it as such, that is, in order to approach an 'other' it is necessary to start by recognizing him/her (or it) as the 'other'. Therefore – and I am conscious that the term I use is perhaps not the most appropriate – a system of thought and beliefs can be approached from and in a cultural space where it has become naturalized only after it has been 'exoticized'. This means that the object (psychoanalysis in this case) has to be approached from a position of permanent perplexity, making a conscious effort 'not to understand' anything *a priori*. This is particularly difficult because we are the 'natives' and therefore the native categories (those originating in psychoanalysis) are part of our everyday life, as I have outlined above.

I would like to suggest – and I know this may sound paradoxical – that to approach a subject like psychoanalysis in a country like Argentina where it has become a central component of everyday culture, we must carry out a two-stage methodological operation. First, we have to see the object as the 'other'; only after this has been achieved can we go back to the object, in a second operation, in an 'ethnographical spirit'. In the words of Brazilian anthropologist Fernanda Peixoto, the object should be approached in this second methodological step by 'taking it seriously', that is, by looking at the multiple dialogues that the field being analysed has established with its own 'others', the discourses and practices with which it debates and interacts.[18] If what we might call an 'anthropological point of view' consists of a dialogue with 'others', whose alterity is recognized in advance, the first methodological step I propose for the study of psychoanalysis consists in recovering its alterity in order to make this dialogue possible. In other words, the incorporation of the native point of view would be, in this case, the second part of the method that would be possible only after we take distance from that native perspective.

The study of the transnational circulation, reception and diffusion of the theory and practice of psychoanalysis creates important methodological challenges, some of which are inherent to the object and unique in many respects. However, some of the difficulties we confront in approaching psychoanalysis historically have to do with

---

18 Fernanda Peixoto, 'El diálogo como forma: Antropología e historia intelectual' ['Dialogue as form. Anthropology and intellectual history'], *Prismas. Revista de historia intelectual* 12 (2008), 17–33.

the fact that, willingly or not, we have internalized and to some extent naturalized categories and forms of thinking originating in it. In that sense, a number of the problems associated with writing the history of psychoanalysis should not be very different from those associated with the task of historicizing other transnational systems of thought or beliefs that have shaped contemporary culture. If this is true, then a space opens up for fruitful comparative work. It would be very interesting, for instance, to compare the forms and circuits of reception, circulation and implantation of two systems of thought and beliefs as different as Marxism and psychoanalysis in one or more cultural space. That would certainly be revealing about the nature of those systems, the articulation of the transnational and the local dimensions, and it would also shed light on the cultural spaces under analysis. But in order to do so, we must first distance ourselves as researchers from the object. Since we are at the same time the scholar and the 'native', the first operation we must perform, before entering into a dialogue with the object, is a kind of 'reverse anthropology' consisting of recognizing it as the 'other'. Doing this requires an attitude of perplexity before the object, and this is bound to be a painful and by no means risk-free operation, since questioning such central elements of the cultural framework in which we live implies, to some extent, questioning constitutive elements of our own subjectivity.

21. In Praise of Ghosts

Uriel Orlow

> Since fate, itself the true order of eternal recurrence, can only be called temporal in an inauthentic, that is parasitical sense, its manifestations seek out time-space. They stand in the narrow frame of midnight, an opening in the passage of time, in which the same ghostly image constantly reappears.
>
> Walter Benjamin, *The Origin of German Tragic Drama*[1]

In the folds of time: *lieux de mémoire* [sites of memory]

In his essay 'Time and the Other', Jean Laplanche describes four levels on which thinking about time usually takes place:

Level I: cosmological time, the time of the world
Level II: perceptual time, the time of our immediate consciousness
Level III: the time of memory, the process of temporalisation of our individual project
Level IV: the time of history, the time of human societies[2]

About the last he writes:

---

1 Walter Benjamin, *The Origin of German Tragic Drama* [*Ursprung des deutschen Trauerspiels* [1928]], trans. by John Osborne (London: Verso, 2003), 135.
2 Jean Laplanche, *Essays on Otherness* [*La Révolution copernicienne inachevée* [1992]], trans. by John Fletcher (London: Routledge, 1999), 238.

Level IV, the time of history, implies not only temporalisation like level III but recapitulation. Without question historical societies may be defined as those whose archives exist, those which have their written memory and not just a memory incorporated into manners, customs, institutions, myths, etc. There can of course be a history of individual temporalisation, in other words a recapitulation of the history of level III. (Laplanche, 238)

The latter, where a historical process of recapitulation is applied to the temporalization of the individual, represents the psychoanalytical case study which Laplanche goes on to discuss in his essay. A similar mechanism, if of a wider span, would be at work in the history of the world (that is, natural or cosmological history) where historical chronology (for example, that of evolutionary theory) is applied to nature and matter. However, beyond the combinatory permutations, what is striking in this model is the spatial metaphor underlying its organization, its topography. The stratification of temporality – if only for the purpose of categorization – does not simply spatialize time by separating different kinds of temporality but also creates an implicit Hegelian hierarchy where history, the time of humanity, towers high *above* the time of the world, as it were, looking down on matter, perception and memory. Henri Bergson's potent critique of the spatialization of time is well known, including his repeated attacks on the misuse of spatial metaphors when talking about temporal phenomena or concepts.[3] But what if thinking time through space did not just mask the true nature of either but, instead, revealed something about their intertwining, an embeddedness that itself needs to be thought further?

Moving in the opposite direction to Laplanche's psychoanalytical case study and taking France as an exemplar, Pierre Nora is concerned with a society whose archives exist, which has its written memory – indeed, more of it than ever before – but which, incorporated into manners, customs, institutions and myths, is disappearing. The broken link between memory and history (between Laplanche's level III and level IV) and the fractured continuity of past, present and future profoundly affects how we *imagine* time and history. Paradoxically, the exponential growth of recording and storage has resulted in an archival heap in front of us, which is so big that it blocks our vision. It is as if we had come full circle and were returning from the idea of a solid, visible, transparent and narratable past to a fractured, invisible and opaque past. Literally mapping this breakdown, Nora proposes

---

3 See Henri Bergson, *Time and Free Will* [*Essai sur les données immédiates de la conscience* (1889)], trans. by F. L. Pogson (London: Dover, 2001).

a cartography of *lieux de mémoire*. They are not historical locations anchored in the continuity of memory but sites *and* instances of memory cast in the discontinuity of history: 'These *lieux de mémoire* are fundamentally remains, the ultimate embodiments of a memorial consciousness that has barely survived in a historical age that calls out for memory because it has abandoned it'.[4] There is a fundamental paradox at the heart of the *lieux de mémoire,* namely that it is precisely because history besieges memory, undermining its spontaneity and deforming, petrifying its living nature, that *lieux de mémoire* exist.

> It is this very push and pull that produces *lieux de mémoire* – moments of history torn away from the movement of history, then returned; no longer quite life, not yet death; [...] only in a regime of discontinuity are such hallucinations of the past conceivable. (Nora, 12, 17)

Café Odeon, Zürich

After 1933. 1965–8. 1955. In the 1920s. Until 4 a.m. At the end of the 80s. At the end of the 60s. So around 1990. 1972. During the Dada-time. After midnight. In the 70s.

We liked it there. Perhaps it was by chance that it had become our meeting place — we all happened to live nearby. For me it was like a little Paris. There was a sense of the foreign there, it was big, it was not provincial. I don't even know whether it still exists.

Die letzten Tage der Menschheit. Im Westen Nichts Neues.

For me it was really a place of free-thinking, of interesting conversations and people. It is, or has become, a kind of myth. It was an erotic place.

At the height of the experience four different cultural magazines were edited at four separate tables. We didn't feel much of this glorious, poetic past. We only knew about the early days, we heard the stories.

Someone rode through the café on a horse. And later someone else on a motorbike. In my generation. Dancing on the tables. For us everything was always already over. But it was great.

---

4 Pierre Nora, 'Between memory and history: les lieux de mémoire', *Representations* (no. 26, Spring 1989), 12.

For the young leftists it became a taboo. People changed.

Among the first reminiscences is Stefan Zweig's description of his encounter with James Joyce. And of course Lenin and Trotsky plotting the revolution at a table nearby. Great modern architects drinking coffee side by side – one creating the structure of a new kind of novel, the other planning a utopian polis.

A photograph of Joyce taken at the meeting of the waters (the two Zürich rivers Limmat and Sihl) in the Platzspitz park which, over half a century later, became the needle-park.

In these great times which I knew when they were this small; and which will be small again, if they still have time.

Klaus and Erika Mann.

Else Lasker-Schüler fled to Zürich in 1933 (as did many others around this time including Thomas Mann, who followed a year later). In 1939 the Swiss officials refused to renew her permit and sent her away. She was one of the few who managed to go to Palestine; others were being sent straight back over the border to Germany to meet certain death in a concentration camp. She died poverty-stricken in Jerusalem a few days before the liberation of Auschwitz in January 1945.

Today I didn't feel like poetry. I read the paper instead.

Have you heard of Klabund, Marianne Werefkin, Alexander Moissi, Emmy Hennings, René Schickele?

Older artists like Varlin. Young artists like Urs Lüthi. The Dadaists of course. Dürrenmatt and Frisch. Bertolt Brecht and Thomas Mann. The American journalist Dorothy Thompson. Mata Hari, Sophie Täuber, Annette Kolb.

They look at us and see us not seeing them.[5]

---

5   Extracts from Uriel Orlow, *Old Haunt*, single channel video with sound, 14' 42", 2009. Around a table an ensemble of five speakers revisit – in Swiss German dialect and accompanied by wine and cigarettes – their memories of the famous Café Odeon in Zürich: a contemporary, not yet crumbled ruin in whose still intact art nouveau interior lie former utopias, stories and characters. *Old Haunt* reimagines this event as a polyphony of names, dates and anecdotes performed

No longer quite life, not yet death...

> Contrary to historical objects (*realia*), *lieux de mémoire* have no referent in reality, or rather they are their own referent: pure, exclusively self-referential signs. [...] this is to suggest that what makes them *lieux de mémoire* is precisely that by which they escape from history. (Nora, 23–4)

What does this mean? How do we understand this notion of temporal excess? And what does this mean for a phenomenology of place and time? *Torn away from the movement of history, then returned; no longer quite life, not yet death...* (Nora, 24) Is this not precisely the definition of haunting? *Lieux de mémoire* are populated by ghosts. Indeed, ghosts are always part of the specificity of place. Places are palimpsestically imbued with former social relations, historical spirits and personified experiences; places are *personed*. The social experience of the physical world haunts a place long after its present; ghosts become the internal lining of its phenomenology. The spectre is a felt presence that is not fully present. It reminds us that the past is unfinished business. Derrida points out: 'Haunting is historical, to be sure, but it is not *dated*, it is never docilely given a date in the chain of presents'.[6] This differentiation is crucial: ghosts belong neither to the past nor present, they are neither absent nor present and thus defy both temporality and ontology. Their appearance is always a reappearance and they only do so in order to disappear again. Phantoms appear as dialectical images 'in which the Then and the Now come together into a constellation like a flash or lightning'.[7] Their historicity echoes Benjamin's conception of images:

> What distinguishes images from 'essences' of phenomenology is their historical index [...] For the historical index of images does not simply say that they belong to a specific time, it says above all that they only arrive at readability at a specific time. Every present is determined by those images that are synchronic with it: every Now is the Now of a specific cognisability [*das Jetzt einer bestimmten Erkennbarkeit*]. (Benjamin, 1: 577–8)

---

by a choir of soliloquists who move through harmony and dissonance. Joined by members of the audience, the *a capella* quintet delves into the past but performs in the present.

6 Jacques Derrida, *Specters of Marx* [*Spectres de Marx* [1993]], trans. by Peggy Kamuf (London: Routledge, 1994), 4.

7 Walter Benjamin, *Gesammelte Schriften*, 14 vols. (Frankfurt am Main: Suhrkamp, 1991), vol. 5, 578.

Ghosts do not claim authenticity or truth: they provide neither an authentic image of history nor one of time. (All they ask for is cognizability: to be recognized at some time.) Their historical index comes out of time, without being anchored in it; they undermine history as progress, dismantle universal history, fracture the continuum of historicism. The logic of haunting disrupts the idea of chronological time, it desynchronizes time. As such, ghosts cut across all four levels of Laplanche's temporal topography: they hover between – as well as connect – the times of the world, perception, memory and history. That ghosts fall below the threshold of what constitutes historical objects (*realia*) is exactly what makes them so important for historical consciousness. The appearance – neither as image nor in the flesh – of something or someone departed makes them a paradoxical incorporation which crosses the boundary of self and world. To be sure, they are figments of our imagination but this does not mean they are pure fantasy. Abraham and Torok stress that the phantom 'works like a ventriloquist, like a stranger within the subject's own mental topography. The imaginings issuing from the presence of the stranger have nothing to do with fantasy strictly speaking'.[8] Phantoms are not to be confused with the return of the repressed. For a phantom is a formation of the unconscious that has never been conscious in the first place. Rather, phantoms are encrypted messages by others: 'What haunt us are not the dead, but the gaps left within us by the secrets of others'. (Nora, 171) What interests me about Abraham's conception of the phantom is that it is transpersonal as well as transgenerational. That is, the phantom appears from a concealment (a repression, a forgetting) by someone else, somewhere else, in another time. As such, it is not only an individual hallucination but can also denote a collective haunting. However, the ghostly economy is different in each case: in familial, individual cases of transgenerational haunting, Abraham and Torok write:

> the 'phantom effect' progressively fades during its transmission from one generation to the next and [...] finally disappears. Yet this is not at all the case when shared or complementary phantoms find a way of being established as social practices along the lines of *staged words*. We must not lose sight of the fact that to stage a word [...] constitutes an attempt at exorcism, an attempt that is to relieve the unconscious

---

8 Nicolas Abraham and Maria Torok, 'Notes on the phantom', in *The Shell and the Kernel* [*L'écorce et le noyau* [1987]], trans. by Nicholas T. Rand (Chicago: University of Chicago Press, 1994), 173.

by placing the effects of the phantom in the social realm. (Abraham and Torok, 176)

This staging or *mise-en-scène* of the phantom represents another, perhaps the final slippage between the temporal and the spatial. By restoring timelessness to time, ghosts represent a kind of staging, where 'history merges into the setting [*Schauplatz*]' (Benjamin, 92). In other words, in the phantom, history appears no longer in its temporal dimension but becomes an image-space, a scene and thus paradoxically a *mise-en-abîme* of time. (This is exactly what Hamlet expresses in his encounter with the ghost when he exclaims – again using a conscious spatial metaphor – that 'the time is out of joint'.) This *mise-en-abîme* allows us to conceive of history no longer as a chain of events in time – bound by chronology, narration and representation – but in terms of resonating events in space, which are evoked through fragments, alluded to in shards of matter, haunted by *revenants*. This ghostly setting, this *lieu de mémoire*, is rarely the stage of history *per se*, rather it is a *Nebenschauplatz*, a minor location, a temporary constellation like that of a café where people hung out, met, talked about ideas and eventually went their different ways. It is a temporally stratified place, which crosses all four levels of time and falls between them.

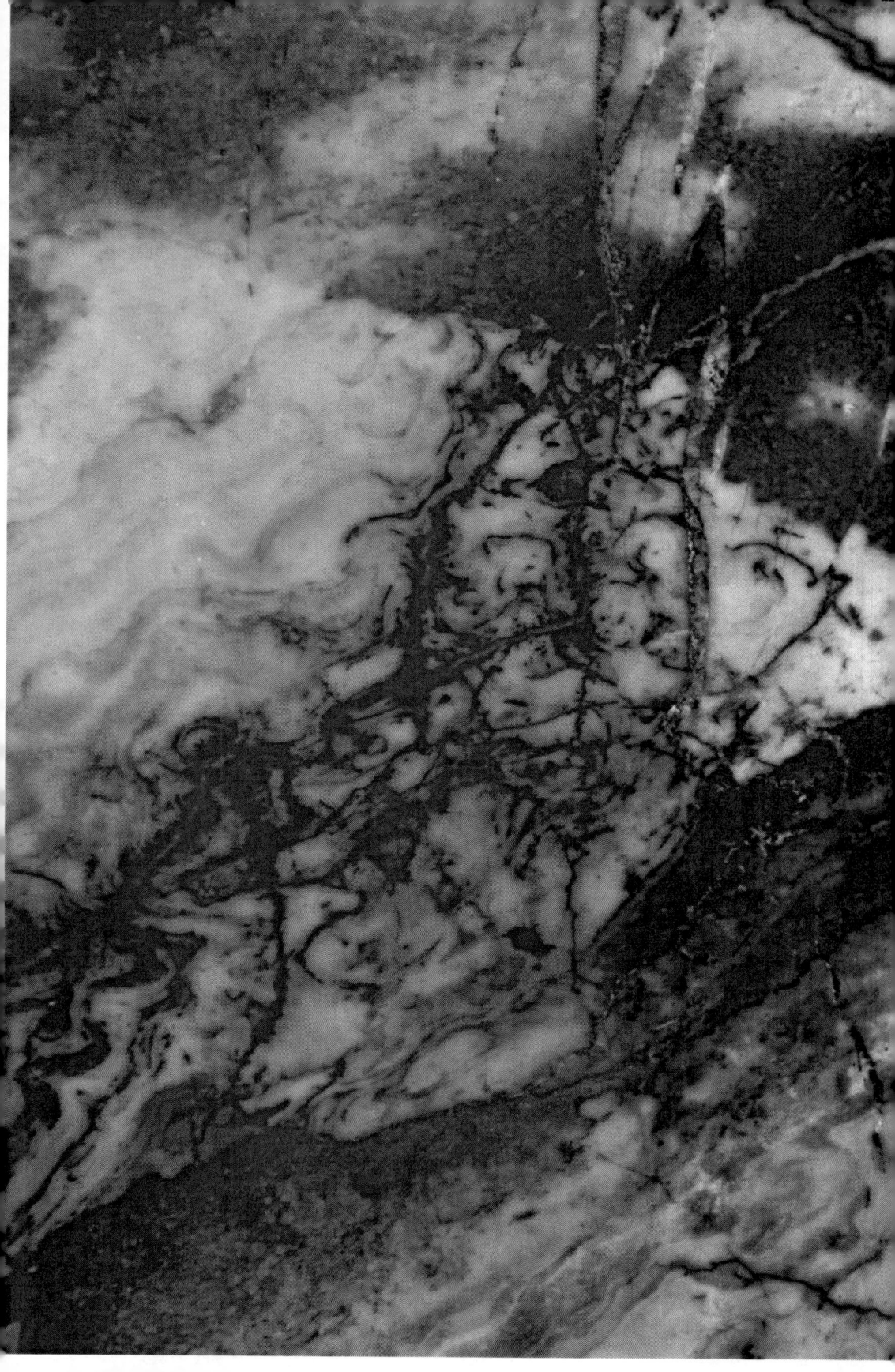

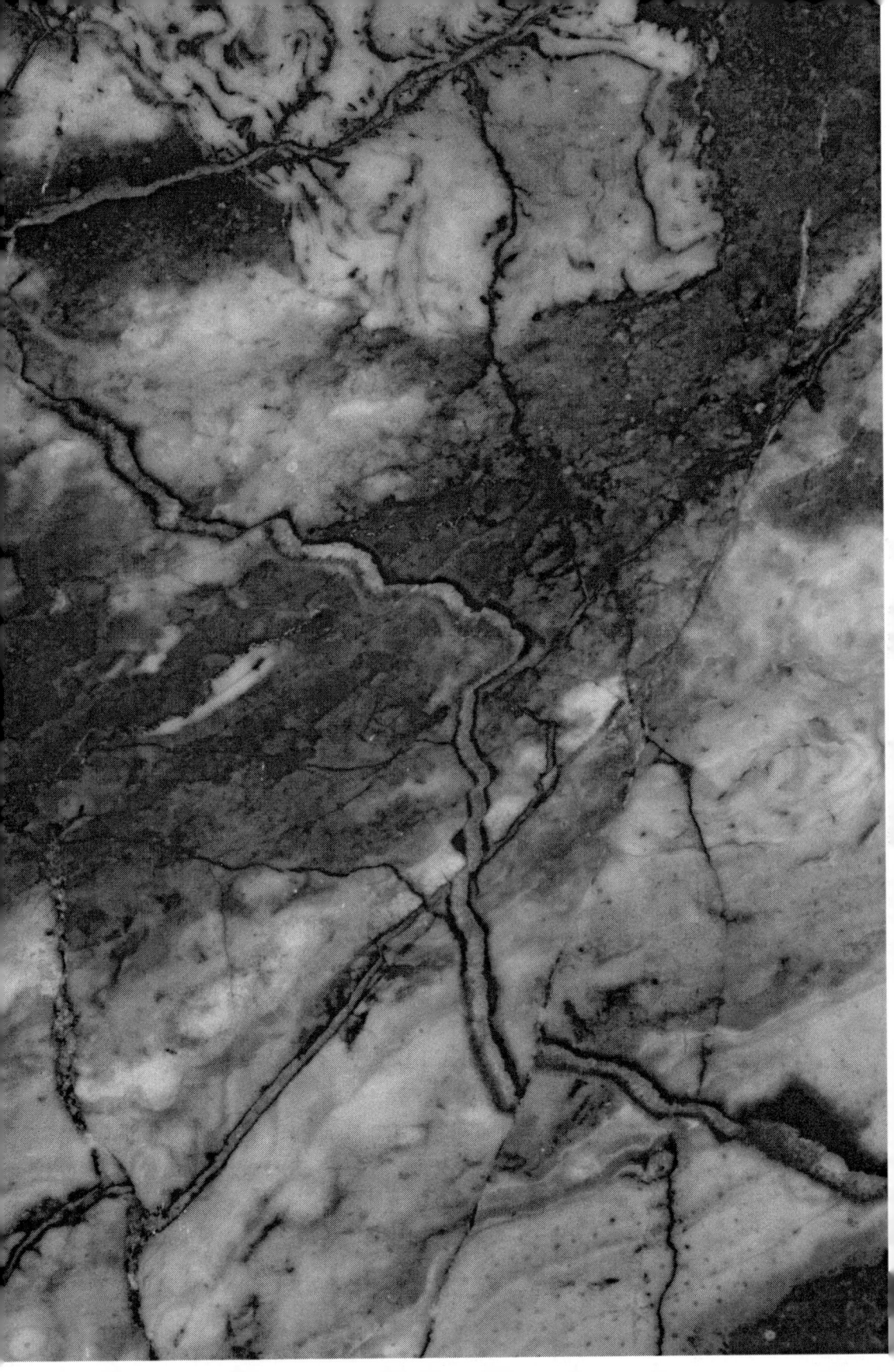

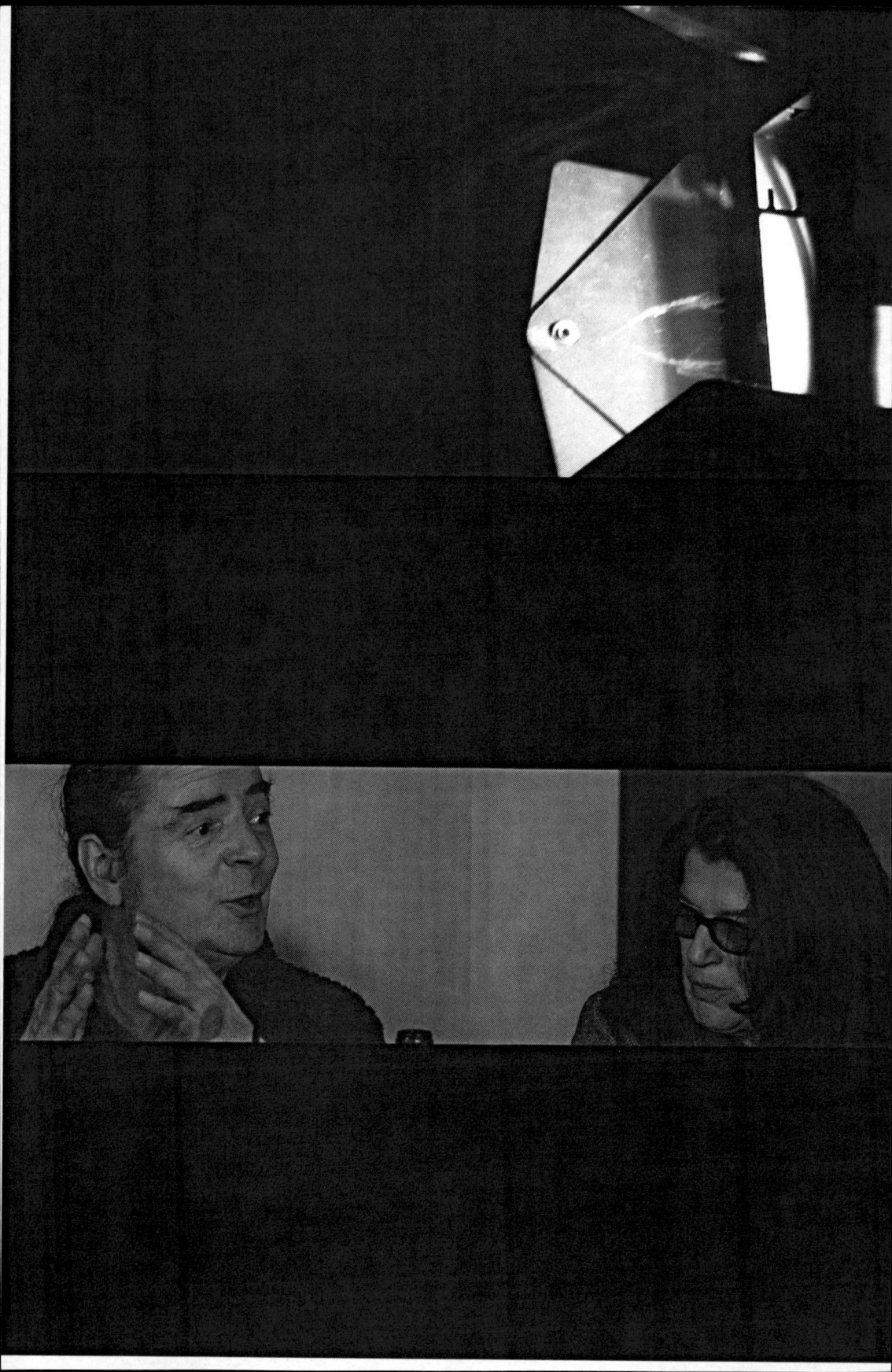

Psychoanalysis in the Italian-Speaking World

22. Family Matters

Lesley Caldwell

Home is Where We Start From – the title of a book by Donald Winnicott – alludes to a non-technical area that he was at pains to insist had a central place in psychoanalytic practice and thought.[1] This extension of psychoanalysis to everyday life remains contentious in some sections of the analytic community, but it is an emphasis gathered together in the art of Marcella Vanzo, where familial encounters and the emotions to which they give rise are presented through a quasi-narrative thread that visualizes an emotional psychological landscape or set of landscapes through the physical spaces constructed by the camera and the temporality offered by the moving image.

The artist describes *On the World of Interiors* as investigating three different human landscapes and the interrelations to which they give rise. Made between 2005 and 2007, the videos offer three visual essays on the family and home. Starting points in nature, sociality, and the landscapes of the mind are connected through the centrality consistently ascribed to relationships, the family and to a place – 'home' – and what it makes available. A sense of enclosure and of enablement, a containment that leads inevitably to relations with the external world, is anchored by what Vanzo calls the 'domestic walls' (this volume, pp. 304 and 307). This implicitly draws parallels with the analytic session and what its given frame enables in the ongoing construction of relations in the transference.

The protagonists in Vanzo's work are the generations of a family the artist has placed in specific locations. In the first segment, *Ama*, the traditionally female activities of weaving, knitting and sewing

---

1   D. W. Winnicott, *Home is Where We Start From: Essays by a Psychoanalyst* (Harmondsworth: Penguin, 1986).

become the life thread of three generations: a woman sits on the floor stitching woollen hair on a doll as her own hair is knitted by her mother. The cycle of generations is recorded through the relations between mothers and daughters and Vanzo describes the work as a 'three-dimensional sculpture' where the female body is the mediator between environment/place and the human.

In the second section, *Limbo*, the artist links a more explicit visual image of the family as the basis of the social and the individual's entry to it, to her anthropological background: the spaces of family and house as the limbo through which all must pass in coming to assume a specific identity/identities. Her own family members provide the cast and the house becomes the theatre in which family dynamics are played out through Vanzo's filming of two ordinary events – a lunch and a family photograph. The soundtrack, provided by the artist's own blood circulation and heartbeat, offers a bodily commentary on the images. In the third part, *Mindfield*, a building site and its infrastructure, shot as if they were the organs of the body, become the location of the mind and its complexity.

The family romance provides a continuing trope of narrative in general and of an art focused on the personal and subjectivity in particular, but in the Italian case the pre-eminence accorded to the family historically and culturally makes a particularity out of a general tendency in the history of the west. In the links with a specific place and the continuing importance of region, town and landscape as signifiers of the artist's own roots and preoccupations, her resort to family members as the only possible protagonists, and in the visual rendering of mother-daughter relationships – a comparatively recent but increasingly important arena for the investigation of Italian familial relations and difficulties – Vanzo draws on the roots of Italian culture and their late modern, gender-aware variants, even as she takes the viewer back to Freud.

Claudio Magris's discussion of identity and selfhood initially seems to look elsewhere, to an Other beyond national borders. He revisits the themes of modern European literature before describing his attempts to interrogate those general preoccupations through the medium of his writerly selves. Like Vanzo, Magris speaks of the issues that preoccupy him through a persistent return to the medium of his own creative work, as an Italian scholar of German culture and as an Italian novelist and thinker. From Hoffmann and Musil, to Svevo, to his own books and his identity as writer, his roots in the borderlands of north-east Italy and his links with his region, 'Identity, writing and uncertainty' draws upon the 19th-century roots of early 21st-century concerns and their theoretical underpinnings in the Freudian texts that have made psychoanalysis a fundamental reference paradigm in the human sciences.

It is the writer and the activity of writing that form the basis for his rumination on issues of identity and the self and their association with place. Location, along with what it connotes, here takes as its establishing conditions, borders, limits and the confusion of languages and cultures that gather around Magris's native Trieste. The shifting allegiances and the impact of the differing state-claims historically made upon Trieste and the areas surrounding it are a distinctive aspect of Magris, the writer and professor who, in leaving the Trieste of family and childhood for the Turin of adulthood and intellectual and political life in 1957, remained committed to both.

His essay's initial references northwards to his work on the literature of the German-speaking countries that border the Italian frontier open a more general discourse that returns to Italy and his own life in the reference to *Verde acqua* (1998),[2] a memoir of the practical and emotional post-World War Two difficulties of its author Marisa Madieri, Magris's late wife. Madieri and her family had to leave Fiume for Trieste in the ongoing conflicts between Slavs and Italians after 1945. In becoming homeless refugees because they were Italian, and in the midst of all the difficulties such a life entails, their Slav and Hungarian origins emerged. The plurality of identities and, in Magris's term, 'selves' encountered and then lived by Madieri and her family and recounted in her memoir, leads Magris himself to Svevo and to Zeno, 'the character that is and is not a self, who is double, multiple and elusive' (this volume, p. 293).

These themes raised by Vanzo and Magris also emerged in the regular meetings of the Italian group over its two-year existence. This group was unusual in comprising a majority of practising analysts: three International Psychoanalytic Association members (two of them Italian), a Jungian and a Lacanian, and four academics, two Italian, one of whom teaches in Italy. The field of Italian studies in the UK has been slow to adopt any sustained interest in psychoanalysis as a methodology and, indirectly, this seemed to produce a certain freedom in approaching the general themes. Two of the papers in the opening conference of the research network, held in November 2006 and entitled 'Freud in Translation, Freud in Transition' had been given by Italian analysts, Jacqueline Amati-Mehler from Rome and

---

2   Marisa Madieri, *Verde aqua* (Torino: Einaudi, 1998).

Giuseppe Civitarese from Pavia, and the latter became part of our ongoing group which from the beginning focused on contemporary areas of interest among practising analysts. Familiar academic references to Freud, and especially to Lacan, were placed in a wide set of psychoanalytic thinkers in the subsequent work of this group.

We began by looking at the psychoanalytic session and at the process of analysis, and this quickly extended to issues of translation, fictionality, the session's 'as-if' quality and how the 'characters' that emerge in any analysis are to be understood. These emphases, fundamental to what is now understood by an analysis, illuminated a different technical approach to transference, and to interpretation and translation, and they emphasized some shared concerns between the practice of psychoanalysis and the work of art. They also provided the framework within which the group tackled what used to be called 'applied psychoanalysis', always with an attention to any cultural and clinical specificity that could be drawn from an Italian dimension.

To hold together psychoanalysis and the specifics of the Italian experience in the clinic and the academy we turned to the body of work Italian analysts have produced in their psychoanalytic societies in recent years. This work has offered a sustained engagement with the use of psychoanalysis in the study of texts and the art object, while also prioritizing parallels, symmetries and asymmetries with clinical practice. These studies have introduced explicitly clinical links between session and narratology, but they continue to maintain a consistent attention to clinical practice itself.

Our emphasis on interdisciplinarity resulted in the decision to read an early academic attempt at cross-disciplinary work, *Il testo moltiplicato* [*The Multiple Text*].[3] In 1982 Mario Lavagetto invited senior scholars to discuss, each from her/his own disciplinary standpoint, Boccaccio's novella 'Lisabetta and the pot of basil' from Day 4 (love stories that end tragically) of the *Decameron*. The tale is set in Messina. A family of three brothers and a sister, Lisabetta, have been made rich by the death of their merchant father, a Tuscan. Their business is managed by Lorenzo, a handsome young man from Pisa with whom Lisabetta falls in love. The brothers discover this and, to protect the family, resolve to kill Lorenzo. The four men go out of Messina together and Lorenzo never returns. Lisabetta is distressed, continually lamenting his absence, but the brothers dismiss her requests for information. Lorenzo appears to her in a dream and tells her of his fate and where he is buried. She goes there with her maid,

---

3 Mario Lavagetto, *Il testo moltiplicato* (Parma: Pratiche editrice, 1982).

finds the body and cuts off the head, brings it back home and plants it in a pot of basil. From then on, she takes this pot of basil everywhere she goes, bathing it with her tears. The girl's beauty disappears, the neighbours comment on her devotion to the plant and the brothers take it away from her. When she falls ill, the brothers discover the head among the basil and bury it. Then, fearing retribution, they leave Messina for Naples. Lisabetta dies of grief.

The precedent of *Il testo moltiplicato* offered a model for our project. The individual papers collected in that book provided one focus, but it was less their content and more what the attempt as a whole was understood as representing that extended the group's work. Lavagetto's choice of text, the historical context of early 1980s Italy, the absence of the contribution of feminist scholars – already anomalous in 1984 – and the event's location, the Istituto Gramsci in Bologna, part of the arena of the culture of the left rather than the academy or a university department, extended the group's initial interest in clinical practice and its associated uses in the study of cultural artefacts to debates about Italian contemporary history and the history of psychoanalysis itself.

The organization of the novella around the family romance led us to consider the significance of the family members who do appear in it (siblings) and those who do not (mother and father). This implies an apparent absence of generational difference alongside the strong presence of the differences between the sexes (Lisabetta and her brothers), and the place of the extra-familial, the quasi-paternal in the figure of Lorenzo (like the father, a Tuscan), the lover of Lisabetta and the administrator of the family business. These were considered in relation to the characteristics of the unconscious – interchangeability of positions, slippage from father to brother, the equivalence of the unconscious with death in Matte-Blanco's account – and the possible implications of Boccaccio's precise specifying of place, from Tuscany, San Gimignano, Pisa, the Florence of the plague from which the initial group departs and the tale's setting in Messina and then Naples. Beyond these details, the parallels and differences between this text and our discussion of it and the process of analysis remained a constant. The experience of the analytic session and of the artwork set in motion a creative process depending on introspection; each may be considered as a container for self-reflection. 'Così come il simbolo artistico produce emozioni, la parola psicoanalitica trasforma, organizzando qualcosa che prima non esisteva nella mente dell'analizzando, innescando un process creativo' ['Just as the artistic symbol produces emotions, words are transformative in psychoanalysis organizing what previously did not exist in the mind of the analysand and triggering a creative process'].[4] The group's continuing absorption in what had begun as an encounter with multidisciplinarity, Lavagetto's studies of the Boccaccio text, saw us increasingly caught up in the text itself, and we briefly considered focusing on *The Decameron* for a year. But the prefiguring of the tale's climax in the loss of the capital letter of the heroine's name (Elisabetta/Lisabetta/L'Isabetta), and the close association between decapitation and *perdere la testa* [losing one's head], not just in terms of control but of passion, irrationality and madness, opened the discussion to a variety of ways of playing with this text. We particularly focused on the similarity of the Italian nouns *testo* [text] and *testa* [head] and the psychological implications of the story's conclusion, Lisabetta's perverse obsession with the head of the dead Lorenzo. At the same time, our discussions of the strength of the cultural resonance of Lavagetto's choice of text as emblematic of 1980s Italy grounded the group's apparently transhistorical fascination with Boccaccio and with the multiple associations the tale evokes.

The initiating conditions for *The Decameron* – a group of Florentine women's flight from the plague, that is, from illness and death – also prompted a discussion of art as confronting the meaning of life through the latter's only real certainty, death. The horror and sheer vividness of the associations to decapitation, a frequent reference in art, encouraged the introduction of other Italian cultural artefacts as the instantiation of a wider interest in themes of beheading and death: representations of Judith and Salomé, Puccini's *Turandot* and, beyond Italy, Conrad's description of the impaled head in *The Heart of Darkness*,[5] and what were at that time recent scenes of Saddam Hussein's execution. There is a historical consistency in the decapitation theme, paralleled by its continuing availability in the unconscious (which is also demonstrated in the patients' material).

The links with castration and the theme of seeing and not seeing in both analysis and the encounter with the world or the text extended our discussion to blindness, to 'writing in the dark' as discussed by Magris, and to our own aesthetic experiences of reading and viewing. The variety of western cultural references, from Oedipus and Tiresias, to Orpheus and his compulsion to look back, his inability to symbolize his desire, his need to see Eurydice literally and concretely

---

4   Antonio Di Benedetto, *Prima della parola. L'ascolto del non detto psicoanalitico attraverso le forme dell'arte* (Milan: Franco Angeli, 2002), 33.
5   Joseph Conrad, *The Heart of Darkness* [1899] (Harmondsworth: Penguin, 1995).

(the basis of his loss), led us to José Saramago's text, *Blindness*.⁶ If Saramago and his illumination and politicization of the theme of blindness and sight provided the occasion for the application of these general themes to particular situations, a determination to attend to 'the Italian element' and where it might reside remained the question that continually hovered: where is Italianness to be located and how is it constituted over time? The last text we examined, Italo Calvino's *Il Barone Rampante* [*The Baron in the Trees*],⁷ was both a return to the family, with its timeless appearances in the unconscious, and to a specifically Italian and regional dimension through the book's focus on childhood and an alternative existence above the ordinary world.

Despite an active concern with the historico-cultural formations that have contributed to the development of psychoanalysis in Italy and an attention to particularity and specificity, both the group's work and that of Claudio Magris and Marcella Vanzo returned over and over to apparently transcultural concerns – the body, life, death, the difference between the sexes and the investigation of the unconscious. These are the very material of clinical practice and of a psychoanalytic approach. To wonder how universal themes manifest themselves culturally and societally, in the multiplicity of forms that constitute, reproduce and reinforce the particularity that is Italy and the Italian, is to continue to explore their articulation in specific texts and practices that have encouraged and shaped the attention of scholars, artist and analysts. Ways of approaching them through the individual pleasure of reading and its parallels with the shared experience of story-telling for Boccaccio's little band, or for the daily exchanges between analyst and analysand, all pose those distinctively modern questions: who is the storyteller? who and what is told? This is the discussion Magris actively pursued, but it is also central to the links between the individual artist or writer's creative process, introspective and self-reflective processes more generally, and the analytic session.

---

6 José Saramago, *Ensaio Sobre a Cegueira* [1985], trans. by Giovanni Pontieri as *Blindness* (London: Harvill, 1998).

7 Italo Calvino, *Il barone rampante* [1957] (Turin: Einaudi scuola, 1957; Milano: Mondadori, 1993), trans. by Archibald Colquhoun as *The Baron in the Trees* (New York: Harvest, 1977).

23. Identity, Writing and Uncertainty

Claudio Magris

At the end of Kipling's famous novel *Kim*, the boy asks himself: 'I am Kim. And what is Kim?'[1] It is not simply the ambiguity of his Anglo-Indian background that makes him ask this question, but his entire being. Something similar happens in Hoffmann's tale 'Der Sandmann' ['The sand-man'] where the protagonist, an unhappy, tormented poet, writes a poem, reads it aloud and then immediately cries out: 'Wessen grauenvolle Stimme ist das?' ['Whose fearful voice is that?'][2] In another of Hoffmann's novels, *Die Elixiere des Teufels*, the main character, Bruder Medardus, repeatedly says: 'Es rief in mir' ['the voice cried out within me'] – and is horrified because he does not know who is speaking within him at that moment.[3]

Examples could proliferate endlessly. Identity seems to exist in the doubting of it. No sooner does it become an object of reflection, no sooner is it established, than it wavers: 'I am Kim. And what is Kim?' Writing seems to be a means of giving it form, but it is also a way of losing it, for there is a yawning gulf between the writing self and the self that is written. When St Augustine begins his *Confessions*,[4] he asks himself what his real self is. He is looking not merely for a psychological, accidental self, but for something essential. Awareness of this otherness, observes Manès Sperber, can also be stimulated by

---

I am indebted to Sharon Kivland, Martin Liebscher and Katia Pizzi for all references.

1 Rudyard Kipling, *Kim* [1901] (Harmondsworth: Penguin, 2000).

2 E. T. A Hoffmann, 'Der Sandmann' in *Die Nachtstücke* [1816] (Frankfurt am Main and Leipzig: Insel, 1986), 36.

3 E. T. A. Hoffmann, *Die Elixiere des Teufels* [1815] (Frankfurt am Main and Leipzig: Insel, 1978).

4 St Augustine, *Confessions*, trans. by Henry Chadwick (Oxford: Oxford University Press, 1991).

physical pain. Having a toothache is enough for us to discover that something exists within us which is not simply *not* us but actually *against* us. We instantly perceive the tooth causing our pain as something foreign, something hostile. Novalis writes that sickness is a kind of transcendence,[5] inasmuch as it transcends, dissolves and transforms the structure of the Self. Equally unknown, and as foreign to us as physical pain, are feelings, obsessions, nightmares, deliria that rise up from the depths within us.

Moreover, when someone says 'I know you', who knows whom? Or if they say 'Be true to yourself', what does that mean? If the self were solid and coherent, it would be impossible to be *un*true to oneself. No: everyone is a Jekyll and Hyde, and also always *other* with regard to themselves – as in Rimbaud's famous saying: 'JE est un autre' ['I is someone else'].[6] Corresponding to this poetic intuition in the specifically psychical field is the case of so-called multiple personality. Thus, one fine day, carpenter Ansel Bourne convinces himself, sometimes at least, that he is shopkeeper Albert Brown; yet, in neither condition is he ever aware of also being – or having been – the other.[7] However, this is merely a case of doubling. There are examples of far more complex structures of the self, capable of harbouring a much higher number of different personalities.

Since the end of the 19th century, at least, literature and philosophy have been thrown into chaos by the presentiment that the self, hitherto believed to be solid and coherent, was breaking up. Bourget, Nietzsche, Musil and other writers would say that everything, even individual unity, was disintegrating into the 'anarchy of atoms'.[8]

---

5 Novalis (pseudonym of Friedrich von Hardenburg), *Novalis' Schriften*, ed. P. Kluckhohn and R. Samuel, 3 vols. (Darmstadt: Wissenschaftliche Buchgesellschaft, 1968), 686: 'Krankheiten, besonders langwierige, sind Lehrjahre der Lebenskunst und der Gemütsbildung'.

6 Arthur Rimbaud, letter of 15 May 1871 to Paul Demeny, reproduced in *Poésies complètes* (Paris: Gallimard, 1963), 219.

7 Ansel Bourne suffered from a probable dissociative fugue. His case was one of the first documented and his nephew, William James, was among the doctors who treated him. A carpenter and evangelical preacher from Rhode Island, he had become known for his account of a partial amnesia, published in 1858. In 1887 he travelled to Pennsylvania where he set up a shop under the name of A. J. Browne. He could, under hypnosis, be induced to assume the personality of either Bourne or Browne. See Michael Kenny, *The Passion of Ansel Bourne: Multiple Personality in American Culture* (Washington: Smithsonian Institution Press, 1986).

8 Friedrich Nietzsche, *Der Fall Wagner*, Kritische Studienausgabe 6 (Munich, Berlin and New York: DTV, de Gruyter, 1999), 27: 'Aber das ist das Gleichniss für jeden Stil der décadence: jedes Mal Anarchie der Atome, Disgregation der

Twentieth-century European literature, from Pirandello to Pessoa, revolves around this theme, experienced now as anguish, now as liberation.

The self becomes a multitude, a fluctuating entity. Moreover, when Nietzsche declared that his *Übermensch* [superman], was none other than Dostoevsky's 'Underground Man', he was saying what some of his interpreters were to say later, namely that *Übermensch* does not mean superman, a super-individual, traditionally an individual of highly developed capacities, but a 'Beyond-man', as Gianni Vattimo has observed,[9] representing a stage of human evolution projected beyond the traditional borders of identity. Plural identity balks at unified consciousness; the Underground Man speaks of conscience as a disease and states that he has no 'character', since character is considered a repressive armour, a type of straitjacket.[10]

Hoffmann's Bruder Medardus is distressed at the loss of himself; he would like to be *one*, to have a precise identity, and when he loses the latter the experience is frightening in the extreme. By contrast, another character in the novel, Schönfeld, finds the same experience to be liberating. In his view consciousness – or rather, identity – is a customs officer who sits aloft and prevents a good number of things from going through which life would otherwise impose on us. Or, he says, it is an army on parade compelled to march in line, while the real self – the mad one – would resemble a carnival, a festival, a throng of people who stroll about wherever they want. Hoffmann suggests that individuals, if they are to grow and live, must learn how to confront their own double, look it in the face rather than eliminate it, complete the odyssey into the abyss of their own unconscious. Often, however, we are too weak and unprepared for this journey, without which we cannot be saved, but which might also prove fatal to us.

Modernity has often been fascinated by the unconscious, as though it were more genuine, more alive, more creative, more real and poetical than the conscious. But the unconscious, Musil wrote, far from being a reserve of primitive yet vital energies, is frequently a mechanical stereotype wherein, rigidly crystallized and stratified, numberless compulsive experiences are deposited, passively endured rather than reworked into truly dangerous fantasies.

Willens, "Freiheit des Individuums", moralisch geredet, - zu einer politischen Theorie erweitert "gleiche Rechte für Alle"'.

9 See Gianni Vattimo, *Dialogo con Nietzsche: Saggi 1961–2000* (Milan: Garzanti, 2001).

10 Fyodor Dostoevsky, *Notes from Underground* [1864], trans. by Michael R. Katz (New York: Norton, 1989).

Nevertheless, they remain falsely seductive and, in reality, banal. It is the conscious Self, with its ironical, never-ending, imperfect yet flexible auto-construction, that is the more genuine creativity. Life is not the quicksand (the unconscious) that wants to suck in Baron Munchhausen: rather, it is the Baron who pulls himself out of that quicksand by the scruff of the neck.

Sometimes the search for identity depends on a process of subtraction: the self is not the sum of things that an individual is and does, of the individual's powers and functions, but rather what remains after setting aside their accidental components. The real self would not be the one that pays taxes, stands in a queue, goes to the dentist, but the one that remains after all that has been discounted. It is also possible that nothing remains, as happens when Peer Gynt removes the layers of an onion only to discover it does not have a nucleus.[11] Oriental philosophies have provided a radical answer to this problem: they affirm that it is not objects and subjects that exist, but facts, relations. When a self looks at a tree, what we have is not a discrete self looking at a tree which is also discrete, but rather the organic occurrence of this looking. This viewpoint – of an identity that is fluid but not dissociated – overcomes the false antithesis between a hyper-compact, paranoiac ego, confined to its own shell, and a schizophrenic dispersion of the self, apparently antithetical but, in reality, complementary to the paranoiac concentration of the ego that still characterizes our age and whose rhizomatic dissemination is only a reactive aspect.

Uncertainty and plurality also distinguish national identities. Musil wrote that the Austrian was an Austro-Hungarian minus the Hungarian, namely the result of a subtraction.[12] Austrian culture elaborated one of the freest images and structures of the Self, making the result not one of repression or a centrifugal explosion of contradictions, but rather an ironical composition of their own. The Triestines, for example, are often alternately fortified, obsessed and blocked by this problem.

Multiple identity may be an addition or a subtraction. It may stimulate nationalist aggression – something that frequently occurs

11   Henrik Ibsen, *Peer Gynt* [1867], trans. by Peter Watts (London: Penguin, 1966).

12   Robert Musil, *Der Mann ohne Eigenschaften* [*The Man without Qualities* [1931–32]], ed. Adolf Frisé, 2 vols. (Reinbek bei Hamburg: Rowohlt, 1978), vol. 1, 170: 'Das österreich-ungarische Staatsgefühl bestand aus einem Ganzen und einem Teil, nämlich aus einem ungarischen und einem österreichisch-ungarischen Staatsgefühl, und dieses zweite war in Österreich zu Hause, wodurch das österreichische Staatsgefühl eigentlich heimatlos war'.

in border territories – or help to overcome particularistic idolatry and *'in mehreren Völkern denken'* ['think in several peoples']. Thus spoke a writer who began to write avant-garde poetry in Hungarian under the name of Reiter Róbert and who later, under the name of Robert Reiter and then Franz Liebhard, wrote traditional poetry in German.

This discovery of a plural identity, of also forming part of another world, likewise applies to Marisa Madieri's case, as recounted in *Verde Acqua*, the story of how, when she was a child, her Italian family was forced to leave Fiume (now Rijeka) immediately after World War Two.[13] This was at the time when, after suffering violence at the hands of the Italians, the Slavs were enjoying the hour of their resurgence and revenge which, like all vengeance, was indiscriminate. In recounting their departure from their native city to experience years of the difficult existence of the marginalized in a refugee camp, Marisa Madieri discovers that the origins of her family – at that moment a family persecuted for being Italian by the Slavs – were also in part Slavic and Hungarian, though this had hitherto been concealed by Italian nationalism. Thus she finds out that she also belongs to the other side, that she forms, to a small degree at least, part of the world that is threatening her. She discovers thus what it is like to have a plural identity, to be an Italian but, so to speak, one with a difference.

Identities, writes Roberto Toscano, cannot be photographed (that is, defined) but only filmed, since they are not static, rigidly fixed once and for all, but rather dynamic, in continuous movement and continuous transformation.[14] Identity is plural, everyone has many: there is religious identity, there is political identity and there is cultural identity. Identity is a matter of doing, not being.

One of the greatest writers to confront all this in depth was Italo Svevo. If there was ever a character who is and is not a self, who is double, multiple and elusive, it is Zeno Cosini.[15] He is a continual laddering of the self, a reboiling of a vital process. Yet, he is a self who, despite his near non-existence, continues to have an irreducible nucleus, is in love with Ada, has his tics, his passions. In this fictional figure, there is a mixture of transience and of a something within this that doggedly resists and seeks to give itself unity – interminable toil, like the endless analysis of which Freud speaks.[16]

13 Marisa Madieri, *Verde Acqua* (Torino: Einaudi, 1987).

14 Roberto Toscano, 'A che cosa servono le diversità', *Reset* 92 (2005), 74–7.

15 Italo Svevo, *La coscienza di Zeno* [1923] in *Tutte le opere*, vol. 1, ed. Nunzia Palmieri and Fabio Vittorini (Milan: Mondadori, 2004).

16 Sigmund Freud, 'Analysis terminable and interminable' ['Die endliche und die unendliche Analyse' [1937]], in *The Standard Edition of the Complete*

Few literary traditions have felt this phenomenon so keenly as Jewish literature (in many countries and many languages). If it has worked out an exceptionally strong and by no means regressive sense of the individual, it is precisely because it has experienced in a radical fashion, not only splitting, division and rupture (which makes a character in one of Singer's novels say: 'every Jew should go to a psychiatrist – every modern Jew, that is'), but also the Jews' resistance to that rupture, constrained to *be* Jews but not *like* Jews. Jewish civilisation has stubbornly resisted this rupture, precisely because it has been taught for hundreds of years to resist violence, trusting in values strongly rooted in the family and the individual. All this has served to produce an individual resistance of almost epic strength. In Joseph Roth's *Hiob* [*Job*], the protagonist Mendel Singer and his wife Deborah have lived in America for years, and when she accuses him 'Du benimmst dich wie ein russischer Jude' ['You behave like a Russian Jew'], he replies 'Ich bin ein russischer Jude' ['I *am* a Russian Jew'].[17] There is another marvellous Jewish story in which a rabbi – by the name of Zussia – says on his deathbed that the Lord will not reprove him for not having been Moses or Abraham, that is, for not having been a great saint prophet, but will say to him: 'Wretch! Why were you not Zussia, why were you not yourself?'

It is irony that can make of the self, however weak, an individual capable of resisting. Irony is a great strength. It allows one to love, to be free to recognize one's own littleness and relativity as well as that of others. *Tristram Shandy* (1759) is perhaps the greatest example, from a poetic point of view, of a self which scarcely exists yet which is also unmistakable.

Identity starts up defence mechanisms, frequently negative and deadly. Kafka showed how disastrous and culpable it is to be, like the protagonist of *The Trial*, condemned to defend oneself.[18] To give another example, in *Die Blendung* [*Auto da fe*],[19] Canetti illustrates this terrible inflexibility: the self that fears to lose itself hardens, seeks to become stone, motionless, unchangeable, essentially not alive,

---

Psychological Works of Sigmund Freud, 24 vols., ed. and trans. by James Strachey et al. (London: The Hogarth Press and the Institute of Psycho-analysis, 1953–74), vol. 23, 209–53.

17 Joseph Roth, *Hiob. Roman eines einfachen Mannes*, in *Werke* [1930], ed. Fritz Hackert, 6 vols. (Cologne, Amsterdam: Kiepenhauer & Witsch; Allert de Lange, 1990), 93.

18 Franz Kafka, *The Trial* [1925], trans. by Idris Parry (London: Penguin, 2007).

19 Elias Canetti, *Auto da Fé* [1935], trans. by C. V. Wedgwood (London: Jonathan Cape, 1971).

because it fears life, which causes identity, every instant, to die and change.

How can we represent this split, united, multiple, divided self, by turns schizophrenic and paranoiac, solid and dissolved?

In the third chapter of his *Kater Murr* [*Tomcat Murr*] Hoffmann imagines that the fragmentary biography of the protagonist, the orchestra conductor Johannes Kreisler, is written on the back of those sheets on which the sly, bourgeois cat Murr has written his own biography. At the beginning of this chapter Hoffmann's narrator announces that he would be delighted were he able to tell the life of his unhappy hero in 'good chronological order' from the moment of his birth onwards.[20] This is impossible, however, because he does not have at his disposal the whole life of his character, complete and well-ordered, but only fragments which he has discovered in fits and starts. He acquires bits and pieces of numerous incidents, but not in the order in which they really took place: rather, they are confused, all jumbled up. For example, he finds out first about an episode belonging to Kreisler's maturity and immediately afterwards one from his childhood. Thus the threads of life and time blend or interweave and at the end our knowledge of Kreisler's biography, far from being greater than at the beginning, is smaller and more confused. All of this does little to simplify the text of the character's biography, but much to obstruct and dislocate. This is typical of what was to become the great 20th-century experimental novel.

A well-ordered and concluded story – a story capable of tracing a complete profile of the protagonist, like a famous bust in some Pantheon – can only be written about Murr the cat. This is because in his age, according to Hoffmann, a complete and harmonious process of personality-growth is no longer possible. *Bildung*, that 'formation' which Goethe and the whole of German classicism pointed to as an ideal that was both possible and essential to attain (both in life and in the art that represents and reproduces it), seems impossible in a society that has become ever more complex, anonymous and impenetrable.

The Self is formed through reduction and subtraction, by way of a renunciation of life and of itself. It begins to feel empty, as happens to Anton Reiser in Karl Philipp Moritz's novel.[21] It refuses all social functions – 'I prefer not to, sir' replies Melville's character Bartleby

---

20 E. T. A. Hoffmann, *Lebensansichten des Katers Murr* [1820] (Düsseldorf: Artemis und Winkler, 2006).
21 Karl Philip Moritz, *Anton Reiser. Ein autobiographischer Roman* [1785], ed. Heinrich Schnabel (Munich: M. Mörike, 1912).

to every request – and above all refuses its own organic evolution:[22] *'Ich habe keine Geschichte'* ['I have no history'], says Grillparzer's Poor Fiddler to the narrator who wants to tell that character's life story.[23]

In Robert Musil's *Der Mann ohne Eigenschaften* [*The Man without Qualities*], Moosbrugger and Clarisse can have no biography because they have no self, they *are* not selves. Madness appears as a mode of subjectivity which no longer lets itself be constricted by the straitjacket of a complete and coherent identity. Writing it is like undertaking a journey into the twisting, turning underworld of multiplicity, more akin to the night-time activity of Penelope than her day-time experiences, unpicking life's fabric rather than weaving it.

A writer obviously feels this problematic relationship between living and writing particularly strongly. Life creates writing, but writing influences and transforms the life that has created it. In one of Svevo's last stories, the old man – who could perhaps be taken for Zeno Cosini living on after writing his ironical autobiography, *La coscienza di Zeno* – comes to think he is no longer the person who lived his life but, rather, the one who wrote it. He also believes certain things in his existence have only become important because (or when) he committed them to paper, not because (or when) he lived them.[24]

The crisis and/or liberation of the self and its fragility along with the crisis of the word, which characterizes so much of the great literature produced at the end of the 19th and during the 20th centuries, are subjects I feel strongly about and are central to my own work as a writer of fiction. I believe *Danubio* [*Danube*] (1986) and *Microcosmi* [*Microcosms*] (1997), for instance, to be attempts to tell the story of a self which is almost non-existent and always on the point of vanishing, like a drop of water that has fallen into other water but in some way continues to have its own individuality. My fiction revolves around the theme of the (horizontal and vertical) borders of the self and those between the true and the false, between the one and the many, the conscious and the unconscious and so on. *Illazioni su una sciabola* [*Inferences on a Sabre*] (1984), dedicated to the grotesque

---

22 Herman Melville, 'Bartleby the scrivener' [1856], in *The Piazza Tales* (Evanston, IL: Northwestern University Press, 1996).

23 Franz Grillparzer, 'The poor player' ['Der arme Spielmann'], in *Sämtliche Werke*, ed. Peter Frank and Karl Pörnacher (Munich: Carl Hanser, 1964), vol. 3, 158.

24 Italo Svevo, *Il vegliardo*, ed. Bruno Maier (Pordenone: Studio Tesi, 1987); this text is also known as *Il vecchione*.

historical event of the brief and chimerical Cossack state created in north-eastern Italy in the last months of World War Two, focuses on a search for genuine identity which is reversed into the most absurd contrivance. In particular, it is founded upon the ambiguity of a desire to believe a false version of the facts even while knowing it to be fake.

In *Danube*, the river is the symbol of the border, of identity and the uncertainty of identity, because it passes through so many boundaries. It is thus also symbolic of the need to cross frontiers and the difficulty of doing so – borders that are not simply national, political and social, but also psychological, cultural and religious. The Danubian voyage is also a voyage into one's own Underworld and into that Babel of today's world which certainly finds a particular symbol in central Europe, but is also a Babel of the contemporary world at large.

The epigraph of *Microcosms* is one of Borges's parables. Borges speaks of a painter who depicts landscapes – mountains, rivers, trees – and in the end realizes that he has painted his own self-portrait and not because he has, in egotistical arrogance, distorted reality, but because his being consists precisely of his way of looking at reality. Our identity is our way of seeing things.

The protagonist's story in *Microcosms* is formed by the concerted plurality of the destinies that cross and merge into his own. The fluctuating narrative derives from a profound sense that the world, and probably humankind with it, has been radically transformed. In the universal empire of computer science and data communication the individual, the self, no longer knows how to distinguish itself from its artificial reproduction, nor how to distinguish its own personal experience from what reaches it via the media, nor whether it is a living person or an artificially constructed replication. Experience seems to belong to everyone and no one, the Self seems to shatter into fragments. Perhaps, far faster than in previous centuries and millennia, an anthropological mutation is taking place which is producing a new type of human being, as yet unknown, general and interchangeable, similar to the ancient figures of myth, who simultaneously are and are not individuals, everyone and no one. *Microcosms*, with its narrative mode, journeys into this mutation and at the same time resists it.

Un altro mare [*A Different Sea*] (1991) is a novel about the border between the genuine and the fake, a novel of identity, of the present in which identity exists and the future into which it throws itself in self-destruction, condemning itself to never truly being. But *A Different Sea* – like other texts – belongs to that writing which Ernesto Sábato defines as nocturnal. He makes a distinction, with which I profoundly agree, between two types of writing, the 'diurnal' and the 'nocturnal'. Authors writing in the diurnal mode, while freely inventing situations and characters and making them speak according to their own logic, nonetheless express in some way a sense of the world which they share; they utter its sentiments and its values. The other writing, the nocturnal, contends with those more disturbing truths that no one dares openly confess, which perhaps are not even noticed, or indeed that the authors themselves reject as shameful and detestable. It often shocks its own author, because it can reveal a state or emotion of which the latter is quite unconscious: feelings or epiphanies which elude the control of consciousness and sometimes go beyond what consciousness would consent to, contradicting the intentions and very principles of the author, immersing themselves in a murky world, very different from the one the writer loves and would like to move and live in. But it is a world into which he must descend every so often and face the serpent-entwined head of the Medusa, which cannot be rendered more presentable at the hairdresser's. It is the meeting with a double, or at least with an unknown component, who speaks with another voice. Real writers let it speak even when they would prefer it to speak of something else and when they feel 'betrayed' in their strong moral convictions by what it is saying. From nocturnal writing – or, as someone has said, from the writing of the left hand, or insomnia – were born a number of my books, *Le voci* [*The Voices*] (1994), *Essere già stati* [*To Have Been*], *Alla cieca* [*Blindly*] (2005), *Lei dunque capirà* [*You Will Understand*] (2006).

In *The Voices* the search for the authentic life takes the form of a man looking for the pure voice. This search for the genuine can be madly transformed into its opposite, the most grotesquely artificial. This play was born both out of a deep obsession with this subject and out of a chance occurrence. I once phoned a friend of mine in Munich; she was out, so it was the answer-phone that replied, in a beautiful voice, deep and velvety, saying that she was not at home and inviting the caller to ring again later. After two hours I did so; she had just got back, and her reply was tired and slovenly: 'hellooo' – and then I told her that I found her recorded voice far more seductive. It was this episode that gave me the idea for the monologue.

The play is about a man who falls in love with the voices of women recorded on the answer-phone. So he calls them – but only when the real women are not at home. He speaks to recorded voices: the women have become pure numbers. His fixation increases to manic proportions; his delirium is by turns tender, violent, desperate, repelling, moving. Here again the language overflows, in his wild monologue, like a river in flood. In his mania there is a real longing for love and a real suffering and fear, but it rebounds on itself: he is simultaneously aggressor and victim.

La Mostra [The Exhibition] (2001), also a play, is violent, visionary and tragicomic. It stages the tiny destiny of a particular man – the Triestine painter Vito Timmel, who died in a lunatic asylum – who strives to forget life and deaden the torment of his suffering in splendid, apathetic, anarchic self-destruction.

During the hallucinatory preparation of an exhibition of his paintings, his existence is reconstructed in fragments through his own words and those of others: friends, jailers, zealous faith-healers, fellow drinkers and fellow artists. The characters are both full-blooded and insubstantial, women poignantly loved and cruelly lost, choruses of voices and bits and pieces that recount the insane truth of the world in an incoherent yet simultaneously dialectal and universal Triestine, in which the fragments and detritus of an entire Central European civilization flow back.

Alla cieca [Blindly] is a novel, a labyrinthine narrative structure, a Jacob's ladder reversed to descend into the nether regions of history and, in particular, the history of the 20th century. In a whirling monologue echoing with many other voices, a man recounts (invents, falsifies, hides, screams out) his life, which has passed through the horror, the hope, the revolutions of the last century and through widely different lands and seas – from the Italo-German territories of the eastern border of Italy to the war in Spain, from the Nazi camps to the Titoist gulags, from the Iceland of a grotesque revolution to the Australia of emigration. This character – who bears the thousand names of illegal immigrants, partisans, revolutionaries, fugitives – identifies himself with many 'doubles', but with one in particular: Jørgen Jørgensen, an early 19th-century adventurer who crossed all the oceans as far as the antipodes. He founded a city there, in which he ended up condemned to hard labour in penitentiaries as terrible as the camps and gulags of the 20th century. The protagonist's journey through the oceans and shipwrecks of history resembles that of the Argonauts in search of the (ever-bloodstained) Golden Fleece.

At once a case history, epic and delirium, life continuously erased and rewritten wherein things and events precipitate as in an abyss, *Alla cieca* is a dogged attempt to escape from the place of existence to find a direction, or at least a final escape route.

Lei dunque capirà, my most recent creative text, is a female monologue. A woman speaks from a mysterious home for the elderly, probably a symbol of the afterlife, of what lies beyond death. She speaks to the equally mysterious head of the institution – head, indeed, of everything, doubtless an allusion to God – and explains why she has decided not to leave the home, to return to life, despite having wanted to, and despite her beloved companion having come down there to fetch her. It is a modern reappraisal of the Orpheus and Eurydice myth, but this time – and I believe for the first time in literature – the words are given to the woman, to Eurydice. It is she who explains, she who has decided. For some years I used to go fairly regularly to a home for the elderly; not for myself, but to visit an old lady. It was in the centre of Trieste and each time I crossed the threshold, going in or coming out, I found myself in a totally different world. Inside, time had other dimensions, a different duration, condensing or expanding in another mode. There were other relationships, other hierarchies, other affections and other enmities; other codes, other lights, other shades. And each time I asked myself, as I entered or left, whether I understood the world and life a bit better inside or out, in front of the mirror or behind it. Hence the reason, given this state of mind, why the woman, in a supreme sacrifice of love, decides not to leave, not to follow the man she loves: in this way she will spare him the terrifying discovery that, even in the afterlife although so different, we do not understand much more than we do here, in life itself.

Lei dunque capirà is the story of a total and failed love, of an acute and rejected union. The woman who speaks out of a mysterious darkness reveals a strength at once tender and merciless in unveiling the greatness and the meanness of life, death and love.

'Caro Cogoi, a dire il vero non sono sicuro, anche se sono stato io a scriverlo, che nessuno possa raccontare la vita di un uomo meglio di lui stesso. Certo, quella frase ha un punto di domanda' ['Dear Cogoi, to be honest with you, I'm not sure, even though I wrote it myself, that a man's life is best told by anyone but himself. To be sure, that sentence has to have a question-mark']. Thus begins my *Alla cieca*.[25] But the whole novel then denies this statement, because it is not known who it is – who we are – the Self that speaks. What is happening in literature, let alone in life, to His Majesty the Self?

In Barcis, a small mountain village in Friuli on the eastern border of Italy, there is an Alpine community with an excellent Record Centre containing the archives of the life and culture of that steep valley in centuries past. Years ago, intrigued by a 19th-century minor poet, I asked one of its employees whether the library had any books by that

---

25 Claudio Magris, *Alla cieca* (Milan: Garzanti, 2007), 9.

poet. 'Who do you represent?' the employee asked me in turn, clearly unable to conceive of anybody being able to look for a book or go for a walk on their own account. The question is difficult. Certainly, there are many categories I could say I legitimately represented: bipeds, teachers, husbands, fathers, sons, travellers, mortals, flat-owners, but...

It may be that, in that isolated province, one facet of the future was revealed to me: a world in which one neither lives nor travels, nor speaks, nor reads, nor desires personally, but always represents something or someone else. It matters little that this other could, on occasion, bear our own name and surname, as in those films in which people play themselves. The self is perhaps destined to become – or has already become – a mere stand-in: the identity card in place of identity. Who knows, it could be a good thing, a liberation from anxiety about the uncertainty of identity, from violent obsession with its compact purity.

In the not-too-distant future perhaps we will only have (or mainly have) 'parallel actions': parallel to others but non-existent, repetitions and copies of originals that do not exist, or people that have left themselves somewhere else. These could also act as placebos to alleviate pain, the disease caused by true life or nostalgia for it. But this does not take account of the destitute, the starving, the fugitives, the wretched of the earth who pour continuously in ever larger numbers onto the roads of the world with their burning wounds, which force us to live truly. 'You do not know who I am' says the bourgeois. The outcast who sleeps on the ground in the streets of the metropolis, where the people know nothing of him and yet are ferociously hostile to him, will still be able to say, with Don Quixote, 'I know who I am', while around him will grow the arrogant chorus of those who will be increasingly compelled to say 'You do not know whom I represent'.

24. On the World of Interiors

Marcella Vanzo

The dimensions of being human engage me, whether in a fictional, real, social, psychological, political, mythological or economic realm. All facets of identity, their implosions and explosions, lie at the core of my work. My background in anthropology instigates many questions about the tenets of objective reality and the margins of objectivity. Therefore I proceed by investigating the cluster of personal and factual circumstances that create the tension of a particular moment.

To date, my work has incorporated performance, usually filmed, since I believe the specificity of film allows a variety of points of views not available otherwise, together with a mix of media specific to each project: photography, installation, drawing, collage and whatever the circumstances and exhibition spaces require.

I am interested in the impact of the work on the viewer: the first seconds of the encounter with the work are of primary importance; I want to trap the viewer, causing her/him to question where reality starts and where the work of art ends. Thus I try as much as I can to mix reality and fiction: a real location, professionals rather than actors: if I want a boxer I will go to the gym and find one. When I needed an auction house, I was lucky enough to work with Sotheby's. Sometimes my work may appear to be documentary narrative (or parodying its form).

Whether I am presenting a fictional or a real situation, I pursue synthesis: my goal is to describe a situation by reducing it to basic visual and audio elements, which produce meaning in the encounter with the attention of the viewer. Time is the means to develop a narrative, which would be impossible otherwise; this is why I decided to change to filming after my initial work with photography.

Video comes to me as an image, an idea to be reproduced by trial and error. Room for improvisation, for surprise, for the unexpected, is fundamental, because on film I can capture a freshness that a scene rehearsed many times does not possess. I work in the way a theatre director would: improvising and trying out ideas, testing the moves, emphasizing actions or minimizing them. Until I am satisfied with the range of possibilities I follow a deductive process that starts with choosing the right performers. I then film them doing whatever action the video requires and I capture all the details and events that I can barely foresee before the camera work begins.

I always do my own editing. To me, editing means sculpting the filmic material by rearranging its visual and temporal depth. I am interested in experimenting with ways of multiplying, dividing or mixing the image, creating a patchwork of pictures that moves, weaving plot, aesthetic and perception – form and function – into a video. I research its relation to space, since it must affect the viewer physically.

Every project is site-specific because I am interested in the stratification of meaning that is made possible by working in a particular location: the flavour, the history, the *taste* of what comes out by layering fictitious images onto an existing place. If I am working in a 'white cube' space, I will give clues that lead to a similar layering of meaning in order to let the materiality of a place add its texture to a situation.

Size matters to me. I work with big projections; the enclosure of an image around the individual in the dark allows the suspension of physicality for a while and draws attention to the video action. In fact, what I want to create is eventually the experience of a situation, something that borrows from all the senses of the viewer in order to arrive at the production of a subjective meaning.

My presentation for the 'Vicissitudes' conference focused on a video trilogy that I had developed between 2005 and 2007, called (mocking the name of a famous magazine) *The World of Interiors*. It takes place within domestic walls. Home is the ideal place for hiding, the location where the most secret fantasies occur. There is nowhere like home. It is the locus of childhood, family, paranoia and theatre. *The World of Interiors* investigates relations between three different human landscapes: *Ama* (2005) describes the deep, underlying relationship with nature; *Limbo* (2006) addresses the inception of human social relationships; *Mindfield* (2007) dwells on the space of the mind. Each captures private situations that are otherwise invisible and reveals a psychic interior reflected inside the physical space of the camera.

Ama

Ama is first of all a real place, the Castello di Ama, a splendid medieval domain in the middle of Chianti, where amazing wine is produced and art collected. As I approached Ama, a latent vision became true: a thick, fast thread; natural and carnal fibres entangled; earth, grass, motherhood, the body like a lawn. A race from the lawn to the body, from nature to culture, from the outside to the inside: a parallel vision of the act of generation, of nature and the female body.

The video opens with a running close-up of grass in the fields, then passes through a country road, a tarmac street, an entrance, a court, the door to a house, runs up a staircase, onto a carpet, into the interior of a room where a woman is sitting on the floor stitching woollen hair on a doll. Her hair is being knitted by an older woman – her mother. For me, this continuous binding stands as a metaphor of the cycle of generations. Actions are carved between mother and daughter: the video is a three-dimensional sculpture, the microscopic vision of a continuous gesture, that of creation, which reconnects the human being to nature. The video unfolds like a dream, leaving viewers with the strong impression of an image that suddenly halts before their eyes, yet lingers in the mind.

In *Ama* the video image is composed of a series of moving fragments. It shows the entire trio – mother, daughter and doll – as if they were a classical painting, yet no one moves. This was the simplest way for me to represent the difference between action, being in the middle of something and reflection, stepping back and staying still so that thought can overcome reality. It is difficult to discern action as a whole, for the very reason that it is taking place as it is being perceived. Every viewer constitutes a fluctuating point of view, arbitrarily registering an action. Vision is a fragment in movement, the bridge that connects a viewer with an action. To look at something is to cross that bridge.

Limbo

This is the reason why I envisaged *Limbo*, the second act of *The World of Interiors*, as a visual investigation of the family as the primal incubator of social relationships. According to the anthropologist Victor Turner, limbo is the moment of initiation when the individual leaves everyday life to enter a ritually coded set of trials that allow him/her to enter a new identity: adult, warrior, parent.[1] In this case, *Limbo* is the place where we learn how to relate to the outside world.

An over-sized fabric playhouse takes up most of the gallery space, leaving just enough room to walk around it. It encloses the video in order to reveal it. Through two case studies – a family portrait and a celebratory lunch – the video observes the interaction of a real family but with the peculiarity that they are all tied together at the wrist. The aseptic environment portrayed is that of a scientific experiment: an empty room filled only with the instruments needed for interaction: a sofa for the family portrait and a dining table, devoid of colour and decoration – in the choice of food as well – in order to focus primarily on the gestures, roles and idiosyncrasies that hold a family together. The performers' faces appear to be those of people bonded by blood-ties; their garments are all the same colour, a most neutral beige, in two styles only: one male, one female. A different plastic prosthesis on each person is the only thing to distinguish them from one another. These objects indicate where the weakness is in everyone, yet at the same time offer a way to overcome it, just like a person's character. They also hint at the hiatus all of us feel between shape and idea, of how things or we ourselves should be and how they – or we – actually are. I worked with my extended family, in order to capture real life-long interactions, which would have been impossible to achieve with actors.

When during rehearsals we took tensions to an extreme, it ended up like an episode of Benny Hill's comedy show, which was not my intention. Therefore, once dressed up and tied up, I allowed any interactions that existed to reveal themselves. Some gentle, yet accurate, acts emerged, such as the young being extremely polite to the old, while being very harsh among themselves; men clearly subjugating women but possibly unaware of what they were doing; people annoyed, yet smiling; and people genuinely smiling.

The pumping of my blood forms the soundtrack, giving it a dark, anguished tone. *Limbo* is a work that reflects on the ambivalence of blood ties, as both a source of strength and an impediment.

On the opening night some viewers left in agony – they could not even watch the whole seven minutes – whereas others complimented me on what a nice family I have. Reactions have continued to be the same. Some of the psychoanalysts who saw *Limbo* at the 'Vicissitudes' conference argued that this was too happy a family to be true. I

---

1   Victor Turner, *The Forest of Symbols: Aspects of Ndembu Ritual* (Ithaca, NY: Cornell University Press, 1967), 93–111.

believe that reactions to *Limbo* depend on viewers' own family ties; however, the aim of my work is to open up and stimulate feelings and reflections, to open doors, rather than to judge situations.

Mindfield

The portrait of the mind as a place in *Mindfield* is that of relentless, continuous work in progress. Ideas, desires and projects direct and manage our minds incessantly, letting them define the reality around each one of us. In order to find a space that could represent the mind, a location for shooting, I did a lot of research, yet I was never satisfied with what I found, since any given place has a precise purpose: a library, an office, a white box: each structure would determine a meaning. I was interested in a place of *becoming*, a place not yet defined by its purpose. Even the house, the setting that I had used so far for my other videos, seemed reductive: the mind goes far beyond domestic walls.

When discussing this issue with an architect friend, she suggested a building-site, a place in constant motion, which would change day by day according to a project, a place with a destination as yet unknown. So I did indeed look for a building site and when I found it, I went back many times while I put the production together, to find out about the enormous amount of work going on there (six floors, 4,000 square metres, 100 workers), the energy that would slowly but surely make something grow.

The grid that encompassed everything, which allowed parts to be built and joined together, worked exactly like the mind: scaffolding once removed would reveal a completed project. For me, that scaffolding represents the space of the mind, a structure necessary in order to lay out reality, something that exceeds our head, which takes over whenever we want to do something; sometimes drains it and directs it towards a precise purpose. That is why I shot the building as if it were the entrails of a human body: tubes, grids, building materials that looked like blood vessels, veins, bones.

The ancient Greeks called the mind *deinos* – marvellous and dangerous at the same time, a tool too often mistaken for the self. This is why I called the video *Mindfield*, a pun which sounds like 'minefield', a dangerous place. Eight performers, their face hidden by a swollen, opaque, macro-cephalous growth, move mysteriously about the huge building-site, directed by the weight of their heads to the entrails of the building, while a soundtrack made of a mix of human and building sounds both orients and disorients the viewer.

While editing, I doubled the video structure into a two-channel projection, which seemed to reproduce better the labyrinthine structure of the mind and the rhythm of its workings.

The mind is the furthest place from home and yet it only exists within one's deepest interiority.

IMAGES:

pp. 310–311, Marcella Vanzo, *Ama*, 2005, light box, 100 x70 cm

pp. 312-313, Marcella Vanzo, *Limbo, still lives*, 2006, colour prints on aluminum, each 50 x 70 cm

pp. 314–315, Marcella Vanzo, *Mindfield*, film stills, 2007, split screen projection (colour, sound, 12:41)

Images courtesy of the artist

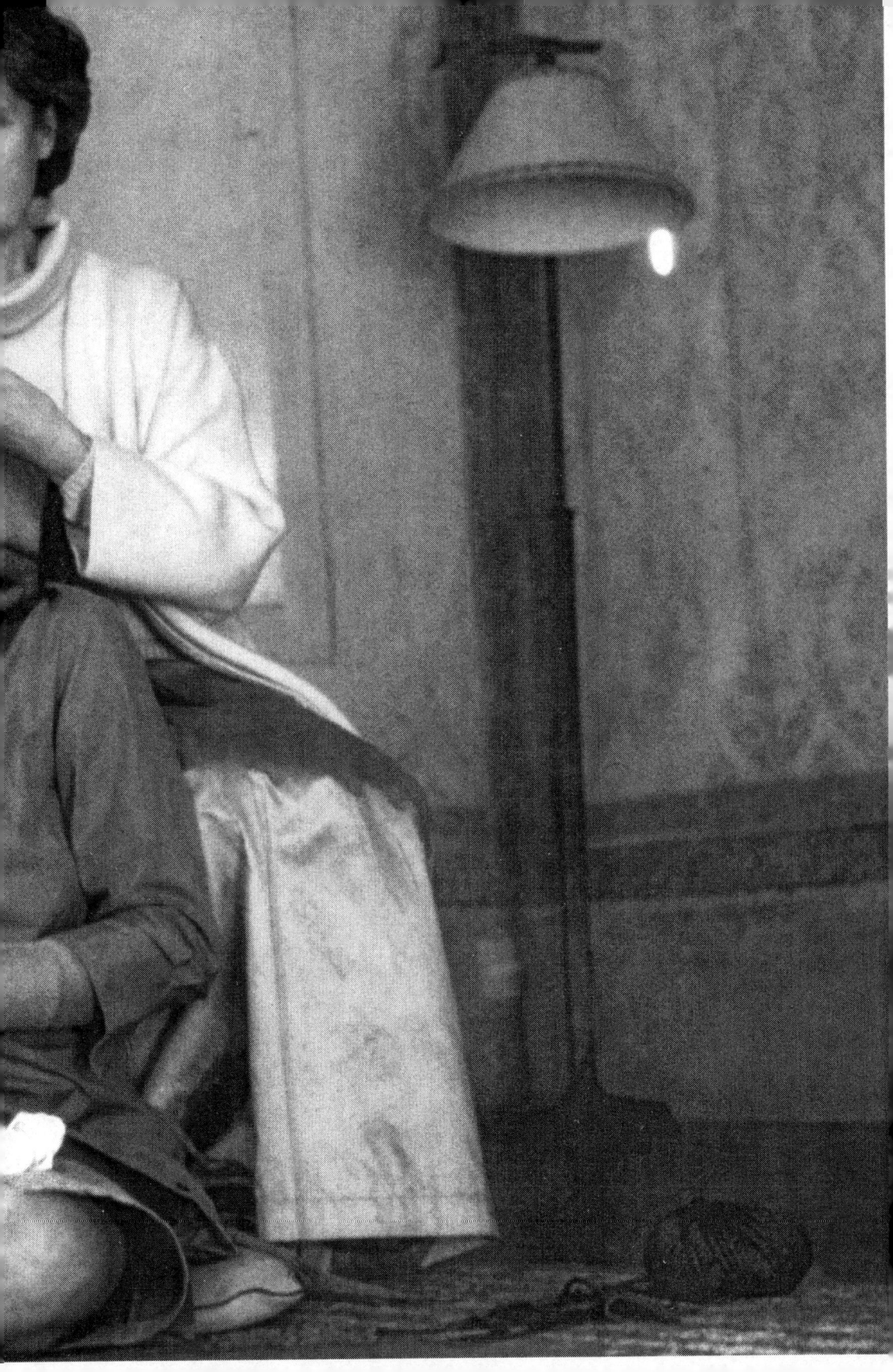

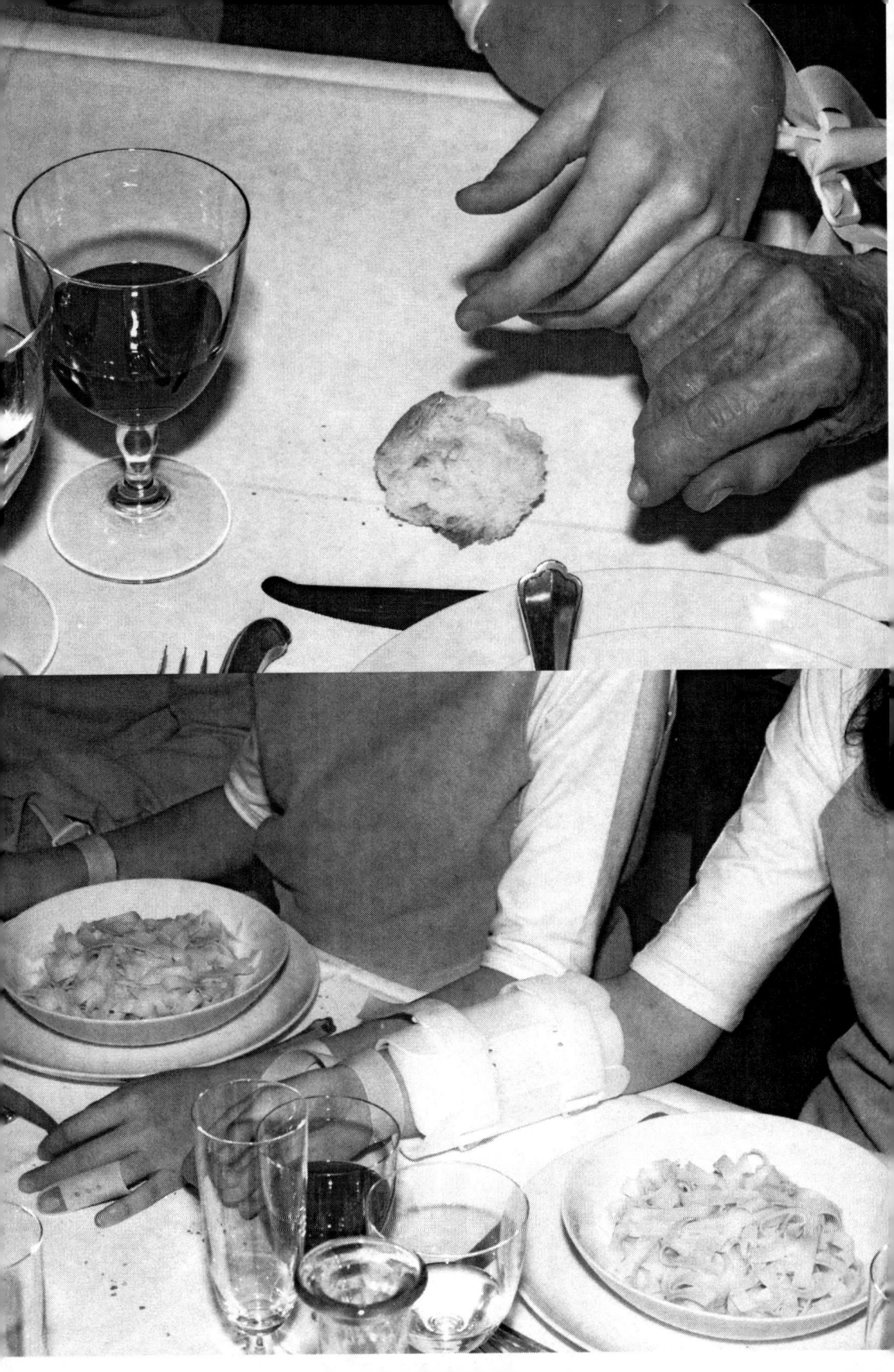

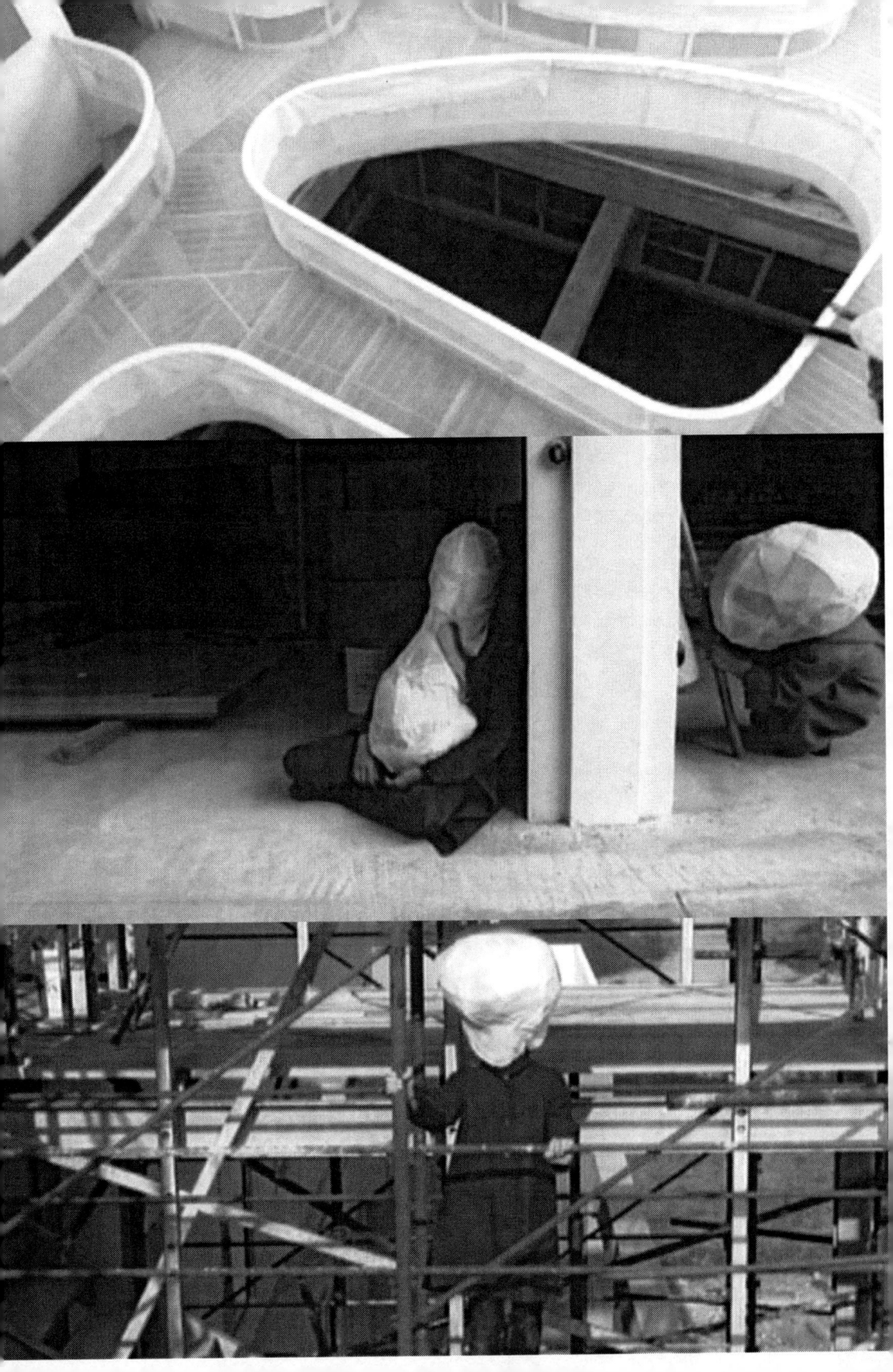

List of Contributors

Christine Anzieu-Premmereur is an adult and child psychiatrist. Trained as a psychoanalyst at the Société Psychanalytique de Paris, she moved to New York in 2000, where she is in private practice as an adult and child psychoanalyst. Christine is a faculty member at the Columbia Psychoanalytic Center for Training and Research, where she is director of the Parent-Infant Psychotherapy Training Program. A member of the New York Psychoanalytic Institute, she is co-director of its Pacella Child Center. She is also Assistant Clinical Professor in Psychiatry at Columbia University. Christine has published two books in French – on play in child psychotherapy and on psychoanalytic interventions with parents and babies – and has written a number of book chapters and papers in English on motherhood, maternal functioning and child development, symbolization process in childhood and techniques of intervention in early childhood.

Julia Borossa is Director of the Research Centre and of the Programmes in Psychoanalysis at Middlesex University. She is the editor of *Sandor Ferenczi: Selected Writings* (1999), and (with Ivan Ward) of *Psychoanalysis, Fascism, Fundamentalism* (2009), and the author of *Hysteria* (2001). Her work on the histories and politics of psychoanalysis has appeared in journals, including *The Oxford Literary Review*, *The Journal of European Studies* and *The Journal of Postcolonial Writing* and several edited collections, most recently in *Psychoanalysis and Politics* (ed. Lene Auestadt, Karnac, 2012) and *The Ethics of Representation in Literature, Art and Journalism: Transnational Responses to the Siege of Beirut* (ed. Caroline Rooney and Rita Sakr, Routledge, forthcoming). She is currently co-editing (with Catalina Bronstein and Claire Pajaczkowska) *The New Klein Lacan Dialogues* (Karnac, forthcoming).

Lesley Caldwell is Honorary Reader in the Psychoanalysis Unit and Senior Research Associate in the Italian department, both at University College London. She is a psychoanalyst of the British Psychoanalytic Association in private practice in London, and an editor for the Winnicott Trust, for whom, with Angela Joyce, she published *Reading Winnicott* (2011). With Helen Taylor Robinson she is joint general editor for the *Collected Writings of Donald Winnicott*. Lesley organizes the interdisciplinary seminar series for the Psychoanalysis Unit and, with Dorigen Caldwell of Birkbeck, the termly lecture series 'On Rome'. She co-edited a special issue of the *Journal of Romance Studies* devoted to the Italian section of the Institute of Germanic & Romance Studies (IGRS) project. Lesley is co-investigator on the Roman Modernities project, funded by the Arts and Humanities Research Council, and consultant to the AHRC workshop, 'La mamma: invention of a stereotype'.

William Cobbing is an artist living and working in London. He studied BA Fine Art at Central Saint Martins College (1997), De Ateliers, Amsterdam (2000), and PhD Fine Art at Middlesex University (2010). His exhibitions include: 'A Secret History of Clay', Tate Liverpool (2004); 'Room with a View', Gemeente Museum, The Hague (2006); Netwerk Centre for Contemporary Art, Aalst, Belgium (2007); 'Man in the Planet', Viafarini DOCVA, Milan (2010); 'Body Gestures', Herzliya Museum of Contemporary Art, Israel (2011); and 'Revolver', Matt's Gallery, London (2012). In 2005–06 William was awarded the Helen Chadwick Fellowship at the Ruskin School University of Oxford and the British School at Rome, leading to the solo exhibition 'Gradiva Project' at the Freud Museum and Camden Arts Centre (2007–08). The cast-iron manhole cover sculptures produced for the project remain on permanent view at these venues.

Juan Cruz is an artist and educator whose work has regularly concerned itself with text and translation as a metaphor for visual representation, and as an embodied and performative process. His recent exhibitions include 'Mensch', Edinburgh International Festival (2009); 'Squatters Murcia', Spain (2008); and solo shows at Galeria Elba Benitez, Madrid (2008); Remise Bludenz, Austria (2007) and Peer, London (2005). Juan Cruz lives and works in Liverpool, where he is Professor of Fine Art and Director of the Liverpool School of Art and Design, Liverpool John Moores University. His work is represented by Matt's Gallery.

List of Contributors

Sander L. Gilman is a distinguished professor of the Liberal Arts and Sciences and Professor of Psychiatry at Emory University. A cultural and literary historian, he has published over 80 books, from *Seeing the Insane* (1982, repr. 1996) and *Jewish Self-Hatred* (1986) to *Obesity: The Biography* and, with Jeongwon Joe, *Wagner and Cinema* (both 2010). He has been a visiting professor at numerous universities in North America, South Africa, the UK, Germany, Israel, China and New Zealand. Sander was awarded a Doctor of Laws (*honoris causa*) at the University of Toronto (1997), elected an honorary professor of the Free University in Berlin (2000), and is an honorary member of the American Psychoanalytic Association (2007).

Jaspar Joseph-Lester is an artist based in London whose work explores the role images play in urban planning, social space and everyday praxis, latterly focusing on conflicting ideological frameworks embodied in urban regeneration projects. He is currently the Dallas Pavilion's lead artist and has recently completed a photo-essay titled 'A guide to the casino architecture of wedding' for the next issue of COLLAPSE: *Philosophical Research and Development*. Author of *Revisiting the Bonaventure Hotel* (Copy Press, 2009), co-editor of *Episode: Pleasure and Persuasion in Lens-based Media* (Artwords, 2008), he is a director of the Curating Video research group, and Reader in Fine Art at Sheffield Hallam University.

Ahuvia Kahane is Professor of Greek and former Director (2005–11) of the Humanities and Arts Research Centre at Royal Holloway, University of London. Among his publications are: *The Interpretation of Order* (1994); *Written Voices, Spoken Signs* (1997); *A Companion to the Prologue to Apuleius' Metamorphoses* (2001); *The Chicago Homer* (online 2001); *Diachronic Dialogues* (2006); *Antiquity and the Ruin* (2010); *Social Order and Informal Codes* (2011, in Hebrew); and *Homer: A Guide to the Perplexed* (2012). *Epic, Novel, and the Progress of Antiquity*, his study of genre, literary history and historical time is forthcoming in 2013. Ahuvia is Senior Associate of the Oxford Centre for Hebrew and Jewish Studies, editor of the *Oxford English Hebrew Dictionary*, and translator of Homer's *Odyssey* into Hebrew (both 1996).

Sharon Kivland is an artist and writer. She is Reader in Fine Art at Sheffield Hallam University, Tutor in Critical Practice at Wimbledon College of Art, University of the Arts London, and a research associate of the Centre for Freudian Analysis and Research, London.

From 2007–10 she was a Visiting Fellow at the IGRS. Her work is represented by DOMOBAAL, London; Galerie Bugdahn & Kaimer, Düsseldorf; and Galerie des petits carreaux, Paris. Her continuing series of books, *Freud on Holiday*, is published by information as material and Cube Art editions.

Herbert Lachmayer is professor at the University of Art and Design in Linz (Austria) and head of the department he founded in 2009, Staging Knowledge – an experimental research practice linking humanities and the arts. At the same university he founded the curriculum Experimental Design in 1991. In Vienna he founded the Da Ponte Research Centre for Applied Humanities and Opera Studies, which produced many exhibitions such as 'Salieri sulle tracce di Mozart', Milan (2004); 'Mozart – Experimental Enlightenment', Vienna (2006); 'Wozu braucht Carl August einen Goethe?', Weimar (2008); 'Haydn Explosiv', Eisenstadt (2009); 'Das Bernhardzimmer', Weimar (2009); 'Phantasy and Pharmacy', Vienna (2010); 'Gustav Mahler – Productive Decadence at the Fin de Siècle Vienna', Berlin (2011). 'Staging Knowledge' is recognized by the Stanford University CA (visiting professor 2009) as a new method of transdisciplinary research combined with artistic creativity. Herbert has published numerous essays and catalogues on the topics of 'taste intelligence' and the content of his exhibitions as well as university curricula.

Zoe Laughlin is a co-founder/director of the Institute of Making and the Materials Library project. She holds a BA in Film and Performance studies from the University of Wales Aberystwyth, an MA from Central Saint Martin's College of Art and Design and obtained a PhD in Materials within the Division of Engineering, King's College London. Working at the interface of the science, art, craft and design of materials, her work ranges from formal experiments with matter to materials consultancy and large-scale public exhibitions and events with partners including Tate Modern, the Hayward Gallery, the Victoria and Albert Museum and the Wellcome Collection.

Stéphane Le Mercier is an artist and curator, teaching at l'Ecole Supérieure d'Art et de Design de Saint-Etienne. He has participated in and curated different projects and international colloquia dealing with the problematics of distribution of published material (such as posters, fliers, free books) in public space. These were: 'Table d'Hôtes', Lyon, in collaboration with Pierre-Olivier Arnaud, collection Frac Rhône-Alpes, (2007–10); 'Le livre d'artiste : Quels projets pour l'Art?', Université de Haute-Bretagne, Rennes 2 (2010); 'Les livres à venir',

Ecole Supérieure des Arts Décoratifs, Strasbourg (2010); 'Exposer]... [Publier', Ecole Supérieure des Beaux-Arts and Carré d'Art, Nîmes (2011). His current artistic projects are: 'avec Excoffon', curated by Gavin Morrison, Galerie Iff, Marseille; University of Nagoya, Komaki, Japan; and Georgia Scherman Projects, Toronto, Canada. His many art books include *Gift*, éditions P, Marseille (2009); *Lectures pour tous*, Incertain Sens, Rennes (2010); and *Corps 72*, Boabooks, Geneva (2011). He is a regular contributor to the review *fondcommun*, Marseille.

Martin Liebscher is Honorary Senior Lecturer at the Centre for the History of Psychological Disciplines and Research Fellow in the German department, University College London. As Philemon editor of C. G. Jung's works, he is currently editing the correspondence between Jung and Erich Neumann. Martin was co-founder and director of the IGRS's Ingeborg Bachman Centre for Austrian Literature. His interests lie in 19th- and 20th-century German philosophy, especially Nietzsche, and in psychoanalysis and psychotherapy (Freud, Jung), especially their history and influence on literature including contemporary Austrian literature (Musil, Bachmann). His publications include *Libido und Wille zur Macht. C. G. Jungs Auseinandersetzung mit Friedrich Nietzsche* (2012); *Thinking the Unconscious. Nineteenth-century German Thought* (co-edited, 2010); *The Racehorse of Genius* (co-edited, 2009); *Kontinuitäten und Brüche* (co-edited, 2006); *Nationalism versus Cosmopolitanism in German Thought & Culture 1789–1914* (co-edited, 2006); and *Nietzsche-Studien. Gesamtregister Bände 1-20 [1972–91]* (2000).

Claudio Magris, as well as being a journalist and novelist, has been professor of modern German literature at the University of Trieste since 1978. Claudio is a member of several European academies and was in the Italian Senate 1994–6. His novels and theatre productions, many translated into several languages, include *Illazioni su una sciabola* (1984); *Danubio* (1986); *Stadelmann* (1988); *Un altro mare* (1991); and *Microcosmi* (1997). He has won many literary prizes including the Erasmus Prize (2001) and the Prince of Asturias Award for Literature (2004). On 18 October 2009, he received the Peace Prize of the German Book Trade at the Frankfurt Book Fair.

Juliet Mitchell has just completed a year as Mellon Visiting Professor at the Courtauld Institute of Fine Art. She teaches and supervises in the PhD programme in theoretical psychoanalysis, which she set up and directed at University College London. Juliet is also a Distinguished Mellon Research Fellow, Department of Psychology,

Witswatersrand, and Senior Research Fellow at the Department of Geography, University of Cambridge, where she is Emeritus Professor of Psychoanalysis and Gender Studies and founder of the Centre for Gender Studies. She is a Fellow of the British Academy and the International Psychoanalytical Association. Her many books include *Women: the Longest Revolution* (1966); *Woman's Estate* (1972); *Psychoanalysis and Feminism* (1974); *Mad Men and Medusas* (2000); and *Siblings: Sex and Violence* (2003).

Mark Nash is Professor and head of department of Curating Contemporary Art at the Royal College of Art, London. He is a curator, film historian and filmmaker, with a specialism in contemporary fine art moving image practices, avant-garde and world cinema. Mark has curated the film element of several international exhibitions including 'Force Fields Phases of the Kinetic' (2000); 'The Short Century: Independence and Liberation Movements in Africa, 1945–1994' (2001); and the Berlin Biennial (2004). He was co-curator of 'Documenta 11' (2002). His recent curatorial projects include an exhibition, 'One Sixth of the Earth: Ecologies of Image', at MUSAC, Spain and ZKM Centre for Art and Media, Germany (2012).

Uriel Orlow is an artist, educator and sometime writer, born in Zurich and based in London, where he is also Senior Research Fellow at the University of Westminster. Uriel's work explores the spatial and imaginary conditions of history and memory, focusing on blind spots of representation and forms of haunting. His work has been exhibited internationally including 'The Deep of the Modern', Manifesta 9; 'Chewing the Scenery', Swiss off-site Pavilion 54th Venice Biennale; 'Essays in Geopoetics', 8th Mercosul Biennial; 'Farewell to Postcolonialism', 3rd Guangzhou Triennial; as well as in group exhibitions and screenings at Tate Modern, Gasworks, Institute of Contemporary Art and Whitechapel Gallery, London; Argos, Brussels; Kunsthalle, Budapest; Oberhausen Short Film Festival, Germany; South African National Gallery, Cape Town; Extra-City, Antwerp; Bétonsalon, Paris; Contemporary Image Collective, Cairo; and Centre d'Art Contemporain, Geneva.

Mariano Ben Plotkin is a researcher for the National Council for Scientific Research at Instituto de Desarrollo Económico y Socia, and Professor of History at the Universidad Nacional de Tres de Febrero in Argentina. He is the author and editor of several books on the history of psychoanalysis and on Argentine cultural and political history including *Freud in the Pampas* (2001, Spanish translation

2003); *Histoire de la psychanalyse en Argentine* (2010); *Argentina on the Couch* (2003); *Transnational Unconscious* (eds. Mariano Plotkin and Joy Damousi, 2009), and *Psychoanalysis and Politics* (eds. Mariano Plotkin and Joy Damousi, 2012). Mariano is also the director of the online journal *CulturasPsi/PsyCultures* (www.culturaspsi.org).

Malcolm Quinn is Associate Dean of Research and Reader in Critical Practice in CCW Graduate School, University of the Arts, London. His current research focuses on identity, taste and governance in the thought of Jeremy Bentham and Adam Smith, with reference to Jacques Lacan's account of the 'utilitarian conversion' in ethics. He is the author (with Professor Dany Nobus) of *Knowing Nothing Staying Stupid: Elements for a Psychoanalytic Epistemology* (2005) and 'Insight and rigour: a Freudo-Lacanian approach', in Biggs and Karlsson (eds.) *The Routledge Companion to Research in the Arts* (2010). His book *Utilitarianism and the Art School in Nineteenth-Century Britain* was published in 2012.

Naomi Segal is Professorial Fellow at Birkbeck, University of London. From 2004 to 2011 she was founding Director of the IGRS; before that, at the University of Reading, she created and directed an MA on The Body and Representation. Since the 1990s, she has served on/chaired numerous national and international committees within the European Science Foundation, Humanities in the European Research Area, the British Academy, Arts and Humanities Research Council and Association of University Professors and Heads of French. Naomi is an Academic Associate of the British Psychoanalytical Society. She has published 77 articles and 12 books, most recently *Consensuality: Didier Anzieu, gender and the sense of touch* (2009); *Indeterminate Bodies* (2003); *Le Désir à l'Œuvre* (2000); and *André Gide: Pederasty & Pedagogy* (1998). Her next major project is a monograph probably to be titled *Eurydice's revenge; or, the haunting of the replacement child*.

Alison Sinclair is Professor of Modern Spanish Literature and Intellectual History at the University of Cambridge. She specializes in 19th- and 20th-century Spanish literature, culture and intellectual history, the history of sexuality in Spain, psychoanalytic approaches to fiction, comparative literature, and the spread of cultural ideas in Europe. Recent books include *Sex and Society in early twentieth-century Spain: Hildegart Rodríguez and the World League for Sexual Reform* (2007); and *Trafficking Knowledge in Early Twentieth-Century Spain: Centres of Exchange and Cultural Imaginaries* (2009). Her AHRC-funded research project, on 'Wrongdoing in Spain 1800–1936: Realities,

Representations, Reactions' (2011–14), focuses on the gap between the historical profile of wrongdoing and its profile in culture, with particular reference to popular culture, and includes the digitization and cataloguing of c. 4,500 items of popular literature in Cambridge University Library and the British Library.

Marcella Vanzo (born in Milan, 1973) works with video, performance and installation, investigating all dimensions of the human being from the mythical to the political. In her work reality and fiction form a tight-knit unity that questions the representation of the everyday world. Her work has been shown in solo and group shows at the Prague Biennale (2011); Performa 09, New York; Fondazione Sandretto Re Rebaudengo, Torino; Walker Art Center, Minneapolis; Museo Reina Sofia, Madrid; Galleria Continua, San Gimignano; and many video festivals. Her awards include the New York Art Residency at Columbia University, New York City and Acacia-Emerging Artist Award, Milan.

Hugo Vezzetti is Professor at the University of Buenos Aires and member of the CONICET (National Research Council, Argentina). His research subjects are the history of psychology and psychoanalysis; history and memory of the recent past; and state terrorism and violence in Argentina. He has been visiting professor at the University of Maryland, the Ecole des Hautes Etudes en Sciences Sociales, Paris and the Ibero-Amerikanische Institut, Berlin. His books are: *La locura en la Argentina* (1983); *Freud en Buenos Aires* (1989); *Aventuras de Freud en el pais de los argentinos* (1996); *Pasado y presente. Guerra, dictadura y sociedad en la Argentina* (2002); and *Sobre la violencia revolucionaria. Memorias y olvidos* (2009).

Andrew Webber is Professor of Modern German and Comparative Culture at the University of Cambridge and a Fellow of Churchill College. He has published widely on German and comparative literary, cinematic and visual cultures, with a strong interest in psychoanalysis. His most recent books are *The European Avant-garde: 1900–1940* (2004) and *Berlin in the Twentieth Century: A Cultural Topography* (2008). He is also editor of a special number of *Paragraph* (32.3, November 2009): *Passage-work: Walter Benjamin between the Disciplines*.

Amy Wygant is a British-based freelance scholar with a long-standing interest in psychoanalysis. In a previous academic career in early modern French studies, she was active as a widely published author of journal articles and monographs – *Towards a Cultural Philology: Phèdre and the Construction of 'Racine'* (1999); *Medea, Magic, and Modernity* (2007); *The Meanings of Magic: From the Bible to Buffalo Bill* (as editor, 2006); and *Seventeenth-Century French Studies* (as journal editor, 2006–11). She served as a network member of the Scottish Institute of Human Relations, and co-founded Women in French in Scotland (WIFIS). She is now writing about cars and food for a more broadly based educated public.

Bibliography

Aberastury Arminda, *Teoría y técnica del psicoanálisis de niños* (Buenos Aires: Paidós, 1962)
Abraham, Nicolas, and Maria Torok, *The Shell and the Kernel* [*L'écorce et le noyau* (1978, 1987) 2001], trans. by Nicholas T. Rand (Chicago: University of Chicago Press, 1994)
—, *L'Écorce et le noyau* (Paris: Flammarion [1978, 1987] 2001)
Alvarez, Agustín, *¿Adónde vamos?* (Buenos Aires: La Cultura Argentina [1904] 1952)
—, *South America. Ensayo de psicología política* (Buenos Aires: La Cultura Argentina [1894] 1918)
Anderson, Perry, 'Components of a national culture', *New Left Review* 50 (July–August 1968), 3–57
Anon., 'Report of the Ninth Psycho-Analytic Congress', *Bulletin of the International Psychoanalytic Association*, vol. 7 (1926), 119–43
Anzieu, Didier, 'La psychanalyse, encore', in *Psychanalyser* (Paris: Dunod, 2000), 257–68
—, *Le Moi-peau* (Paris: Dunod [1985] 1995)
—, *Les Enveloppes psychiques* (Paris: Dunod [1987, 1996] 2000)
—, *Psychic Envelopes*, trans. by Daphne Briggs (London: Karnac Books, 1990)
—, *The Skin Ego*, trans. by Chris Turner (New Haven: Yale University Press, 1989)
Argentine Psychoanalytic Association, 'Historia de APA', at www.apa.org.ar/apa/historia/
Assmann, Aleida, Jan Assmann and Christof Hardmeier (eds.) *Schrift und Gedächtnis: Beiträge zur Archäologie der literarischen Kommunikation* (Munich: Fink, 1983)
Augustine, *Confessions*, trans. by Henry Chadwick (Oxford: Oxford University Press, 1991)
Balint, Michael 'On the Psycho-Analytic Training System', *International Journal of Psychoanalysis* 29 (1948), 163–73

Bann, Stephen and J. E. Bowlt (eds.) *Russian Formalism: A Collection of Articles and Texts in Translation* (Edinburgh: Scottish Academic Press, 1973)
Baumeyer, Franz, 'The Schreber case', *International Journal of Psychoanalysis*, vol. 37 (1956), 61–75
Bayky, C. A., Sven Beckert, Matthew Connelly, Isabel Hofmeyr, Wendy Kozol and Patricia Seed, 'AHR conversation: on transnational history', *American Historical Review*, vol. 111, no. 5 (December 2006), 1441–64
Benedetto, Antonio, *Prima della parola. L'ascolto del non detto psicoanaltico attraverso le forme dell'arte* (Milan: Franco Angeli, 1982)
Benjamin, Walter, *Gesammelte Schriften* (Frankfurt am Main: Suhrkamp, 1991)
—, *The Arcades Project* (*Das Passagen-Werk* [1982]), ed. Roy Tiedemann, trans. by Howard Eiland and Kenneth McLaughlin (Cambridge, MA: Harvard University Press, 1999)
—, *The Origin of German Tragic Drama* [*Ursprung des deutschen Trauerspiels* (1963)], trans. by John Osborne (London: Verso, 2003)
Berger, Peter, 'Towards a sociological understanding of psychoanalysis', *Social Research*, 32 (1965), 25–41
Bergson, Henri, *Le rire. Essai sur la signification du comique* (Paris: Alcan [1900] 1924)
—, *Time and Free Will* [*Essai sur les données immédiates de la conscience* (1889)], trans. by F. L. Pogson (London: Dover, 2001)
Berman, Emanuel, *Impossible Training: A Relational view of Psychoanalytic Education* (Hillsdale, NJ: Analytic Press, 2004)
Bettelheim, Bruno, *Freud and Man's Soul* (London: Chatto and Windus, 1983)
Bion, Wilfred, *Second Thoughts: Selected Papers on Psycho-Analysis* (London: Karnac, 1967)
Bird, Jon, *Gradiva Project*, ed. William Cobbing (London: Camden Arts Centre, 2007)
Birksted, J. K., *Le Corbusier and the Occult* (London and MA: MIT Press, 2009)
Blake, Peter, *Le Corbusier. Architecture and Form* (London: Penguin Books, 1960)
Blaser, Werner, *Nature in Buildings: Rudolf Steiner in Dornach 1913–1925* (Basel: Birkhauser, 2002)
Bleger, José, *Psicoanálisis y dialéctica materialista* (Buenos Aires, Paidós, 1958)
—, *Psicohigiene y psicología institucional* (Buenos Aires: Paidós, 1966)

Boccaccio, Giovanni, *Decameron*, ed. Branca Vittore (Milan: Mondadori [c. 1353] 1985)

Borossa, Julia, 'Narcissistic wounds, race and racism: a comment on Frantz Fanon's critical engagement with psychoanalysis', in *Narcissism: A Critical Reader*, ed. Anastasios Gaitanidis and Polona Curk (London: Karnac, 2007), 113–26

Bourdieu, Pierre, 'Une interprétation de la théorie de la religion selon Max Weber', *Archives européennes de sociologie*, vol. 12, no. 1 (1971), 3–21

Bourriaud, Nicolas, *Relational Aesthetics* [*L'Esthétique relationnelle* (1998)], trans. by Simon Pleasance and Fronza Woods with the participation of Mathieu Copeland (Dijon: Presses du réel), 2002

Bowlby, John, *Attachment and Loss*, vol. 3: *Loss: Sadness & Depression* (London: Hogarth Press, 1980)

Braddock, Louise and Michael Lacewing, *The Academic Face of Psychoanalysis* (London: Routledge, 2007)

Breton, André, 'Interview du Professeur Freud à Vienne', *Littérature*, Nouvelle Série 1 (1922), 19

Breuer, Josef, 'Fräulein Anna O.' ['Fräulein Anna O.' (1893)], in *The Standard Edition of the Complete Psychological Works of Sigmund Freud*, ed. and trans. by James Strachey *et al.*, 24 vols. (London: The Hogarth Press and the Institute of Psycho-Analysis, 1953–74), vol. 2, 21–47

Bunge, Carlos O., *Nuestra América. Ensayo de psicología social* (Buenos Aires: A. Moen y Hermanos Editores [1903] 1911)

Butler, Judith, *Antigone's Claim: Kinship Between Life and Death* (New York: Columbia University Press, 2000)

—, *Excitable Speech: A Politics of the Performative* (New York: Routledge, 1997), 103–26

Calvino, Italo, *Il barone rampante* [*The Baron in the Trees*] (Turin: Einaudi scuola, 1957)

Canetti, Elias, *Auto da Fé* [*Die Blendung* (1935)], trans. by C. V. Wedgwood (London: Jonathan Cape, 1971)

Carus, Carl Gustav, *Psyche – Zur Entwicklungsgeschichte der Seele* (Pforzheim: Flammer und Hoffmann, 1846)

Castoriades, Cornelius, 'Psychoanalysis and politics', in *World in Fragments. Writings on Politics, Society, Psychoanalysis, and the Imagination*, ed. and trans. by David Ames Curtis (Stanford, CA: Stanford University Press, 1997), 125–36

—, *The World in Fragments* (Stanford, CA: Stanford University Press, 1997)

Chasseguet-Smirgel, Janine, 'The triumph of humor', in *Fantasy, Myth and Reality: Essays in Honor of Jacob Harlow* , ed. H. P. Blum (New York: International Universities Press, 1988)

Chateaubriand, François-René de, 'Voyage au Mont-Blanc; paysages de montagnes', in *Œuvres complètes de M. le vicomte de Chateaubriand* (Paris: Pourrat Frères [1806] 1836), vol. 13

Conrad, Joseph, *The Heart of Darkness* (Harmondsworth: Penguin [1899] 1995)

Dagfal, Alejandro, 'Paris-London-Buenos Aires: the adventures of Kleinian psychoanalysis between Europe and South America', in *The Transnational Unconscious: Essays in the History of Psychoanalysis and Transnationalism*, ed. Joy Damousi and Mariano Plotkin (London: Palgrave Macmillan, 2009), 179–98

Damousi, Joy and Mariano Plotkin (eds.) *The Transnational Unconscious: Essays in the History of Psychoanalysis and Transnationalism* (London: Palgrave Macmillan, 2009)

Danto, Elizabeth Ann, *Freud's Free Clinics: Psychoanalysis and Social Justice, 1918–1938* (New York: Columbia University Press, 2005)

Deleuze, Gilles and Félix Guattari, *L´Anti-Œdipe. Capitalisme et Schizophrénie* (Paris: Minuit, 1972)

Derrida, Jacques, *Archive Fever: A Freudian Impression* [*Mal d'Archive: une impression freudienne* (1995)], trans. by Eric Prenowitz (Chicago, University of Chicago Press, 1995)

—, *Given Time. I. Counterfeit Money* [*Donner le temps* (1991)], trans. by Peggy Kamuf (Chicago, Chicago University Press 1994)

—, *Specters of Marx* [*Spectres de Marx* (1993)], trans. by Peggy Kamuf (London: Routledge, 1994)

Descartes, René, *Discours de la méthode: Von der Methode des richtigen Vernunftgebrauchs und der wissenschaftlichen Forschung* [*Discours de la méthode pour bien conduire sa raison et chercher la vérité dans les sciences* (1673)], ed. and trans. by Lüder Gäbe (Hamburg: Meiner, 1997)

Deutsch, Helene, 'The Training Institute and the Clinic', *International Journal of Psychoanalysis* 13 (1932), 255–7

Dimler, G. Richard, S. J., *Studies in the Jesuit Emblem* (New York: AMS Press, 2007)

Dostoevsky, Fyodor, *Notes from Underground* [*Zapiski iz podpolya* (1864)], trans. by Michael R. Katz (New York: Norton, 1989)

Elias, Norbert, *The Germans: Power Struggle and the Development of Habitus in Nineteenth and Twentieth Centuries* [*Studien über die Deutschen* (1989)], trans. with introduction by Eric Dunning and Stephen Mennell (New York: Columbia University Press, 1996)

Ellenberger, Henri, *The Discovery of the Unconscious: The History and Evolution of Dynamic Psychiatry* (New York: Basic Books, 1970)

Evans, Jo, *Julio Medem*, Critical Guides to Spanish and Latin American Texts and Films, 71 (London: Grant & Cutler, 2007)

Falzeder, Ernst (ed.) *The Complete Correspondence of Sigmund Freud and Karl Abraham 1907–1925*, trans. by Caroline Schwarzacher (London: Karnac, 2002)

Fanon, Frantz, *Black Skin, White Masks*, trans. by Charles Lam Markmann (New York: Pluto Press, 1986)

—, *Peau noire, masques blancs* (Paris: Seuil, 1952)

—, *The Wretched of the Earth* (*Les Damnés de la terre* [1961]), trans. by Constance Farrington (New York: Grove, 1965)

Forrester, John, *Dispatches from the Freud Wars. Psychoanalysis and its Passions* (Cambridge, MA: Harvard University Press, 1997)

Foucault, Michel, 'What is an author?' ['Qu'est-ce qu'un auteur ?' (1969)], *Screen* (1979) 20 (1): 13–34

—, *Histoire de la sexualité*, t.1, *La Volonté de savoir* (Paris: Gallimard, 1976)

—, *Surveiller et Punir* (Paris: Gallimard, 1975)

Freud, Sigmund and Josef Breuer, *Studies on Hysteria* [*Studien über Hysterie* (1895)], in *The Standard Edition of the Complete Psychological Works of Sigmund Freud*, ed. and trans. by James Strachey et al., 24 vols. (London: The Hogarth Press and the Institute of Psycho-Analysis, 1953–74), vol. 2

Freud, Sigmund, 'Das Unbehagen in der Kultur' (1930), in *Gesammelte Werke*, 19 vols. (Frankfurt am Main: S. Fischer, 1968), vol. 14, 419–596

—, 'Das Unbehagen in der Kultur' [1929/30], in *Studienausgabe Bd. IX: Fragen der Gesellschaft, Ursprünge der Religion*, (Frankfurt am Main: Fischer, 1974), 191–270

—, 'Der Wahn und die Träume in W. Jensen's "Gradiva"' (1907), in *Gesammelte Werke*, vol. 7, 29–122

—, *Das Unbehagen in der Kultur* (Vienna: Internationaler Psychoanalytischer Verlag, 1930)

—, Das Unheimliche' [1919], in *Studienausgabe Bd. IV* (Frankfurt am Main: Fischer, 1974), 241–75

—, *Der Mann Moses und der Monotheismus* (1939), *Gesammelte Werke*, vol. 16, 101–246

—, *Die Traumdeutung* (Vienna & Leipzig: Franz Deuticke, 1900)

—, *Letters of Sigmund Freud 1873–1939*, ed. Ernst L. Freud (London: The Hogarth Press, 1961)

—, *Obras completas*, trans. by José Luis Etcheverry, 24 vols. (Buenos Aires: Amorrortu, 1974–85)

—, *Obras completas*, trans. by Luis López-Ballesteros and Ludovico Rosenthal, 22 vols. (Buenos Aires: Santiago Rueda, 1952–6)
—, *Obras completas*, trans. by Luis López-Ballesteros y de Torres (Madrid: Biblioteca Nueva, 17 vols., 1922–34)
—, *Psychoanalysis and Faith: The Letters of Sigmund Freud and Oskar Pfister*, trans. by Ernst Mosbacher (London: Hogarth Press and the Institute of Psychoanalysis, 1963)
—, *Sigmund Freud, Oskar Pfister: Briefe 1909–1939*, ed. Ernst L. Freud and Heinrich Meng (Frankfurt am Main: S. Fischer, 1963)
—, *The Complete Letters of Sigmund Freud to Wilhelm Fliess, 1887–1904* (Cambridge, MA and London: Belknap Press, 1985)
—, *The Standard Edition of the Complete Psychological Works of Sigmund Freud*, ed. and trans. by James Strachey *et al.*, 24 vols. (London: The Hogarth Press and the Institute of Psycho-Analysis, 1953–74)
Garber, Marjorie, 'Good to think with', *Profession* (2008), 11–20
García Lorca, Federico, 'Teoría y juego del duende' ['Theory and play of the *Duende*'], lecture given in Buenos Aires and Havana, repr. in García Lorca, *Obras completas*, ed. Arturo del Hoyo, 2 vols. (Madrid: Aguilar [1954], 1980), vol. 1
Germani, Gino, *Política y sociedad en una época de transición* (Buenos Aires: Paidós, 1962)
Goethe, Johann Wolfgang von, 'Julius Cäsars Triumphzug – gemalt von Mantegna' ['The triumphs of Caesar – painted by Mantegna' (1822)], in *Werke. Hamburger Ausgabe*, ed. Erich Trunz, 14 vols. (Munich: C. H. Beck, 1999), XII, 182–202
Grant, Catherine, 'Hal Foster in conversation with Catherine Grant', *Immediations*, 2: 1 (2008)
Greve, Germán, 'Sobre psicología y psicoterapia de ciertos estados angustiosos', in *Revista de Psicoanálisis*, III ([1910], 1945), 203–13
Grillparzer, Franz, *Sämtliche Werke*, ed. Peter Frank and Karl Pörnacher (Munich: Carl Hanser, 1964)
Grinker, Roy R. Sr., 'The history of psychoanalysis in Chicago, 1911–1975', *Annual of Psychoanalysis*, 23 (1995), 155–95
Grosz, Elizabeth, *Becomings: Explorations in Time, Memory, and Futures* (Ithaca, NY: Cornell University Press, 1999)
Grünbaum, Adolf, *The Foundations of Psychoanalysis: A Philosophical Critique* (Berkeley, CA: University of California Press, 1984)
—, *Validation in the Clinical Theory of Psychoanalysis: A Study in the Philosophy of Psychoanalysis* (Madison, CN: International University Press, 1993)
Habermas, Jürgen, *Knowledge and Human Interests* [*Erkenntnis und Interesse* (1968)], trans. by Jeremy J. Shapiro (Boston, MA: Beacon Press, 1972)

Hale, Nathan G., *Freud and the Americans: The Beginnings of Psychoanalysis in the United States, 1876–1917* (Oxford and New York: Oxford University Press, 1971)
—, *The Rise and Crisis of Psychoanalysis in the United States: Freud and the Americans, 1917–1985* (Oxford: Oxford University Press, 1995)
Harrison, Lucy, Sharon Kivland, Nina Papaconstantinou, *A Reader* (London: DOMOBAAL EDITIONS, 2003)
Heath, Stephen, 'Cinema and psychoanalysis: parallel histories', in *Endless Night: Cinema and Psychoanalysis – Parallel Histories*, ed. Janet Bergstrom (Berkeley: University of California Press, 1999), 25–57
Heath, Stephen, Colin MacCabe and Christopher Prendergast (eds.), *Signs of the Times: Introductory Readings in Textual Semiotics* (Cambridge: Granta, 1971)
Heidegger, Martin, 'The origin of the work of art' ['Der Ursprung des Kunstwerkes' (1935–6)], in *The Continental Aesthetics Reader*, ed. Clive Cazeaux (London: Routledge, 2000)
Heinrich, Klaus, 'Festhalten an Freud. Eine Heine-Freud-Miniatur zur noch immer aktuellen Rolle des Aufklärers Freud' ['Cleaving to Freud: a Heine-Freud Miniature on the ever-new role of Freud as Enlightener'], *Zeitschrift für psychoanalytische Theorie und Praxis*, 3 (2007), 365–87
Hernández, José, *Martín Fierro* (Buenos Aires: Centro Editor de América Latina [1872, 1879] 1979)
History of Psychiatry, 'Unsung heroes – Frantz Fanon his life and work', vol. 7 part 4 no. 28 (December 1996)
Hoffmann, E. T. A, *Die Elixiere des Teufels* (Frankfurt am Main and Leipzig: Insel [1816] 1978)
—, *Die Nachtstücke* (Frankfurt am Main and Leipzig: Insel [1816] 1986)
—, *Lebensansichten des Katers Murr* (Düsseldorf: Artemis und Winkler [1820] 2006)
Hoffmann, Kathryn, *Society of Pleasures: Interdisciplinary Readings in Pleasure and Power During the Reign of Louis XIV* (New York and Basingstoke: St. Martin's Press and Macmillan, 1997)
Horstmann, Claude, *Die Landschaft ist nicht die Lösung* [*Landscape is Not the Solution*], (Nürtingen: Stiftung Domnic, 2004)
Hudson, Guillermo Enrique [William Henry], *Allá lejos y hace tiempo*, trans. by Juan Antonio Brusol (Buenos Aires: Guillermo Kraft, 1958)
—, *Far Away and Long Ago: A History of My Early Life* (London: J. M. Dent [1918] 1939)

Huet, Pierre-Daniel, *A Treatise of Romances and their Original* (London: printed by R. Battersby for S. Heydrick, 1672), *Early English Books Online*, www.eebo.chadwyck.com

—, *Traité de l'origine des romans* (Paris: Dessessarts [1670] 1798–9), http://gallica2.bnf.fr/ark:/12148/bpt6k650112

Ibsen, Henrik, *Peer Gynt*, trans. by Peter Watts (London: Penguin [1867] 1966)

Ingenieros, José, 'La formación de la raza argentina', in *Sociología Argentina* [*Argentine Sociology*] (Buenos Aires: Elmer [1915] 1957)

Iriye, Akira and Pierre-Yves Saunier (general eds.), *Dictionary of Transnational History*, (London: Palgrave Macmillan, 2009)

Isaacs, Susan, 'The nature and function of phantasy', *International Journal of Psychoanalysis* 29 (1948), 73–97

Jameson, Fredric, 'Imaginary and symbolic in Lacan: Marxism, psychoanalytic criticism, and the problem of the subject', in *Literature and Psychoanalysis*, ed. Shoshana Felman (Baltimore, MD: Johns Hopkins University Press, 1982), 381–2

Jauch, Pia, *Damenphilosophie und Männermoral: Von Abbé de Gérard bis Marquis de Sade* [*Ladies' Philosophy and Men's Morality: From the Abbé de Gérard to the Marquis de Sade*] (Vienna: Passagen, 1990)

Jensen, Wilhelm, *Gradiva. Ein pompejanisches Phantasiestück* [*Gradiva: A Pompeiian Fancy*] (Dresden and Leipzig: Reißner, 1903)

Kafka, Franz, *The Trial* (*Der Prozeß* [1925]), trans. by Idris Parry (London: Penguin, 2007)

Kant, Immanuel, *Kritik der reinen Vernunft* [*Critique of Pure Reason*] (Riga: Johann Friedrich Hartknoch, 1781)

—, ‚Was ist Aufklärung?' ['What is Enlightenment?'], *Berlinische Monatsschrift 2, (1784), 481–94*

Kernberg, Otto F., 'Perspectives on psychoanalysis: impossible training', *Journal of the American Psychoanalytic Association* 54 (2006), 281–6

Kipling, Rudyard, *Kim* (Harmondsworth: Penguin [1901] 2000)

Kivland, Sharon, *L'Esprit d'escalier* (York: information as material, 2007)

Klein, Melanie, 'Bemerkungen über einige schizoide Mechanismen' [1946] ['Notes on some schizoid mechanisms'], in *Das Seelenleben des Kleinkindes und andere Beiträge zur Psychoanalyse*, ed. Hans A. Thorner (Stuttgart: Klett-Cotta, 1983), 131–63

Lacan, Jacques, 'Le fantasme au-delà du principe de plaisir', in *Les Formations de l'inconscient* (Paris: Seuil, 1998), 233–48

—, 'Of the gaze as *objet petit a*' ['Du regard comme objet petit a'], in *The Four Fundamental Concepts of Psycho-analysis* (*Les quatre concepts fondamentaux de la psychanalyse* [1973]), ed. Jacques-Alain Miller, trans. by Alan Sheridan (London: Vintage, 1998), 65–119

—, 'The Mirror Stage as formative of the function of the I as revealed in psychoanalytic experience' ['Le stade du miroir. Théorie d'un moment structurant et génétique de la constitution de la réalité, conçu en relation avec l'expérience et la doctrine psychanalytique' (1936)], trans. by Alan Sheridan in *Écrits: A Selection* (W. W. Norton: New York, 1977), 1–7

—, *Écrits* (Paris: Seuil, 1966)

—, *Écrits: A Selection*, ed. and trans. by Bruce Fink (New York: Norton, 2002)

—, *Le séminaire, Livre VII: L'éthique de la psychanalyse* (Paris: Seuil, 1986)

—, *Le Séminaire. Livre XVII. L'envers de la psychanalyse, 1969–70*, ed. Jacques-Alain Miller (Paris: Seuil, 1991)

—, *Les complexes familiaux dans la formation de l'individu* (Paris: Navarin [1938] 1984)

—, *Television* [*Télévision* (1974)], ed. Joan Copjec, trans. by Denis Hollier, Rosalind Krauss, Annette Michelson (New York: W. W. Norton, 1990)

—, *The Other Side of Psychoanalysis: The Seminar of Jacques Lacan Book XVII* [*Le Séminaire. Livre XVII. L'envers de la psychanalyse, 1969–1970* (1998)], ed. Jacques-Alain Miller, trans. with notes by Russell Grigg (New York and London: W. W. Norton, 2007)

—, *The Seminar of Jacques Lacan. Book I. Freud's Papers on Technique. 1953–1954* [*Le Séminaire I* (1975)], ed. Jacques-Alain Miller, trans. by John Forrester (New York: W. W. Norton, 1991)

—, *The Seminar, Book VII: The Ethics of Psychoanalysis 1959–60*, ed. Jacques-Alain Miller, trans. by Dennis Porter (London and New York: Routledge, 1992)

Laclau, Ernesto, *On Populist Reason* (London: Verso, 2007)

Langer, Marie, 'El niño asado y otros mitos sobre Eva Perón', in *Fantasías eternas a la luz del psicoanálisis* (Buenos Aires: Hormé [1957] 1966)

—, *Maternidad y sexo. Estudio psicoanalítico y psicosomático* (Buenos Aires: Paidós, 1951)

Laplanche, Jean and Jean-Bertrand Pontalis, 'Fantasy and the origins of sexuality', *International Journal of Psychoanalysis*, 49 (1968), 1–18

Laplanche, Jean, *Essays on Otherness* [*La Révolution copernicienne inachevée* (1992)], ed. and trans. by John Fletcher (London: Routledge, 1999)

Lavagetto, Mario, *Il testo moltiplicato* (Parma: Pratiche editrice, 1982)

Liddell, Henry George and Robert Scott (with the assistance of Henry S. Jones), *A Greek-English Lexicon*, 9th edn. (Oxford: Oxford University Press, 1996)

Machado, Danuza, 'A little object', Danuza Machado interviewed by Alex Potts, *AN Visual Arts* (September 1997), 10–13

Madieri, Marisa, *Verde Aqua* (Turin: Einaudi, 1998)

Magris, Claudio, *Alla cieca* (Milan: Garzanti, 2007)

Makari, George, *Revolution in Mind: The Creation of Psychoanalysis* (New York: Harper/Harper Collins, 2008)

Malinowski, Bronislaw, *Sex and Repression in Savage Society* (New York: Harcourt Brace, 1927)

Mann, Thomas, *Joseph and his Brothers* [*Joseph und seine Brüder*, 1933–42], trans. by John E. Woods (New York: Alfred A. Knopf, 2005)

Mannoni, Octave, *Prospero and Caliban: The Psychology of Colonization*, trans. by Pamela Powesland (London: Methuen, 1956)

Marinelli, Lydia, and Andreas Mayer, *Dreaming by the Book. Freud's 'The Interpretation of Dreams' and the History of the Psychoanalytic Movement* [*Träume nach Freud. Die 'Traumdeutung' und die Geschichte der psychoanalytischen Bewegung* (2002)], trans. by Susan Fairfield (New York: Other Press, 2003)

Martin, Margot. 'The rhetoric of *mouvement* and passionate expression in seventeenth-century French harpsichord music', *Seventeenth-Century French Studies*, 31 (2009), 137–9

Martínez Estrada, Ezequiel, 'Sobre *Radiografía de la Pampa*', in *Leer y escribir* (México: Moritz, 1969)

—, *Radiografía de la pampa* [*Radiography of the Pampas*], Critical Edition by Leon Pollmann (México: Fondo de Cultura Económica [1933] 1996)

Mattenklott, Gert, 'Mantegnas "Doppelleben" als Muster für Goethes späte Ästhetik', in *Bausteine zu einem neuen Goethe*, ed. Paolo Chiarini (Frankfurt am Main: Athenäum, 1987), 135–47

Mauss, Marcel, *The Gift: Form and Reason for Exchange in Archaic Societies* [*Essai sur le don* (1950)], trans. by W. D. Halls (London: Routledge 2001)

Mayerfeld Bell, Michael, 'The ghosts of place', *Theory and Society* (vol. 26, no. 6, December 1997)

McGowan, Todd, 'Looking for the gaze: Lacanian film theory and its vicissitudes', *Cinema Journal*, 42.3 (Spring 2003), 27–47

Melville, Herman, *The Piazza Tales* (Evanston: Northwestern University Press [1856] 1996)

Meyer, Catherine (ed.) *Le Livre noir de la psychanalyse: Vivre, penser et aller mieux sans Freud* (Paris: Arènes, 2005)

Mitchell, Juliet, 'Procreative mothers (sexual difference) and child-free sisters (gender)', in *The Future of Gender*, ed. J. Browne (Cambridge: CUP, Cambridge 2007)
—, *Mad Men and Medusas: Reclaiming Hysteria and the Effects of Sibling Relations on the Human Condition* (London: Allen Lane & Penguin, 2000)
—, *Siblings, Sex and Violence* (Cambridge: Polity, 2003)
Moritz, Karl Philip, *Anton Reiser. Ein autobiographischer Roman*, ed. Heinrich Schnabel (Munich: M. Mörike [1785] 1912)
Morra, Joanna, *Gradiva Project*, ed. William Cobbing (London: Camden Arts Centre, 2007)
Musil, Robert, *Der Mann ohne Eigenschaften*, ed. Adolf Frisé, 2 vols. (Reinbek bei Hamburg: Rowohlt, 1978, repr. 1987)
Nash, Mark, *Screen Theory Culture* (London: Palgrave 2008)
Nietzsche, Friedrich, 'On the genealogy of morals', trans. by Walter Kaufmann and Reginald J. Hollingdale, in *On the Genealogy of Morals and Ecce Homo* (New York: Vintage, 1967), 15–167
—, 'Zur Genealogie der Moral', *Kritische Studienausgabe*, 15 vols. (Berlin, Munich: de Gruyter, DTV, 1988), vol. 5, 245–412
—, *Der Fall Wagner*, Kritische Studienausgabe 6 (Munich, Berlin and New York: DTV, de Gruyter [1888] 1999)
Nobus, Dany and Malcolm Quinn, *Knowing Nothing, Staying Stupid: Elements for a Psychoanalytic Epistemology* (London: Routledge, 2005)
Nora, Pierre, 'Between memory and history: *Les Lieux de Mémoire*', trans. by Marc Roudebush, *Representations* no. 2 (Spring 1989)
Novalis [Friedrich von Hardenburg], *Novalis' Schriften*, ed. Paul Kluckhohn and Richard Samuel, 3 vols. (Darmstadt: Wissenschaftliche Buchgesellschaft, 1968)
Nunberg, Hermann and Ernst Federn (eds.), *Minutes of the Vienna Psychoanalytic Society*, trans. by Margarete Nunberg, 4 vols. (New York: International University Press, 1962–75)
Ornston Jr., Darius Gray, 'How standard is the *Standard Edition*', in *Freud in Exile: Psychoanalysis and its Vicissitudes*, ed. Edward Timms and Naomi Segal (New Haven, CT and London: Yale University Press, 1988), 196–209
Osborne, Charles, *W. H. Auden: The Life of a Poet* (London: Eyre Methuen, 1980)
Peixoto, Fernanda,'El diálogo como forma: Antropología e historia intelectual', *Prismas. Revista de historia intelectual*, vol. 12 (2008), 17–33
Pichon Rivière Enrique and Ana Quiroga, *Psicología de la vida cotidiana* (Buenos Aires: Galerna, 1970)

—, Enrique, *Del psicoanálisis a la psicología social*, 2 vols. (Buenos Aires: Galerna, 1970)
—, Enrique, *Teoría del vínculo* (Buenos Aires: Nueva Visión, 1979)
Plotkin Mariano, *Argentina on the Couch. Psychiatry, State and Society, 1880 to the Present* (Albuquerque: University of New Mexico Press, 2003)
Plotkin, Mariano and Sergio Visacovsky, 'Saber y autoridad en las intervenciones de los psicoanalistas en torno a la crisis en la Argentina', *Estudios Interdisciplinarios de América Latina y El Caribe*, vol. 18, no. 1 (2007)
—, *Freud in the Pampas: The Emergence and Development of a Psychoanalytic Culture in Argentina* (Stanford, CA: Stanford University Press, 2001)
Ponce, Aníbal, 'La divertida estética de Freud', *Revista de Filosofía*, IX, vol. 17 (1923)
—, 'Madame Sokolnicka y el psicoanálisis francés', *El Hogar* (10 May 1929)
—, *Apuntes de viaje* (Buenos Aires: El Ateneo, 1942)
Protokolle der Wiener Psychoanalytischen Vereinigung, ed. Hermann Nunberg and Ernst Federn, 4 vols. (Frankfurt am Main: S. Fischer, 1967–75)
Rascovsky, Arnaldo, *El filicidio* (Buenos Aires: Orion, 1973)
Rimbaud, Arthur, *Poésies complètes* (Paris: Gallimard, 1963)
Rose, Jacqueline, *States of Fantasy* (Oxford: Clarendon Press, 1998)
Roth, Joseph, *Hiob. Roman eines einfachen Mannes*, in *Werke*, ed. Fritz Hackert, 6 vols. (Cologne, Amsterdam: Kiepenhauer & Witsch; Allert de Lange [1930] 1990)
Roudinesco, Élisabeth and Michel Plon, *Dictionnaire de la psychanalyse* (Paris: Fayard, 1997)
—, *La Bataille de cent ans : Histoire de la psychanalyse en France*, 2 vols. (Paris: Fayard, 1986 and 1994)
Rousseau, Jean-Jacques, *Du contrat social ou Principes du droit politique* (Amsterdam: Chez Marc Michel Rey, 1762)
—, *Émile ou de l'éducation* (Paris: Garnier-Flammarion, 1966)
Roussillon, René, 'La fonction symbolisante de l'objet, *Revue française de psychanalyse*, vol. LXI, no. 2 (avril-juin 1997), 399–415
Sábato, Ernesto, *On Heroes and Tombs* [*Sobre Héroes y Tumbas* (1961)], trans. by Helen R. Lane (Boston, MA: David R. Godine, 1981)
—, *The Angel of Darkness* [*Abaddón el Exterminador* (1974)], trans. by Andrew Hurley (New York: Ballantine, 1991)
—, *The Tunnel* [*El Túnel* (1948)], trans. by Margaret Sayers Peden (New York: Ballantine, 1991)

Said, Edward, *Freud and the Non-European* (London: Verso, 2003)
Saramago, Jose, *Blindness* [*Ensaio Sobre a Ceguera* (1985)], trans. by Giovanni Pontieri (London: Harvill, 1998)
Sarmiento, Domingo F., *Conflictos y armoniás de las razas en América* (Buenos Aires: La Cultura Argentina [1883] 1915)
—, *Facundo* (Buenos Aires: Centro Editor de América Latina [1845] 1979)
Sayers, Janet, *Mothering Psychoanalysis: Helene Deutsch, Karen Horney, Anna Freud and Melanie Klein* (Harmondsworth: Penguin, 1991)
Sbriglio, Jacques, *Le Corbusier's Unité d'Habitation in Marseille* [*Le Corbusier, l'Unité d'habitation de Marseille* (1992)], trans. by Sarah Parsons (Basel: Birkhauser, 2004)
Schacht, Lore, 'La capacité d'être surpris', *Journal de la psychanalyse d'enfant*, no. 29 (2001) 195–214
Schorske, Carl, *Fin-de-Siècle Vienna: Politics and Culture* (New York: Vintage Books, 1981)
Schreber, Daniel Paul, *Memoirs of a Nervous Illness* [*Denkwürdigkeiten eines Nervenkranken* (1903)], ed. and trans. by Ida Macalpine and Richard A. Hunter (London: W. M. Dawson & Sons, 1955)
Séchaud Evelyne, 'Didier Anzieu: penser les pensées', in *Didier Anzieu: le Moi-peau et la psychanalyse des limites*, ed. Catherine Chabert, Dominique Cupa, René Kaës, René Roussillon (Paris: Eres, 2007), 11–30
Segal, Leon, 'La radiografía de la pampa: un saber espectral', in Ezequiel Martínez Estrada, *Radiografía de la pampa* Critical Edition by Leon Pollmann (México: Fondo de Cultura Económica [1933] 1996)
Segal, Naomi, *Consensuality: Didier Anzieu, Gender and the Sense of Touch* (Amsterdam and New York: Rodopi, 2009)
Shelford, April G. *Transforming the Republic of Letters: Pierre-Daniel Huet and European Intellectual Life* (Rochester, NY: University of Rochester Press, 2007)
Smithson, Robert, *Robert Smithson: The Collected Writings*, ed. Jack Flam (Los Angeles: University of California Press, 1996)
Stavrakakis, Yannis, *Lacan and the Political* (London and New York: Routledge, 1999)
Steiner, Riccardo, '"Die Weltmachstellung des Britischen Reichs": notes on the term "standard" in the first translations of Freud', in *Freud in Exile: Psychoanalysis and its Vicissitudes*, ed. Edward Timms and Naomi Segal (New Haven, CT and London: Yale University Press, 1988), 181–95
—, *It's a New Kind of Diaspora. Explorations in the Sociopolitical and Cultural Context of Psychoanalysis* (London: Karnac, 2000)

Svevo, Italo, *Il vegliardo*, ed. Bruno Maier (Pordenone: Studio Tesi, 1987)
—, *La coscienza di Zeno* in *Tutte le opere*, vol. 1, ed. Nunzia Palmieri and Fabio Vittorini (Milan: Mondadori [1923] 2004)
Szasz, Thomas S., 'Psycho-analytic training – a socio-psychological analysis of its history', *International Journal of Psychoanalysis* 39 (1958), 598–613
Timms, Edward and Naomi Segal, *Freud in Exile: Psychoanalysis and its Vicissitudes* (New Haven and London: Yale University Press, 1988)
Toscano, Roberto, 'A che cosa servono le diversità', *Reset* 92 (2005)
Turkle, Sherry, *Psychoanalytic Politics: Jacques Lacan and Freud's French Revolution* 2nd edn. (London: Free Association Books, [1978] 1992)
Turner, Victor, *The Forest of Symbols. Aspects of Ndembu Ritual* (Ithaca, NY: Cornell University Press, 1967)
Ulla, Noemí, *Tango, rebelión y nostalgia* (Buenos Aires: Jorge Álvarez, 1967)
Vattimo, Gianni, *Dialogo con Nietzsche: Saggi 1961–2000* (Milan: Garzanti, 2001)
Verhaeghe, Paul, 'Psychotherapy, psychoanalysis, and hysteria', *The Letter*, vol. 2 (1994), 47–68
Vezzetti, Hugo, 'Freud en langue espagnole', *Revue Internationale d'Histoire de la Psychanalyse* (Paris: PUF, 1991), vol. 4
—, 'El psicoanálisis en el siglo', *Punto de Vista*, 88 (August 2007)
—, 'Elizabeth I, Lady Macbeth, Eva Perón', *Punto de Vista*, 52 (August 1995)
—, 'From the psychiatric hospital to the street: Enrique Pichon Rivière and the diffusion of psychoanalysis in Argentina', in *Argentina On the Couch. Psychiatry, State and Society, 1880 to the Present*, ed. Mariano Plotkin (Albuquerque, NM: University of New Mexico Press, 2003)
—, 'Las promesas del psicoanálisis en la cultura de masas', in *Historia de la vida privada en la Argentina*, ed. Fernando Devoto and Marta Madero, vol. III (Buenos Aires: Taurus, 1999)
—, *Aventuras de Freud en el país de los argentinos* (Buenos Aires: Paidós, 1996)
—, *Freud en Buenos Aires, 1910–1939*, 2nd edn. (Bernal: Universidad de Quilmes [1989] 1996)
Vidler, Anthony, *The Architectural Uncanny: Essays in the Modern Unhomely* (Cambridge, MA: MIT Press, 1992)

Visacovsky, Sergio, 'Origin stories, invention of genealogies and the early diffusion of Lacanian psychoanalysis in Argentina and Spain (1960–1980)', in *The Transnational Unconscious*, ed. Damousi and Plotkin, 227–56

Warburg, Aby, *Der Bilderatlas MNEMOSYNE* [*The Picture Atlas Mnemosyne* (1924–9)] ed. Manfred Warnke and Claudia Brink (Berlin: Akademie Verlag, 2000)

Webber, Andrew, 'Pan-Dora's box: fetishism, hysteria and the gift of death in Die Büchse der Pandora', *International Journal of Psychoanalysis*, 87 (2006), 273–86

—, *Berlin in the Twentieth Century: A Cultural Topography* (Cambridge: Cambridge University Press, 2008)

Weber, Max, *Ensayos sobre sociología de la religión* [*Gesammelte Aufsätze zur Religionsoziologie* (1920–1)], trans. by José Almaraz and Julio Carabaña (Madrid: Taurus, 1986)

White, T. H., *The Once and Future King* (New York: Ace Books [1958] 1987)

Wilbur, Shawn, '*Paul Virilio: Speed, Cinema, and the End of the Political State*', *Speed* (electronic journal), 1997, 1 (4): 1–10 (originally posted online in 1994)

Wilden, Anthony, *System and Structure – Essays in Communication and Exchange* (London: Tavistock, 1972)

Williamson, Beth L., 'William Cobbing: Gradiva Project', *The Art Book*, vol. 15, Issue 3 (August 2008)

Winnicott, D. W., *Playing and Reality* (New York: Routledge [1971] 2002)

—, *Psycho-Analytic Explorations*, ed. Clare Winnicott, Ray Shepherd and Madeleine Davis, (London: Karnac, 1989)

—, *The Child, the Family, and the Outside World* (Harmondsworth: Penguin, 1964)

—, *The Family and Individual Development* (London: Tavistock, 1965)

Winnicott, Donald W., *Home is Where We Start From* (Harmondsworth: Penguin, 1986)

Wygant, Amy, 'Relevance and its discontents: teaching Sofia Coppola's *Marie Antoinette*' *Teaching the Early Modern Period*, ed. ed. Derval Conroy (Basingstoke: Palgrave Macmillan, 2011)

—, *Towards a Cultural Philology: Phèdre and the Construction of 'Racine'* (Oxford: Legenda, 1999)

Žižek, Slavoj, '*Objet a* in social links', in *Jacques Lacan and the Other Side of Psychoanalysis*, ed. Justin Clemens and Russell Grigg (Durham, NC: Duke University Press, 2006), 107–28

—, 'The Hitchcockian blot', in *Looking Awry: an Introduction to Jacques Lacan through Popular Culture* (Cambridge, MA: MIT Press, 1991), 88–106

Zweig, Stefan, *Die Heilung durch den Geist: Anton Mesmer, Mary Baker-Eddy, Sigmund Freud* (Frankfurt am Main: Fischer Verlag [1931] 1982)

Index

Aberastury, Arminda, 140, 140n
Abraham, 294
Abraham, Karl, 101n, 205
Abraham, Nicolas, 57, 57n,
 268–69, 268n
Acconci, Vito, 147–49, 147n,
 149n
Alexander, Franz, 102–03
Almodóvar, Pedro, 60
Althamer, Pawel, 147n
Althusser, Louise, 28
Altounian, Janine, 58, 59
Alvarez, Agustín, 135, 135n
Amati-Mehler, Jacqueline, 284
Anderson, Perry, 28, 28n
Anzieu, Didier, 57–58, 57n,
 61–62, 67–69, 70n, 75
 Le Moi-peau, 67n
 Les Enveloppes psychiques, 67n,
 68
Anzieu-Premmereur, Christine,
 55, 56, 61, 63–75, 317
Arendt, Hannah, 26
Aristotle, 206
Arndt, Gertrud, 219
Asher, Michael, 147, 147n
Assmann, Aleida, 212, 212n
Assmann, Jan, 212, 212n

Auden, W. H., 180, 180n

Bal, Mieke, 246
Baldessari, John, 36, 36n, 149
Balint, Michael, 103, 103n
Ballesteros, Luis López, 127,
 127n, 134n
Balza, Martín, 250
Bann, Stephen, 28, 29n
Barbour, Lindy, 97, 98n
Barthes, Roland, 28
Basserman, Helen Vianna, 128
Bate, David, 14, 22
Baumeyer, Franz, 171–72, 171n,
 176–79, 177n, 181–83
Bayky, C. A., 255n
Beardsworth, Richard, 61
Beck, Orit, 128
Beckert, Sven, 255n
Beckett, Samuel, 71
Benedict, Ruth, 106
Benjamin, Walter, 242–43, 242n,
 247–48, 248n, 263, 263n,
 267–69, 267n
Berg, Alban, 220
Berger, Peter, 260, 260n
Bergson, Henri, 57, 57n, 264,
 264n

Berman, Emanuel, 105, 105n
Bettelheim, Bruno, 127, 127n
Bion, Wilfred, 16, 70, 70n,
Bird, Jon, 229, 229n
Bleger, José, 133, 133n, 144, 144n
Boccaccio, Giovanni, 284–87
Borges, Jorge Luis, 297
Borossa, Julia, 55– 62, 317
Bourdieu, Pierre, 253, 253n
Bourelly, Anne-Marie Augustina, 60
Bourget, Paul, 290
Bourne, Ansel, 290, 290n
Bourriaud, Nicolas, 36n
Bowlt, J. E., 29n
Braddock, Louise, 23n
Brecht, Bertolt, 11, 35, 266
Breton, André, 220, 220n, 229, 229n
Breuer, Josef, 56n, 125, 125n
Briggs, Daphne, 67n
Brill, A. A, 41
Browne, J., 186n
Brücke, Ernst, 101
Brusol, Juan Antonio, 137n
Bunge, Carlos Octavio, 135, 135n
Burgin, Victor, 29, 31
Butler, Judith, 162, 162n, 244, 245n
Byron, George Gordon, Lord, 187

Caldwell, Lesley, 281–87, 318
Calvino, Italo, 287, 287n
Canetti, Elias, 294, 294n
Caprotti, Federico, 226
Carus, Carl August, 210n
Castoriadis, Cornelius, 97, 97n, 161–62, 161n, 162, 162n
Cavalli, Alessandra, 15
Cazeaux, C., 36n

Chasseguet-Smirgel, Janine, 70–71, 71n
Chateaubriand, François-René de, 81, 81n
Civitarese, Giuseppe, 284
Cobbing, William, 203, 207, 225–31, 318
Colloredo, Hieronymus von, 214
Connelly, Matthew, 255n
Conrad, Joseph, 286, 286n
Cooper, David, 32
Copernicus, Nicolaus, 212, 221–22, 259
Cruz, Juan, 125–26, 129–30, 145–49, 318
Csabai, Márta, 14, 22

D'Argens, Jean-Baptise de Boyer, Marquis de, 215
Da Ponte, Lorenzo, 213
Dachy, Vincent, 25, 44, 44n
Dagfal, Alejandro, 256n
Dalí, Salvador, 28, 229n
Damousi, Joy, 250n, 253n
Danto, Elizabeth Ann, 100n
Darrieussecq, Marie, 59, 59n
Darwin, Charles, 221–22
Deleuze, Gilles, 140, 140n
Derrida, Jacques, 25, 25n, 28n, 227, 227n, 267, 267n
Descartes, René, 96, 160, 216, 216n
Deutsch, Helene, 100, 100n
Di Benedetto, 286n
Di Cori, Paola, 15
Diderot, Denis, 24
Dimler, G. Richard, S. J., 93n
Dostoevsky, Fyodor, 291, 291n
Dreyer, Carl, 22, 30–31
Durr, Jason, 33
Dürrenmatt, Friedrich , 266

Einstein, Albert, 104
Eitingon, Max, 99–100
Elias, Norbert, 254, 254n
Ellenberger, Henri, 251, 251n
Ernst, Max, 28, 229n
Etcheverry, José L., 127n, 134
Eurydice, 286, 300
Evans, Jo, 127, 128n

Fanon, Frantz, 22, 33–34, 33n, 57, 57n, 58–59, 58n, 59n, 244, 244n
Ferenczi, Sándor, 105, 180, 185
Flechsig, Paul Emil, 163–64, 167, 169–71, 178–80, 183, 187
Fleischl-Marxow, Ernst, 219
Fliess, Wilhelm, 186, 205, 205n
Fontana, Lucio, 114
Forrester, John, 41n, 251n, 252, 258–59, 258n
Foster, Hal, 21–22, 22n
Foucault, Michel, 36, 36n, 138, 138n, 213, 213n
Fowler, Luke, 32n
Freud, Julius, 186
Freud, Martha, 101, 225
Freud, Sigmund, 12–15, 19, 20n, 21, 24, 24n, 25, 27, 29, 31, 33, 33n, 34, 40, 40n, 41, 41n, 56, 56n, 57, 60–61, 63–64, 63n, 64n, 65, 65n, 67, 70, 75, 81, 95–97, 95n, 96n, 97, 99, 100, 100n, 101, 101n, 103, 105, 125–26, 125n, 127, 127n, 130, 131–38, 132n, 133n, 134n, 140, 140n, 144, 144n, 160, 161–63, 167–78, 167n, 169n, 170n, 172m, 177n, 180–87, 183n, 186n, 203–07, 203n, 204n, 205n, 206n, 209–12, 212n, 215–22, 215n, 216n, 217n, 222n, 225–31, 225n, 226n, 227, 242–45, 244n, 245n, 250, 252, 254, 256–60, 256n, 282, 284, 293, 293n, 294n
'A child is being beaten', 245n
'Analysis of a phobia in a five-year-old boy' ('Little Hans'), 183, 183n
'Analysis terminable and interminable', 293n
'Constructions in analysis', 169, 169n, 174, 184, 207, 207n
'Creative writers and daydreaming', 12, 126, 126n, 169, 169n
'Delusions and dreams in Jensen's *Gradiva*', 203–05, 203n, 207, 226n
'Femininity', 170n, 174-75
'Mourning and melancholia', 127, 127n
'Negation', 95n
'On narcissism', 184
'On the history of the psychanalytic movement', 132, 132n, 134
'Psycho-analytic notes on an autobiograophical account of a case of paranoia' (Schreber case), 167n
'The splitting of the ego in the process of defence', 184
'The uncanny', 215n, 217n
'"Wild" psycho-analysis', 96n, 97
An Autobiographical Study, 259
An Outline of Psycho-Analysis, 172, 172n, 184

Civilization and its Discontents,
  144n, 161, 161n, 204, 204n,
  212n
*Group Psychology and the
  Analysis of the Ego,* 161,
  184
Humour, 64n
*Introductory Lectures on
  psycho-analysis,* 19, 20n, 24,
  33n, 212n, 222n
*Jokes & their Relation to the
  Unconscious,* 15, 63n, 70
Moses and Monotheism, 168,
  173, 184, 185, 206, 207n
*New Introductory Lectures on
  psycho-analysis,* 24, 24n
*Project for a Scientific
  Psychology,* 65, 65n
Studies on Hysteria, 56n, 125n
The Interpretation of Dreams,
  14, 40, 40n, 41, 168, 216n,
  252, 256n, 258
*Three Essays o the Theory of
  Sexuality*, 41, 41n, 167
Totem and Taboo, 60, 60n, 161,
  184, 244n
Frisch, Max, 266
Furlong, Bill, 14, 22

García Lorca, Federico, 129,
  129n, 146, 146n
Germani, Gino, 139, 141–43,
  143n
Giampieri-Deutsch, Patrizia, 15
Gilman, Sander L., 98, 99–107,
  319
Goethe, Johann Wolfgang von,
  214, 214n, 216, 216n, 295
Gould, Polly, 14, 22, 25–26
Greve, Germán, 132–33, 133n,
  138
Grigg, Russell, 23, 23n

Grillparzer, Franz, 296, 296n
Grinker, Roy R., 102, 102n
Grosz, Elizabeth, 160n
Grubrich-Simitis, Ilse, 168
Grünbaum, Adolf, 251n
Guattari, Félix, 140, 140n
Guggenheim, Willy (Varlin),
  266

Habermas, Jürgen, 251n, 253n
Hale, Nathan, 134, 134n
Hall, Kirsty, 95, 95n
Haneke, Michael, 58
Harrison, Lucy, 14, 22, 24, 39n
Haselden, Francis Baptiste, 39
Haydn, Joseph, 214
Heath, Stephen, 28, 28n, 245,
  245n
Hegarty, Frances, 14, 22
Hegel, Georg Wilhelm Friedrich,
  162, 264
Heidegger, Martin, 36–37, 36n
Heinrich, Klaus, 211, 211n, 215n,
  217n, 218n
Hennings, Emmy, 266
Hesiod, 216
Hidalgo, Alberto, 138
Hill, Benny, 306
Hitchcock, Alfred, 28
Hoffmann, E. T. A., 282, 289,
  289n, 291, 295, 295n
Hoffmann, Kathryn, 94n
Hofmannsthal, Hugo von, 220
Hofmeyr, Isabel, 255n
Horney, Karen, 100, 103
Horstmann, Claude, 81n
Hudson, William Henry, 136,
  136-37n
Huet, Pierre-Daniel, 93–96, 93n,
  98
Humboldt, Wilhelm von, 99, 107

Index

Hutchins, Robert Maynard, 98, 102

Ibsen, Henrik, 292n
Ifode, Mariama, 131n
Ingenieros, José, 133, 136, 136n, 139
Ingres, Jean Auguste Dominique, 219
Iriye, Akira, 255n
Isaacs, Susan, 245, 245n
Isherwood, Christopher, 180

Jacob, 182
Jacobs, Amber, 60
James, William, 290n
Jameson, Fredric, 30–31, 30n
Janet, Pierre, 133
Jankélévitch, Samuel, 40
Jauch, Pia, 210n
Jensen, Wilhelm, 81, 203–05, 209, 211, 220, 225, 227
Jones, Ernest, 13, 102
Jørgensen, Jørgen, 299
Joseph-Lester, Jaspar, 14, 22, 161, 163–66, 189–92, 319
Joyce, James, 266
Judith, 286
Julien, Isaac, 33, 33n, 58, 58n, 59
Jung, Carl Gustav, 15, 137, 180, 185, 186, 250, 283

Kafka, Franz, 294, 294n
Kahane, Ahuvia, 159–66, 319
Kant, Immanuel, 216, 216n, 217n
Kelly, Mary, 29, 31
Kennedy, Michael, 26
Kernberg, Otto, 105–06, 106n
Kipling, Rudyard, 289, 289n
Kivland, Sharon, 11–16, 14, 19–20, 22, 23, 34–35, 34n, 39–45, 39n, 242–43, 242n, 246, 247, 289n, 319–20
Klabund (Alfred Henschke), 266
Klein, Melanie, 130, 140–42, 142–43n, 172–73, 211n, 256
Kolb, Annette, 266
Kozol, Wendy, 255n
Kraepelin, Emil, 101–02
La Mettrie, Julian Offray de, 215
Lacan, Jacques, 15, 23, 23n, 25, 26, 26n, 28, 28n, 29, 29n, 30, 31, 32, 34, 35, 41, 41n, 43, 43n, 57, 57n, 60, 96, 128, 130, 133, 140n, 144, 162, 162n, 206, 245, 245n, 255, 256, 260, 283, 284
  'The mirror stage as formative of the function of the I as revealed in psychoanalytic experience', 29, 29n
  Seminar VII (Ethics of Psychoanalysis), 162, 162n
  Seminar XVII (The other side of psychoanalysis), 23–24, 23n, 43n
  Television, 26, 26n
  The Four fundamental Concepts of Psycho-analysis, 245n
Lacewing, Michael, 23n
Lachmayer, Herbert, 207, 209–23, 320
Laclau, Ernesto, 159n
Lagache, Daniel, 133
Laing, R. D., 32, 32n, 97
Langer, Marie, 140, 140n, 142, 142n, 143
Laplanche, Jean, 57, 57n, 245, 245n, 247, 263–64, 263n, 268
Large, Duncan, 206
Lasker-Schüler, Elsa, 266
Laughlin, Zoe, 98, 109–15, 320

Lavagetto, Mario, 284–86, 284n
Le Corbusier (Charles-Édouard Jeanneret), 165, 165n, 189–92
Le Mercier, Stéphane, 55, 56, 61, 77–82, 320–21
Le Witt, Sol, 114
Leibovich de Duarte, Adela, 106
Lenin, Vladimir Ilyich, 266
Lewis, Mark, 14, 22
Lichtenstein, Roy, 219
Liebscher, Martin, 127, 203–07, 289n, 321
Lipski, Ed, 147
López-Ballesteros y de Torres, Luis, 127, 127n
Lüthi, Urs, 266

MacCabe, Colin, 28, 28n
MacCannell, Juliet Flower, 161
McGowan, Todd, 245, 245n
Machado, Danuza, 34–35, 35n
Mack, Michael, 206
Madieri, Marisa, 283, 283n, 293, 293n
Madonna, 143
Magris, Claudio, 282–83, 286, 287, 289–301, 321
Mahler, Gustav, 220
Makari, George, 100n
Malinowski, Bronisław, 244, 244n
Manacorda, Francesco, 34
Mann, Erika, 266
Mann, Klaus, 266
Mann, Thomas, 182, 182n, 266
Mannoni, Oscar, 244, 244n
Marinelli, Lydia, 40n
Martin, Margot, 94n
Martin, Tim, 24
Martínez Estrada, Ezequiel, 135–37, 135n, 136n, 139–40, 141

Marx, Karl, 22, 28, 144, 160, 253, 262,
Masotta, Oscar, 133
Masson, André, 229n
Mata Hari (Margarethe Zelle), 266
Mattenklott, Gert, 216n
Mauss, Marcel, 25, 25n
Mayer, Andreas, 40n
Mead, Margaret, 106
Medeiros, Paulo de, 127
Medem, Carlos, 128, 130
Melville, Herman, 295–96, 296n
Metastasio (Pietro Antonio Domenico Trapassi), 213
Meyer, Catherine, 253n
Michelson, Annette, 26n, 28
Miller, Jacques-Alain, 23, 255
Mitchell, Juliet, 161, 163–65, 167–88, 241, 321–22
Moissi, Alexander, 266
Moritz, Karl Philipp, 295, 295n
Morlock, Forbes, 14, 22, 25
Morra, Janne, 229–31, 229n
Morris, Simon, 14, 23
Moses, 294
Mozart, Wolfgang Amadeus, 11, 214
Musil, Robert, 220n, 221, 282, 290, 291–92, 292n, 296
Mussolini, Benito, 226

Nash, Mark, 21–22, 27–37, 58n, 322
Nelson, Mike, 147, 147n
Nietzsche, Friedrich, 160, 205–06, 206n, 290, 290–91n
Nobis, Margit, 219
Nobus, Dany, 22, 22n
Nora, Pierre, 247, 264, 265n, 267–68

Novalis (Friedrich von Hardenberg), 290, 290n
Nunberg, Hermann, 100

Oedipus, 139, 188, 220, 286
Orlow, Uriel, 242, 246–48, 263–69, 322
Ornston, Darius Gray Jr., 14, 14n
Orpheus, 286
Ortega y Gasset, José, 127
Osborne, Dora, 203, 204, 204n

Pabst, G. W., 205
Papaconstantinou, Nina, 39n
Pappenheim, Bertha, 125
Parr, Martin, 114
Pavey, Liz, 14, 23
Pavlov, Ivan, 101–02
Peixoto, Fernanda, 261, 261n
Perón, Eva, 142–43
Perón, Juan, 130, 141–43
Pessoa, Fernando, 128, 291
Pfister, Oscar, 206
Picard-Drillien, Anne-Marie, 57n, 60
Pichon Rivière, Enrique, 130, 133, 133n, 139, 140–42, 140n, 141n
Pirandello, Luigi, 291
Pizzi, Katia, 289n
Plotkin, Mariano Ben, 242, 246–48, 246n, 249–62, 322–23
Polanszky, Rudolf, 219
Politzer, Georges, 133, 133n
Ponce, Aníbal, 133, 133n
Pontalis, Jean-Bertrand, 245, 245n
Popper, Karl, 253n
Prendergast, Christopher, 28, 28n
Proust, Marcel, 211
Puccini, Giacomo, 286

Quinn, Malcolm, 14, 19–26, 43, 323
Quiroga, Ana, 141n

Rachel, 182
Racine, Jean, 60, 94n
Rainer, Yvonne, 28
Rank, Otto, 206
Rascovsky, Arnaldo, 140, 140n
Richards, Mike, 128
Rimbaud, Arthur, 290, 290n
Róbert, Reiter, 293
Rorty, Richard, 259
Rose, Jacqueline, 163, 163n
Rosenthal, Ludovico, 134, 134n
Roth, Joseph, 294, 294n
Roudinesco, Élisabeth, 56, 56n, 134, 134n, 258, 258n
Rousseau, Jean-Jacques, 161, 215, 215n
Ruprecht, Lucia, 203–05, 205n
Ruscha, Ed, 36, 36n

Sábato, Ernesto, 297–98
Sachs, Hanns, 205
Sade, Donatien Alphonse François, Marquis de, 215
Said, Edward, 244, 244n
St Augustine, 289, 289n
Salomé, 286
Saramago, José, 287, 287n
Sarmiento, Domingo F., 135, 135n, 136, 136n, 139, 141
Saunier, Pierre-Yves, 255n
Sayers, Janet, 142n
Schickele, René, 266
Schneider, Monique, 60
Schnitzler, Arthur, 220
Schorske, Carl, 259, 259n
Schreber, Anna (later Jung), 170–72, 172n, 176, 181

Schreber, Daniel Gottlob, 163, 176
Schreber, Daniel Gustav, 163, 169-70, 171, 172, 172n, 176–79, 181, 183
Schreber, Daniel Paul, 163–64, 167n, 167–88
Schreber, Klara (later: Krause), 170, 172, 178
Schreber, Sabine (wife of Daniel Paul), 171, 177, 181, 182
Schreber, Sidonie, 170, 172, 175–76, 179–81, 183
Séchaud, Evelyne, 70, 70n
Seed, Patricia, 255n
Segal, Leon, 136n
Segal, Naomi, 11, 11–16, 13n, 14n, 30, 57n, 69n, 131n, 209n, 323
Sehgal, Tino, 147n
Shaw, Becky, 25
Shelford, April, 93n
Siebers, Johan, 206
Sierra, Santiago, 147n
Silverman, Kaja, 246
Sinclair, Alison, 125–30, 323–24
Smithson, Robert, 24–25, 228, 228n
Solms, Mark, 24
Sperber, Manès, 289
Spielberg, Steven, 14
Stavrakakis, Yannis, 162, 162n
Steiner, Riccardo, 13n, 134, 134n
Steiner, Rudolph, 163
Stern, Alfred K., 103
Stokes, Adrian, 31
Strachey, James, 29, 41, 127, 130, 134, 226n
Surprenant, Céline, 15, 60
Svevo, Italo, 282, 283, 293, 293n, 296, 296n
Symons, Morwenna, 209n

Szasz, Thomas, 104, 104n

Tanning, Dorothea, 28
Täuber, Sophie, 266
Thompson, Dorothy, 266
Timerlake, John, 25
Timms, Edward, 13n, 14n
Tiresias, 286
Torok, Maria, 57, 57n, 268–29, 268n
Toscano, Roberto, 293, 293n
Tosquelles, François, 33
Trotsky, Leon, 266
Turkle, Sherry, 252, 252n
Turner, Victor, 305–06, 306n

Uden, Joel, 147
Ulla, Noemí, 132n

Vanzo, Marcella, 281–83, 287, 303–08, 324
Vattimo, Gianni, 291, 291n
Verhaeghe, Paul, 162, 162n, 163
Vezzetti, Hugo, 125, 125n, 128, 130, 131–43, 324
Vidler, Anthony, 244
Visacovsky, Sergio, 250n, 256, 256n
von Held, Phoebe, 14, 23, 24

Wagner-Jauregg, Julius, 101
Wallace, Alfred Russel, 221–22
Warburg, Aby, 165, 165n, 218, 218n
Webber, Andrew, 203–04, 204n, 205, 205n, 241–48, 324
Weber, Guido, 170
Weber, Max, 253, 253n
Werefkin, Marianne, 266
West, Franz, 219
White, T. H., 96, 96n
Wilbur, Shawn, 78, 78n

Wilden, Anthony, 29, 29n
Williamson, Beth, 229, 229n
Winnicott, Donald W., 64–66, 64n, 66n, 68n, 69, 73n, 140n, 164, 169, 173, 174–75, 182, 187, 187n, 281, 281n, 282
Wood, Sarah, 14, 23
Wygant, Amy, 93–98, 324–25

Zemlinsky, Alexander von, 220
Ziehen, Theodor, 101–02
Žižek, Slavoj, 32, 32n, 35, 245, 245n
Zweig, Stefan, 138, 138n, 266

Lightning Source UK Ltd.
Milton Keynes UK
UKOW032356110113

204749UK00008B/331/P